East Germany

WORLD BIBLIOGRAPHICAL SERIES

General Editors:
Robert L. Collison (Editor-in-chief)
Sheila R. Herstein
Louis J. Reith
Hans H. Wellisch

VOLUMES IN THE SERIES

VOLUME 77

East Germany

The German Democratic Republic

Ian Wallace
Compiler
with the assistance of
Douglas Burrington
David Childs
Michael Dennis
Marianne Howarth
Martin Kane
Derek Lewis
Stuart Parkes

CLIO PRESS

OXFORD, ENGLAND · SANTA BARBARA, CALIFORNIA
DENVER, COLORADO

British Library Cataloguing in Publication Data

Wallace, Ian, *1942-*
East Germany: (German Democratic Republic)
– (World bibliographical series; v. 77).
1. Germany (East) – Bibliography
I. Title   II. Series
016.9431   Z2250

ISBN 1–85109–023–1

Clio Press Ltd.,
55 St. Thomas' Street.
Oxford OX1 1JG, England.

ABC-Clio Information Services.
Riviera Campus, 2040 Alameda Padre Serra.
Santa Barbara, Ca. 93103, USA.

Designed by Bernard Crossland
Typeset by Columns Design and Production Services, Reading, England
Printed and bound in Great Britain by
Billing and Sons Ltd., Worcester

.943

CEN

14. APR. 1987

THE WORLD BIBLIOGRAPHICAL SERIES

This series will eventually cover every country in the world, each in a separate volume comprising annotated entries on works dealing with its history, geography, economy and politics: and with its people, their culture, customs, religion and social organization. Attention will also be paid to current living conditions – housing, education, newspapers, clothing, etc. – that are all too often ignored in standard bibliographies; and to those particular aspects relevant to individual countries. Each volume seeks to achieve, by use of careful selectivity and critical assessment of the literature, an expression of the country and an appreciation of its nature and national aspirations, to guide the reader towards an understanding of its importance. The keynote of the series is to provide, in a uniform format, an interpretation of each country that will express its culture, its place in the world, and the qualities and background that make it unique.

SERIES EDITORS

Robert L. Collison (Editor-in-chief) is Professor Emeritus, Library and Information Studies, University of California, Los Angeles, and is currently the President of the Society of Indexers. Following the war, he served as Reference Librarian for the City of Westminster and later became Librarian to the BBC. During his fifty years as a professional librarian in England and the USA, he has written more than twenty works on bibliography, librarianship, indexing and related subjects.

Sheila R. Herstein is Reference Librarian and Library Instruction Coordinator at the City College of the City University of New York. She has extensive bibliographic experience and has described her innovations in the field of bibliographic instruction in 'Team teaching and bibliographic instruction'. *The Bookmark*, Autumn 1979. In addition, Doctor Herstein co-authored a basic annotated bibliography in history for Funk & Wagnalls *New encyclopedia*, and for several years reviewed books for *Library Journal*.

Louis J. Reith is librarian with the Franciscan Institute, St. Bonaventure University, New York. He received his PhD from Stanford University, California, and later studied at Eberhard-Karls-Universität, Tübingen. In addition to his activities as a librarian, Dr. Reith is a specialist on 16th-century German history and the Reformation and has published many articles and papers in both German and English. He was also editor of the *American Society for Reformation Research Newsletter*.

Hans H. Wellisch is a Professor at the College of Library and Information Services, University of Maryland, and a member of the American Society of Indexers and the International Federation for Documentation. He is the author of numerous articles and several books on indexing and abstracting, and has also published *Indexing and abstracting: an international bibliography*. He also contributes frequently to *Journal of the American Society for Information Science, Library Quarterly*, and *The Indexer*.

For my mother

Contents

Contents

Contents

Introduction

East Germany or, to give the country its official name, the German Democratic Republic (GDR) was founded on the 7th October 1949 in what had been the Soviet Zone of Occupation since the end of the Second World War. In the almost forty years which have followed, it has become an increasingly well-established and successful member of the international community – a country which has developed into the Soviet Union's most important ally in the Eastern Bloc, whose athletic prowess is familiar to millions of television viewers all over the world, and whose economic growth can, without exaggeration, be described as truly impressive.

However, it is probably true to say that the most widespread perception of the GDR in the West, and most notably in the English-speaking world, continues to be grounded in that mixture of hostility and ignorance so dangerously fostered by the Cold War in East-West relations which developed soon after 1945. The hostility grew most obviously from the conflict between the GDR and the Federal Republic of Germany (FRG). Each claimed to be exclusively the 'true' representative of the German people but, more importantly for non-Germans, each was also seen to stand for the values, respectively, of 'communism' and the 'Western democracies'. The ignorance both followed from, and reinforced, the hostility, as the physical and psychological barriers of the Cold War (symbolized most starkly by the erection in 1961 of the ugly Wall which divides East from West Berlin) rapidly made first-hand information about, and experience of, the GDR a rare commodity for Westerners.

The 'policy of strength' which West Germany's Chancellor, Konrad Adenauer, pursued in his so-called Hallstein Doctrine played an important part in this process. Its aim was to deny West German recognition to the GDR – and to see that as many countries of the world as possible followed suit. In effect, the

GDR was to be turned into an international pariah whose existence was not acknowledged outside of the Soviet sphere of influence. In Ernst Richert's phrase, it was to become 'ein Staat, der nicht sein darf' (roughly, a state with no right to exist).

Notwithstanding this, apparently against all the odds, the GDR did not collapse. Indeed, eventually, it became clear that Adenauer's policy, far from fatally undermining the GDR and thus opening the way to a reunification of the two Germanies on West German terms, was having the effect of making the two states grow further apart as contacts between the two populations grew more tenuous with the passage of time. It was against this background, and in the wake of the policy of détente towards which the superpowers had felt their way in the 1960s, that Adenauer's bankrupt 'policy of strength' was replaced by Willy Brandt's *Ostpolitik* (policy towards the East), with its emphasis on contact and dialogue with the Eastern Bloc, and with the GDR in particular. This led, in 1972, to the conclusion of a momentous Basic Treaty between the two German states. Although Brandt here stopped short of *de jure* recognition of the GDR, preferring only a *de facto* acknowledgement of the second German state's existence, other countries had no such inhibitions once the process of dialogue was under way. Diplomatic recognition by a succession of countries followed in the early 1970s. The international outcast had become 'the state that came in from the cold' (Jonathan Steele).

The 1970s, then, were characterized by a basically more open attitude in the GDR towards the outside world in general, and towards its arch-enemy, the Federal Republic, in particular. Naturally, the old suspicions did not disappear overnight. The GDR remained convinced that the West Germans' new and more conciliatory policy did not mean they had given up their fundamental objective of reuniting the two Germanies in one capitalist state. This helps to explain why the GDR, for both political and economic reasons, went along with the development of closer intra-German ties, while at the same time vigorously pursuing its *Abgrenzungspolitik* – its policy of demarcation, or delimitation, by which it insisted on the many factors which marked off the two German states as utterly distinct and separate entities. Nevertheless, Westerners certainly found it much easier than hitherto to travel to, and within, the country, as journalists, academics, and even ordinary tourists discovering a part of pre-war Germany from which they had been largely cut off. An obvious consequence of these developments has been that the old ignorance of everyday life in the GDR has begun to recede as curiosity about, and experience of, the country has grown over the last fifteen years, not least in the English-speaking countries. Not surprisingly, perceptions of the country have, as a result, become more richly varied and differentiated than in the early post-war years, and there is now far less of a tendency among serious commentators simply to condemn the GDR as an oppressive Soviet satellite.

Having said that, the overwhelmingly predominant image of the GDR which is projected in our mass media continues to be that of a particularly inhuman prison from which daring members of the population are prepared to risk life and limb to escape. There is, of course, some truth in this, as the sections on escapes and dissent in this bibliography show. However, it is not the whole story. A central aim of the bibliography is, therefore, to point the general reader towards written evidence of various kinds which indicates that the truth about the GDR is far more complex than this simplistic image would suggest.

Of course, the bibliography can present only a selection from the considerable body of literature which is now available on the GDR. Emphasis has been given to recent publications, but early studies of lasting merit, or of significant documentary value, have also been included where this may help the reader to form a fuller picture of the GDR. It should be stressed that, in selecting items for inclusion, I have focused specifically on the GDR and on the Soviet Zone of Occupation out of which it grew. In other words, studies on pre-1945 Germany have been excluded, as have, works on the Federal Republic of Germany, except where these, have an obvious relevance to the study of the GDR. This very particular focus on the GDR also explains, for instance, why certain dictionaries, but not others, have been selected for inclusion. Readers with an interest in the Federal Republic and pre-1945 Germany are referred to the forthcoming volume in the World Bibliographical Series entitled *West Germany*.

The general aim has been to cover as many significant areas in GDR life as possible. Naturally, the need to be selective has been one inhibiting factor in this respect. Another has been the relative lack of attention which, despite the growing volume of literature devoted to the GDR in recent years, has been accorded to certain important subjects. Two such areas are transport and planning, although in the latter case an important study has just been published as this volume goes to press: Roy E. H. Mellor, 'The German Democratic Republic', in: *Planning in Eastern*

Introduction

Europe, edited by Andrew H. Dawson (London, Sydney: Croom Helm, 1987, p. 139-66). Where possible, preference has been given to works written in English. Nonetheless, the need to keep an English-speaking readership in mind has had to be balanced against the importance of reflecting the considerable body of literature on the GDR which has been produced in the Federal Republic of Germany and, indeed, in the GDR itself. This, in turn, has involved taking some care to avoid focusing solely, or even primarily, on the literature produced in either of the two Germanies. I hope that the critical reader will judge the bibliography a success in this very sensitive part of its endeavours.

Each entry is accompanied by an annotation which attempts, with varying degrees of brevity, to indicate the kind of information contained in the item under review. In many instances, the annotation will also offer a critical assessment of the item's significance as a contribution to the study of the GDR. By their very nature, such assessments do not lay claim to represent the only possible view of the matters in question; rather they are intended to give the reader a flavour of the issues which exercise serious students of the GDR, in the hope that his curiosity will be sufficiently aroused to make him wish to read further.

It should be noted that the terms 'East Germany', 'German Democratic Republic' and 'GDR' are used interchangeably. The same applies to 'West Germany', 'Federal Republic of Germany' and 'FRG'. Purists may object to such a proliferation of names. My defence is that this practice reflects what happens in the world at large and, by natural extension, in the body of literature on which the bibliography is based.

Finally, my sincere thanks go to Dr. Robert G. Neville of Clio Press for his untold patience and skill in dealing with a 'rogue' manuscript which made excessive demands on his considerable editorial abilities. I would also like to express my gratitude to those colleagues – Douglas Burrington, David Childs, Michael Dennis, Marianne Howarth, Martin Kane, Derek Lewis and Stuart Parkes – who kindly agreed, at much shorter notice than they would have certainly liked, to make significant contributions to sections of this volume, which would otherwise not have been so well covered.

Ian Wallace
Loughborough University of Technology, Leicestershire
January, 1987

Major Publishing Houses in the GDR

Akademie-Verlag, 108 Berlin, Leipziger Strasse 3-4.

Aufbau-Verlag, 108 Berlin, Französische Strasse 32.

VEB Bibliographisches Institut, 701 Leipzig, Gerichtsweg 26.

Buchverlag Der Morgen, 108 Berlin, Johannes-Dieckmann-Strasse 47.

VEB Deutscher Verlag der Wissenschaften, 108 Berlin, Johannes-Dieckmann-Strasse 10.

VEB Domowina, 86 Bautzen, Tuchmacherstrasse 27.

VEB Fotokinoverlag, 7031 Leipzig, Karl-Heine Strasse 16.

VEB Friedrich Hofmeister Musikverlag, 701 Leipzig, Karlstrasse 10.

VEB Greifenverlag, 682 Rudolstadt, Heidecksburg.

Henschelverlag, Kunst und Gesellschaft, 104 Berlin, Oranienburger Strasse 67–68.

VEB Hinstorff Verlag, 25 Rostock, Kröpeliner Strasse 25.

VEB Lied der Zeit, Musikverlag, 102 Berlin, Rosa-Luxemburg-Strasse 41.

Mitteldeutscher Verlag Halle-Leipzig, 401 Halle (Saale), Thälmannplatz 2.

Tribüne Verlag und Druckereien des FDGB, 1193 Berlin-Treptow, Am Treptower Park 28–30.

VEB Verlag Enzyklopädie, 701 Leipzig, Gerichtsweg 26.

VEB Verlag für Bauwesen, 108 Berlin, Französische Strasse 13-14.

VEB Verlag für Buch- und Bibliothekswesen, 701 Leipzig, Gerichtsweg 26.

Major Publishing Houses in the GDR

Verlag der Nation, 104 Berlin, Friedrichstrasse 113.

Verlag Neue Musik, 108 Berlin, Leipziger Strasse 26.

Verlag Neues Leben, 108 Berlin, Behrenstrasse 40-41.

Verlag Rütten & Loening, 108 Berlin, Französische Strasse 32.

Verlag Volk und Welt, 108 Berlin, Glinkastrasse 13-15.

Verlag der Weltbühne, 1056 Berlin, Karl-Liebknecht-Strasse 29.

Volk und Wissen, Volkseigener Verlag, 108 Berlin, Lindenstrasse 54a.

The Country and Its People

1 **The GDR: Moscow's German ally.**
David Childs. London: George Allen & Unwin, 1983. 346p. map.
bibliog.
Childs attempts 'a comprehensive study of the GDR'. The first third of his book is
devoted to a survey of the GDR's (mainly political) history. Individual chapters
then deal with the following subjects: the Socialist Unity Party (Sozialistische
Einheitspartei Deutschlands, SED); the constitution; the economy; education;
intellectuals; the mass media; women; the military; and foreign relations. Childs
emphasizes the GDR's achievements in many fields (notably the economy, social
services and sport) but he is equally explicit in his criticism of some negative
features, especially the 'credibility gap' separating the leaders from the led, the
'façade' of the multi-party system, and the 'sullen, bitter, alienated and angry'
mood he finds among many East Germans. The book has two indexes and a
section of thumb-nail biographies of leading GDR personalities.

2 **Honecker's Germany.**
Edited by David Childs. London, Boston, Sydney: Allen & Unwin,
1985. 201p. map. bibliog.
This volume is divided into eleven chapters, each devoted to one aspect of the
GDR: the Socialist Unity Party (SED); the constitution; the economy; the
education system; the Church; the significance of East German intellectuals in
opposition; youth; the country's naval build-up; relations with the USSR; and
relations with the United States. A further chapter offers a comparative analysis
of two important prose works of the 1980s by women writers: *Kassandra* by
Christa Wolf; and *Amanda* by Irmtraud Morgner.

1

The Country and Its People

3 **The new Germans: thirty years after.**
John Dornberg. New York: Macmillan, 1975. 293p.
Despite an emphasis on West German affairs, the GDR receives attention in this critique of post-war Germany which is written in an engaging pictorial style by a German-born American journalist. The topics covered include: the GDR's alleged mute anti-semitism in the form of its anti-Israel policy; the popular wave of support for the Czech reformists in 1968; the morale and class-structure of the National People's Army; the apparent emancipation of women; and the liberalization of attitudes towards sexual morality. The education system is seen as achievement-orientated but more efficient and socially more equitable than the FRG's, while the miracle of economic recovery earns honest respect. Considerable attention is accorded to literature and cultural policy (especially the work of Stefan Heym, 'a Marxist who drinks his socialism pure'), while East-West German relations merit a detailed review written in trenchant journalistic style, in which inter-German tensions come 'all wrapped together in a soccer ball'.

4 **German Democratic Republic.**
In: *Countries of the world and their leaders yearbook 1983*. Detroit, Michigan: Gale, 1983, p. 511–17. map. bibliog.
An expanded version of data provided by the US State Department in its information series entitled *Background Notes on Countries of the World*, this digest of basic facts about the GDR is so compiled that 'the student, traveler, or businessperson can answer most common questions' about the country and travel inside it 'without a multi-source research effort'.

5 **The German Democratic Republic.**
In: *The Europa year book 1986: a world survey*. London: Europa, 1986. vol. 1, p. 1,099–120.
A comprehensive, yet concise introduction to fundamental aspects of the GDR. An initial survey of the country's history is followed by notes on its government, defence, economic affairs, transport and communications, social welfare, education and tourism. A detailed statistical survey is also included, as is a summary of the constitution. The leading figures in government and political organizations are listed and the addresses of foreign embassies in the GDR together with the names of the ambassadors are also supplied. Additional information (including useful names and addresses) is provided on the following: the judicial system; religion; the press; publishing houses; radio and television; finance; trade and industry; transport; tourism; and atomic energy.

6 **German Democratic Republic.**
In: *The world of learning 1986*. London: Europa, 1986, 36th ed.
p. 455–64.
Provides basic information on academies, learned societies, libraries and archives, museums and art galleries, universities and colleges, including their addresses, the names of their principal members, and details of any publications which they produce.

7 **The GDR: twenty years on.**
Peter Johnson. *GDR Monitor*, no. 5 (summer 1981), p. 21–26.

Peter Johnson, who as a journalist covered numerous events in the GDR in the late 1950s and 1960s, compares the East Germany of 1981 with the one he knew shortly before the building of the Berlin Wall. He looks at conditions of housing, the domestic economy and farming and recounts many observations, often from East Germans themselves who give their views on what they consider to be the best and worst aspects of their country. Johnson concludes that GDR citizens have accommodated themselves to the régime but feel in some respects more dissatisfied than they were prior to the building of the Wall.

8 **East Germany: a country study.**
Edited by Eugene K. Keefe. Washington, DC: Department of the Army, 1982. 348p. bibliog. (Area Handbook Series).

A well-presented general survey of the GDR by a group of specialists whose initial readers will be members of the US armed forces. Five chapters cover: the historical setting; the society and its environment; the economy; government and politics; and national security. There is a useful brief sketch of the Council for Mutual Economic Assistance (Comecon) and another of the Warsaw Pact. There is also a good bibliography and a glossary. The volume is nicely illustrated with sketches and photographs, though most of the latter are official GDR material. The book opens with a chronology of important events starting with 'Germanic tribes settled in Germania. Roman army defeated by Germans at Battle of Teutoburg Forest in A.D.9' and ending with the GDR 'admitted to United Nations (1973).' The useful historical chapter is perhaps unfair to the Germany of pre-1914 in that its cultural and educational achievements are not mentioned. The Weimar Republic, on the other hand, is privileged with a section on Weimar Culture. The anti-Nazi resistance (other than the July plotters) could have done with three or four sentences and to write that 'the SED polled approximately 50 per cent of the vote in each state in the October 1946 elections' is not quite accurate. Despite these, and some other points, this is a commendable attempt to present a realistic picture of the GDR. Would a book published under the imprint of the Soviet armed forces on, say, West Germany be as fair as this?

9 **The German Democratic Republic: the search for identity.**
Henry Krisch. Boulder, Colorado; London: Westview Press, 1985. 194p. map. bibliog.

Presents a comprehensive overview of the GDR, focusing in successive chapters on: the history and geography of the country; its political system (including the armed forces); its foreign policy; its relationship with the Federal Republic of Germany and with the German past; its economic achievements; the way in which society is managed (with particular reference to 'problem areas' such as the Church, the unofficial peace movement, and dissent in, for example, the cultural domain); and its social policy regarding women and youth and in the spheres of education and sport. In a concluding chapter, Krisch argues that 'the basic requirements of international acceptance, minimal domestic legitimacy, and steady economic growth' have been successfully achieved and that the problems which the GDR faces in the near and middle-term future are those resulting from this very success. He asserts that a stable GDR is likely to be maintained but that

3

the task of its political leadership remains 'to convince the GDR population that socialism with a German face is an acceptable way of life'. The volume is illustrated with 21 tables, 20 photographs, and 1 figure.

10   **The German Democratic Republic: a developed socialist society.**
Edited by Lyman H. Legters.   Boulder, Colorado: Westview Press, 1978. 285p. bibliog.

This book sets out to dispel 'some of the outworn myths and distortions' which, as the editor rightly notes, still affect the way in which the GDR is commonly judged. The contributors, eleven American academics and one West German, focus attention on a number of centrally important areas: changing perceptions of the GDR; the rôle of the state; the New Economic System; participation and ideology; official nationalism; intellectuals and system change; literature and political culture; foreign policy; détente and the military; international political communication; and the GDR after Ulbricht.

11   **German Democratic Republic.**
In: *The statesman's year-book: statistical and historical annual of the states of the world 1985–1986*. Edited by John Paxton. London: Macmillan, 122nd edition, 1985, p. 511–16. bibliog.

Provides facts, figures and names and covers several subjects including: history; area and population; climate; constitution and government; defence; international relations; the economy; energy and natural resources; agriculture; industry and trade; communications and transport; religion, education and welfare; and diplomatic representatives.

12   **German Democratic Republic.**
In: *The international year book and statesman's who's who 1986*. Researched by Mervyn O. Pragnell, Ann Patricia Rogers. East Grinstead, England: Thomas Skinner Directories, 1986. 34th ed. p. 206–09.

Supplies basic facts about the GDR.

13   **The GDR: the history, politics, economy and society of East Germany.**
Eberhard Schneider, translated from the German by Hannes Adomeit, Roger Clarke.   London: Hurst, 1978. 121p. bibliog.

This compact study contains chapters on nine aspects of the GDR: economic geography; history; state and Party structure; economy; education and training; social and trade union policy; ideology and society; foreign policy; and the German problem. He adopts 'a composite approach' to his presentation, 'combining the analysis and interpretation of the GDR as seen from within the system with a critical appraisal from a vantage point outside it.' This makes for an extremely readable and comprehensive account, although there is necessarily a lack of detail in a work of such brevity.

14   **The GDR today: life in the 'other' Germany.**
Hanns Werner Schwarze, translated and adapted from the German
by John M. Mitchell.   London: Wolff, 1973. 128p.

In its original German version, this book was written in 1970 in an attempt to
remove some of the ignorance about the GDR among West Germans, and others,
which was then perceived as one of the consequences of the intense Cold War.
Schwarze writes, not as an academic, but as a reputable television journalist
specializing in GDR affairs. In his preface to this English edition he says his book
may have contributed to 'the fact that a growing number of West Germans now
adopt a more realistic attitude to the GDR.'

15   **German Democratic Republic.**
Michael Simmons.   In: *Europe Review 1986*. Saffron Walden,
England: World of Information, 1986, p. 70–75. maps.

In a compact review of the GDR's performance in 1984 and early 1985, Simmons
stresses: the country's new self-assurance (as evidenced in visits to, or by, leading
political figures in Western countries); its 'intriguingly assertive' reappraisal of
German history; its uncertain relationship with the Church and with the
campaigners for disarmament and peace; the emigration of significant numbers of
GDR citizens to West Germany in 1984; the country's excellent economic and
industrial performance and its attempts further to improve it; and its special
trading relationship with West Germany. Key facts and indicators, together with a
useful business guide directory, are included in tabular form.

16   **Wissenschaft und Gesellschaft in der DDR.** (Science and society in
the GDR.)
Edited by Rüdiger Thomas, introduced by Peter Christian
Ludz.   Munich: Carl Hanser Verlag, 1971. 316p.

Contains contributions by several leading scholars and specialists on the GDR.
Ludz introduces the volume with a call for a critical and positive model of analysis
instead of the traditional normative anti-totalitarian model. Rüdiger Thomas
reviews the history of ideology, Manfred Rexin examines the development of
science and research policy in the GDR and Ludwig Bress considers the economic
system. Further studies consider sociology and social psychology, history, the
legal and educational systems, cultural politics and the depiction of the GDR's
history in its own schoolbooks. The general theme of this wide-ranging, detailed
and in-depth study of many aspects of the GDR is that this Marxist-Leninist
society must be taken seriously in its advances in academic, social and technological
fields.

17   **DDR.** (The GDR.)
Klaus Ullrich (et al.).   Leipzig, GDR: F. A. Brockhaus, 1986.
6th ed. 340p.

Presents good quality colour photographs depicting a wide variety of aspects of
East German life. The accompanying text is in German, Russian, French and
English.

5

18 **Überflug. Die DDR aus der Vogelperspektive.** (A bird's-eye view of the GDR.)
Lothar Willmann, text by Werner Rietdorf, Horst
Baeseler. Munich-Pullach, FRG: Verlag Ludwig Simon, 1983.
192p.

An excellent selection of aerial photographs which reflect the variety of rural and urban landscapes in the GDR.

19 **The GDR in the 1970s.**
Hartmut Zimmermann *Problems of Communism*, vol. 27, no. 2 (March/Apr. 1978), p. 1–40.

This extensive and informative survey begins with a long section devoted to the final years of the Ulbricht era. It then looks at developments in the 1970s ranging over a large number of areas including ideology, the economy, social and cultural policy and education. The general impression given is that the 1970s marked a turning point in that more low-key, less utopian, policies were pursued in many fields following Erich Honecker's coming to power in 1971. The number of students, for instance, was reduced as the vision of a scientific-technological revolution faded, whilst the ideal of a united socialist Germany gave way to the doctrine of 'delimitation'. The defensive term 'actually existing socialism' sums up the mood. Zimmermann does not feel able to draw easy conclusions. He sees many complexities in the situation in the GDR but foresees – correctly – a general pattern of continuity.

Geography

General

20 **Lake Stechlin: a temperate oligotrophic lake.**
Edited by S. Jost Casper. Dordrecht, The Netherlands; Boston, Massachusetts; Lancaster, England: Dr W. Junk, 1985. 553p. maps. bibliog. (Monographiae Biologicae, vol. 58).
Published to mark the Silver Jubilee of the setting up in 1959 of the GDR's Limnological Research Station at Lake Stechlin at Neuglobsow near Rheinsberg (north of Berlin), this volume brings together some of the most important papers to have been produced by researchers in order to present 'a first survey of the limnology of Lake Stechlin and its surroundings'. The book has four main parts: the historical background; the hydrographical, hydrometereological and chemical background; the biological background; and the metabolism of the Lake Stechlin area. There is an appendix in which taxa observed in the Lake Stechlin area are listed.

21 **The two Germanies: a modern geography.**
Roy E. H. Mellor. London; New York; Hagerstown, Maryland; San Francisco; Sydney: Harper & Row, 1978. 461p. 83 maps. bibliog.
Mellor provides a regional geographical study of both Germanies on the grounds that 'it seems unreal to study one in isolation from the other', largely for historical reasons but also because eventual reunification remains a possibility. Within this comparative approach, the author devotes individual chapters to: the state and population; industry; agriculture and forestry; and transport and the tertiary sector in the GDR. One chapter deals with Berlin, and a prognosis for the future of the two Germanies is added in a postscript. Overall, the book provides a very full and readable account.

22 **Eastern Europe.**
Norman J. G. Pounds. London: Longmans, 1969. 912p. bibliog.
This voluminous study of the geography of Eastern Europe (as defined by the
post-war re-drawing of political boundaries) includes a chapter on East Germany
(p. 189–294) describing in full the GDR's: physical boundaries; landform regions;
climate; vegetation; soils; population and settlement characteristics; agriculture;
industrial development; transport structure; and trade patterns. There is also a
brief section on West Berlin. The general conclusion is that the GDR is a strong
industrial nation by East European standards with creditable capital investment,
but with a poorly managed agricultural sector. The bibliography is arranged
thematically.

23 **Eastern Europe.**
David Turnock. Boulder, Colorado: Westview Press; Folkestone,
England: Dawson, 1978. 278p. maps. bibliog. (Studies in Industrial
Geography.)
In a review of the industrial geography of Eastern Europe, Turnock considers
various aspects of the GDR, including its system of economic planning, post-war
development and trade, as well as its utilization of human and industrial
resources. Attention is also given to problems of pollution and the environment.
The interesting, and perhaps surprising, conclusion is that recent economic
progress is not an intrinsically 'communist' achievement and would have
proceeded along much the same lines regardless of the political – not industrial-
geographical – motivation of 'ideology'. It is asserted that, given the large-scale
problems of industrialization in post-war Eastern Europe, similar policies on the
location of key industries, the concentration of modern technology and the
restriction of consumer goods may well have been pursued under non-communist
governments.

Maps and atlases

24 **Guide to atlases: world, regional, national and thematic; an
international listing of atlases published since 1950.**
Gerard L. Alexander. Metuchen, New Jersey: Scarecrow Press,
1971. 671p.
The main purpose of this book is to provide a listing of 'all atlases published since
1950, by whom and where, of what area, what type, in what language, and of
what size and date'. The section on Germany is on p. 297–312; the book is well
indexed. A supplement was published in 1977 by the same author and publisher,
in which atlases which appeared between 1971 and 1975 are listed; the section on
Germany is on p. 123–29.

25 **Berlin Hauptstadt der DDR. Buchplan.** (Berlin, capital of the
GDR: plan of the city in book form.)
Berlin (East), Leipzig, GDR: VEB Tourist Verlag, 1980. 64p. ca.
1:25,000.

A very handy plan of Berlin (East) in booklet form which includes a useful index
of street names as well as a plan of the city railway system. A section of valuable
information for the tourist is to be found on p. 52–64.

26 **Berlin Stadtplan.** (Berlin: plan of the city.)
Berlin (East), Leipzig, GDR: VEB Tourist Verlag, 18th ed. 1985.
1:25,000

A fold-out plan of Berlin (East) which includes, in English, a short history of the
city and information on the sights to see. An index of street names is provided for
easy referencing.

27 **DDR Verwaltungskarte** (GDR administrative map.)
Berlin (East), Leipzig, GDR: VEB Tourist Verlag, 1981. Scale
1:200,000.

A series of fourteen maps (of which eight had been published by 1981) showing
the regions into which East Germany is divided.

28 **German Democratic Republic.**
Bern: Kümmerly & Frey, 1986. 1:500,000.

A general road map in an easy-to-handle form.

29 **Kreishandkarten.** (District maps.)
Gotha, GDR: Verlag Hermann Haack, 1984-87. Scale 1:100,000.

A series of 191 maps showing the local districts into which the GDR is divided.

30 **International maps and atlases in print.**
Edited by Kenneth L. Winch. London, New York: Bowker,
1976. 2nd ed. 866p. maps. bibliog.

Section 430.2 (p. 124–25) is devoted to the GDR and includes maps in several
languages (German, English, French, Spanish, Russian, Czech and Polish) and of
various categories (general; town plans; official surveys; political and administrative; physical; geological; biogeographical; human; economic; and atlases).

Tourism and Travel Guides

31 **Reisen zu Luther. Wirkungs- und Gedenkstätten.** (Trips to Luther: places he lived, memorials.)
Paul Ambros, Udo Rössling, introduction by Gerhard Brendler. Berlin (East), Leipzig, GDR: VEB Tourist Verlag, 1983. 208p. bibliog.
A very useful guide for anyone wishing to trace Martin Luther's life in what is today the territory of the GDR. Twenty-six major places are listed and discussed alphabetically, and a further forty-eight excursions to places of relatively less importance are suggested. The book is well illustrated with photographs and some town plans. There is also a chronological table and two indexes.

32 **Weimar: Bilder einer traditionsreichen Stadt.** (Weimar: pictures of a town rich in tradition.)
Klaus G. Beyer, text by Herbert Greiner-Mai. Berlin (East), Weimar, GDR: Aufbau Verlag, 1979. 162p. of photographs (unnumbered) and 41p. of notes on the photographs.
Presents over a hundred and fifty photographs, many in colour, which provide an excellent insight into Weimar's cultural riches.

33 **Reisen zu Goethe. Wirkungs- und Gedenkstätten.** (Trips to Goethe: places he lived, memorials.)
Ingrid Burghoff, Lothar Burghoff, with an introduction and chronological table by W. Hecht. Berlin (East), Leipzig, GDR: VEB Tourist Verlag, 1982. 248p. map. bibliog.
An alphabetical listing of thirty-six places in the GDR where Johann Wolfgang von Goethe lived, or which he visited. The entries are well written and informative and the volume includes numerous photographs and some town plans.

34 **Deutsche Demokratische Republik. Verkehr.** (German Democratic
Republic: communications.)
Gotha, Leipzig, GDR: VEB Hermann Haack, 1979. 5th ed. 228p.
20 maps. 35 town plans. 18 'special maps'.
Provides all the basic information needed by the traveller in the GDR, including
lists of interhotels, petrol stations, airports and details about traffic signs.

35 **Fodor's Germany West and East 1986.**
Andrea Dutton (et al.). London, Sydney, Auckland: Hodder &
Stoughton, 1986. 534p. 4 maps. 6 town plans.
Under a tenth of this travel guide is devoted to East Germany, undoubtedly a
reasonable reflection of the limited extent to which the country has developed its
potential as a tourist attraction. In this respect, the guide rightly refers to East
Germany as 'a Sleeping Beauty, waiting for a prince to bring her wonders to life'.
The reader will find here a highly compressed but generally reliable introduction
to much that the GDR has to offer the visitor, written in an eminently readable
style.

36 **Sanssouci: Schlösser Gärten Kunstwerke.** (Sanssouci: castles,
gardens, works of art.)
Hans-Joachim Giersberg (et al.). Karl-Marx-Stadt, GDR:
Druckhaus Karl-Marx-Stadt, 12th ed., 1984. 136p.
This volume contains lavish colour photographs of Georg Wenzeslaus
Knobelsdorff's (1699–1753) magnificent Sanssouci Palace in Potsdam, now
lovingly restored. The accompanying text provides an informative and scholarly
guide.

37 **Literatur: Dichter, Stätten, Episoden.** (Literature: writers, places
and episodes.)
Herbert Greiner-Mai in collaboration with Wolfgang Schneider
and Horst H. Müller. Berlin (East), Leipzig, GDR: VEB Tourist
Verlag, 1985. 280p. 18 maps. bibliog.
This attractively produced and highly informative book represents the first
attempt to provide, for those tourists with an interest in German literature, a
comprehensive guide to the places in the GDR where some of Germany's greatest
writers (as well as some from abroad) lived and worked. In all, 211 such places
are introduced in alphabetical order, and their importance for particular writers is
succinctly outlined. Particular attention is paid to the major centres – Berlin
(East), Dresden, Leipzig, Weimar and Jena. Cross-referencing is made easy by
the inclusion of indexes. The book ends with: a list of all literary museums in the
GDR; a list of all theatres which boast a permanent company of their own; and
eighteen pages of maps which together cover the whole of the GDR. The text is
excellently illustrated by 105 colour photographs and 23 town plans, or maps,
showing centres of literary significance. This volume is essential reading for any
tourist with an appreciation of Germany's rich literary achievements.

Tourism and Travel Guides

38 **Ausflugsatlas. Umgebung von Berlin.** (Excursions in the vicinity of
Berlin.)
Erich Hobusch.   Berlin (East), Leipzig, GDR: VEB Tourist
Verlag, 3rd ed., 1984. 284p.

A valuable guide for the tourist who wishes to discover the area around East
Berlin on foot, by car, by bicycle, or by boat. Places to visit are listed
alphabetically and each is described in some detail (in German only). The volume
is liberally sprinkled with maps, town plans and colour photographs.

39 **Städte, die keiner mehr kennt. Reportagen aus der DDR.** (Towns
which nobody knows any more: reports from the GDR.)
Marlies Menge, with photographs by Rudi Meisel and a foreword
by Günter Kunert.   Munich: Hanser, 1979. 119p.

Menge, a well-known West German journalist, and her photographer colleague
Meisel, record the impressions left on them by numerous visits to the GDR. As
this title indicates, the emphasis is on the places which West Germans may have
heard of but have never seen, such as Perleberg, Ludwigslust, Zittau, Wittenberg,
Neuruppin, Güstrow and Warnemünde. The text focuses on aspects of everyday
life and on 'human interest' stories. The volume is superbly illustrated by Meisel's
photographs, many of which are in full-colour and are spread over two large
pages.

40 **Frommer's dollarwise guide to Germany.**
Darwin Porter, assisted by Danforth Prince.   New York: Simon &
Schuster, sponsored by Lufthansa, 1986. 518p.

The GDR is dealt with on p. 462–512 of this recommended guide book which
contains basic information for the tourist in East Germany.

41 **Travel guide: German Democratic Republic.**
Dresden, GDR: Zeit im Bild Publishing House, 1983. 216p. maps.

An attractively produced but inexpensive guide in English to the GDR. The
country is divided into ten sections and each is discussed in turn. The informative
text is interspersed with numerous photographs, many of them in high-quality
colour. A highly recommended volume.

42 **Eurorail guide: how to travel Europe and all the world by train.**
Kathryn Saltzman Turpin, Marvin L. Saltzman.   Malibu,
California: Eurail Guide Annual, 1986. 16th ed. 816p. maps.

A useful companion for the rail-user in East Germany (p. 456–64) and in Eastern
Europe generally (p. 448–94). It includes the departure and arrival times and
other details of trains running between major centres in the GDR, as well as
information about international trains running to and from the country.

Travellers' Accounts and Descriptions of East Germany by GDR Citizens, Émigrés from the GDR and Westerners

Accounts by GDR citizens

43 **So sehe ick die Sache: Protokolle aus der DDR.** (That's how I see it: reports from the GDR.)
Gabriele Eckart.   Cologne, FRG: Kiepenheuer & Witsch, 1984. 270p.

This is a series of edited interviews given by a variety of East Germans living and working in an agricultural community. Originally meant to be published in the GDR, they were thought by the authorities to be too critical and publication was abandoned. Seeing the author as an official GDR interviewer, the subjects probably engaged in self-censorship. The comments are, therefore, not very shocking to a Western reader but the volume remains of considerable interest.

44 **Die Pantherfrau. Fünf Frauen in der DDR.** (The panther woman: five women in the GDR.)
Sarah Kirsch.   Reinbek, FRG: Rowohlt, 1978. 121p.

A collection of interviews with a variety of GDR women recorded and edited by Sarah Kirsch (a leading GDR poet) before she left the country in 1977 to live in the West.

45 **Reise nach Rostock, DDR.** (Trip to Rostock, GDR.)
Irene Runge.   Frankfurt am Main, FRG: Suhrkamp, 1971. 343p.

In the summer of 1970 Irene Runge spent three weeks in and around Rostock recording individual interviews and group discussions with a wide variety of GDR citizens. In this book she presents the reader with selected transcripts of those recordings, arranging them around a number of themes in such a way that a

13

picture of the GDR's development emerges. As Runge frankly admits, the people she talked to emphasized what was new and positive in the GDR and were not inclined to reveal to a reporter from West Germany what their major problems and criticisms were. In this respect both Maxie Wander in *Guten Morgen du Schöne* (q.v.) and Gabriele Eckart in *So sehe ick die Sache* (q.v.) were more successful.

Accounts by émigrés from the GDR

46 Twelve years: an American boyhood in East Germany.
Joel Agee.   New York: Farrar Straus Giroux, 1981. 324p.

As the stepson of the well-known GDR writer Bodo Uhse and his American wife Alma, Joel Agee spent twelve years in the GDR, from the family's return to Europe after years of exile in Mexico (1948) until the breakdown of his parents' marriage and Alma's return to the United States (1960). In some ways his boyhood in the GDR reads like a boyhood anywhere – friendships, escapades at school, puberty and its problems, adolescent love – but some aspects (his conflic with the Free German Youth (FDJ) – the only youth organization permitted in the GDR and one to which the Party looks for its future members; his awareness of the often tense relations between Germans and Russians; the impact of Joseph Stalin's death in 1953; de-Stalinization; the Hungarian Revolution of 1956; and the official campaign against rock and roll) afford valuable insights into life in the GDR at the time. Given Bodo Uhse's position among the (privileged) cultural élite, it is no surprise that intellectuals such as J. R. Becher (the GDR's Minister of Culture), Wolfgang Harich and Walter Janka – both imprisoned in the 1950s for 'dissidence' – Erwin Strittmatter and Stephan Hermlin play a brief, but often revealing, part in these memoirs.

47 **Die da drüben: Sieben Kapitel DDR.** (On the other side: seven views of the GDR.)
Irene Böhme, with illustrations by Wasja Götze.   Berlin (West): Rotbuch, 1983. 3rd ed. 134p.

The author, once a student of journalism and then of drama in Leipzig, worked for eight years on the cultural weekly *Sonntag* and for ten years at the *Volksbühne* theatre in East Berlin before moving to West Berlin in 1980. This book represents her personal, highly perceptive account of several aspects of GDR life which are central to her own experience. She discusses how people in the GDR typically see visitors from West Germany and vice versa, her basic point being that Germans in East and West are growing ever further apart because of the different sociopolitical systems in which they live. Of equal interest are her comments on the relationship of the GDR worker to his or her job (it is the worker and not the customer who is king, for example, in a standard restaurant); the role of the state and of the Party; the part played by women; the significance of certain 'rules of the game' in the GDR (the importance of bartering, of one's class pedigree, of education, and of 'socialist consciousness'); and the treatment of creative artists. The main value of the book lies in the way it presents a frank and, the reader feels, honest picture of life in the GDR, often with a sharp eye for the conflict between ideology and reality.

48 **In welchem Land lebt Mephisto? Schreiben in Deutschland.** (In which land does Mephistopheles live? Writing in Germany.) Siegmar Faust. Munich, Vienna: Olzog, 1980. 186p.

A student of the University of Leipzig and at the Johannes R. Becher Institute of Literature, Siegmar Faust was a member of the Socialist Unity Party of Germany (SED) in 1965–68 before being imprisoned for anti-state incitement and finally expelled to West Germany in 1976. In this autobiographical volume, he recounts his experiences and contacts with other intellectual figures in the GDR and documents his conflicts with official state institutions from the university to the state police itself. An interesting account for those interested in cultural politics in the GDR. It also includes fascinating insights into the results of the Bitterfeld Way (the name given to a concerted, but largely unsuccessful attempt in the late 1950s to overcome the gap separating writers and workers) and into the ways in which Party functionaries operate.

49 **Ich bin Bürger der DDR und lebe in der Bundesrepublik: 12 Interviews.** (I am a citizen of the GDR and live in the Federal Republic: twelve interviews.) Edited by Barbara Grunert-Bronnen, with a foreword by Uwe Johnson. Munich: Piper, 1970. 130p. (Serie Piper, vol. 3).

This collection of interviews with twelve GDR citizens – eight men and four women, all aged between twenty-five and thirty-eight years and currently living in West Germany – offers a revealing insight into the feelings and thoughts of a particular group of émigrés: those who left the GDR because they felt let down by the country but who nevertheless retain enough respect for its positive aspects to make a return a distinct possibility. The interviews, which were conducted in 1969, can be seen as a useful corrective to the widespread impression that all GDR émigrés look on their country of origin as a detested prison which they are fortunate to have exchanged for a life of freedom in the West.

50 **Beyond the Berlin Wall: by refugees who have fled to the West.** As told to Erika von Hornstein, translated from the German by Lawrence Wilson, with an introduction by John Mander. London: Oswald Wolff, 1962. 254p.

The major part of this book consists of refugees' own descriptions of the events in their lives that led them to leave the GDR. They possess, therefore, considerable human interest, besides presenting a bleak picture of a repressive society. In her foreword, Erika von Hornstein gives some historical background to the refugee question, whilst John Mander considers the wider implications of a volume made up of a limited number of individual experiences. If he is correct in saying that they should not be dismissed as unreliable, his conclusion, written after the erection of the Berlin Wall, can be seen with hindsight to be wrong. Contrary to his prediction, the population has not indulged in large-scale passive resistance but come to some kind of accommodation with the régime.

51 **Vom 'Grossen Knast' ins 'Paradies'? DDR-Bürger in der Bundesrepublik. Lebensgeschichten.** (Out of the 'Big Prison' into 'Paradise'? GDR citizens in the Federal Republic: the story of their lives.)
Horst-Günter Kessler, Jürgen Miermeister. Reinbek, FRG: Rowohlt Taschenbuch Verlag, 1983. 222p.

Examines, and demolishes, one of the clichés about the two German states, i.e., that the West is a 'paradise' and the East is a 'living hell'. Its editors have interviewed a range of people of all ages and from all walks of life – a tramp, a social worker, a criminal, a lawyer and a schoolgirl – from among the three million people in all who have left the GDR for the West, either legally or illegally. Only a minority have found the promised land; more typical is a cautious reaction to their new environment. The interviews are supported by background historical information on the still considerable annual flow of refugees and on the impressions of West German teenagers of the GDR ('the GDR to me is a foreign country').

52 **Das rote Kloster: Eine deutsche Erziehung.** (The red monastery: a German education.)
Brigitte Klump. Hamburg, FRG: Hoffmann und Campe, 1985. 3rd ed. 335p.

Brigitte Klump's autobiography, dealing essentially with the period between 1953 and 1957 when she was a student in the Faculty of Journalism at the Karl-Marx-University in Leipzig, presents an insider's view of the 'red monastery'. This is the nickname attached to the Faculty on the grounds that it is only formally a part of the University and in fact operates, according to Klump, under the direction of the Central Committee of the Socialist Unity Party (SED) with the purpose of educating those selected to become an important part of the GDR's ruling élite. Her account includes valuable portraits of some of the most important people she encountered in the Faculty (for example, Reiner Kunze and Helga Nowak, both of whom now live as writers in West Germany; and Klaus Höpcke, currently the GDR's Deputy Minister for Culture) and also through her connection with the Berliner Ensemble (Helene Weigel, Wolf Biermann and Wieland Herzfelde). Klump's highly personal view of events, made all the more readable by her frequent use of direct speech and by the intrinsically dramatic nature of much of her material (notably the attempts by the State Security Police, or Stasi, to pressure her into becoming an informer), give this book an immediacy and feeling of authenticity which make it a valuable addition to the literature about the 1950s. Brigitte Klump moved from the GDR to West Berlin in 1957.

53 **Child of the revolution.**
Wolfgang Leonhard, translated from the German by C. M. Woodhouse, introduction by Edward Crankshaw. London: Collins, 1957. 447p.

A slightly abbreviated version of the German original (which appeared as *Die Revolution entlässt ihre Kinder* in 1955), this book contains Leonhard's account of how he, a convinced Marxist-Leninist brought up in the Soviet Union (1935–45), became so disillusioned with developments in Germany that he abandoned his career as a privileged Party functionary in the GDR and fled to Tito's Yugoslavia in 1949. Leonhard was part of the National Committee for Free Germany and one of the 'Ulbricht Group' which in May 1945 returned from exile in Moscow to set about building up a communist-dominated régime in the Soviet Zone. He therefore speaks with the authority of an 'insider'. His narrative makes for gripping reading, not least because he attempts to present each incident 'exactly as I saw it and reacted to it and felt it at the time' rather than colouring it with the judgements of hindsight. Some of his allegations are highly damaging, for example, Walter Ulbricht is quoted as saying of newly established local government that 'it's got to look democratic, but we must have everything in our control'.

54 **Die unglaubwürdige Gesellschaft.** (The unbelievable society.)
 Franz Loeser. Cologne, FRG: Bund-Verlag, 1984. 236p.

The author is a former professor at the Humboldt University in East Berlin who, because of his personal history and high political profile, was well-connected. Originally from Breslau, as a boy he went to England as a refugee, later serving as a soldier in the British Army in World War II. After 1945 he studied in both Britain and the United States where, he says, he was a victim of McCarthyism. In 1956, with the help of Harry Pollitt, Secretary of the British Communist Party, he went 'home' to the GDR. He appears to have finally fallen out with the Socialist Unity Party (SED) over the issue of nuclear war and whether it could be won by the 'socialist camp': Loeser believes there would be no winners. Loeser made his break in 1983 in New York, in a country whose system of society he had spent a good deal of energy denouncing. In the book he tells us that he has come to the conclusion that US bourgeois democracy is far more real than the GDR's version of 'socialist democracy'. He paints a very gloomy picture of the SED leaders as a self-perpetuating bureaucracy with little grasp of reality, the prisoners of their own propaganda. Their decisions, according to Loeser, are often irrational, based on dogma, political expediency or just personal whim. Parts of the book are lively and amusing; other parts aggressive and angry. Loeser wishes to be known as a democratic socialist who would argue the GDR has social and economic achievements to its credit but needs to be drastically reformed. The book is a mixture of biography, reminiscence, and analysis and puts forward a programme of essential reforms for the GDR. It should make Western visitors to the GDR consider, next time they meet an SED Party-liner, whether he really believes what he is saying. Loeser turned his back on 'real existing socialism' in September 1983, so the book is very relevant to the GDR as it exists today. He is a witness who cannot be ignored.

55 **Sag nie, du gehst den letzten Weg. Ein deutsches Leben.** (Never say you are taking the final way: a German life.)
 Franz Loeser. Cologne, FRG: Bund-Verlag, 1986. 235p.

This is the second book written by Franz Loeser [see also *Die unglaubwürdige Gesellschaft* (q.v.)] since his decision to break with the GDR in 1983. In this volume, he describes episodes in the different stages of his life. He starts in 1938 when, as a thirteen-year-old, he witnessed his father, a lawyer, being beaten up and arrested by the Nazis on 'Strasse der SA' in his hometown, Breslau. Most of Loeser's family, including his father, mother and younger brother, were victims of

17

the holocaust. He was lucky enough to be sent to England where he attended a Quaker school in Kent and was influenced by a left-wing teacher. He tells how he became a Marxist-Leninist and joined the Free German Youth (FDJ) organized by German communists in London. Loeser joined the British Army Medical Corps, was promoted to sergeant, and served in North Africa, Europe and, during the occupation of Japan, Hiroshima. In post-war America, he studied at the University of Minnesota but was forced to leave for Britain during the McCarthy purge. He studied and worked as a shop assistant and then teacher in Manchester, took part in communist activities and emigrated to the GDR in 1956. We learn of his contacts with Paul Robeson, of the unreal world of Walter Ulbricht and of the difficulties of being an academic in the GDR. This is a serious, emotional book, enlivened by its author's sense of fun and by some interesting photographs. However, one feels much has been kept back, and many difficult questions are not dealt with. What did Loeser think of the 20th Congress of the Communist Party of the Soviet Union (CPSU) in 1956 and the Hungarian Revolution (1956)? Was it not clear to him at an early stage that the great majority of the GDR people reject the régime? What did he think, or do, about the persecution of other Socialist Unity Party (SED) intellectuals?

56 **Durch die Erde ein Riss. Ein Lebenslauf.** (A rent through the earth: a life.)
Erich Loest. Hamburg, FRG: Hoffmann und Campe, 1981. 414p.

Inevitably, the main focus of Erich Loest's autobiography – which takes its title from a mawkish poem on the death of Joseph Stalin by Johannes R. Becher – is the author's fall from political grace which led, in 1957, to his being sentenced to seven years in prison for forming a supposedly counter-revolutionary group. However, the volume also provides an account of his youthful involvement with Nazism, his enthusiasm after the war for communist ideals, and the subsequent disillusionment which was triggered off by the abortive uprising of 17 June 1953. For all that has happened to Loest, this is an ironical, not a bitter book. The text is punctuated with examples of his earlier work, the cool prose of the present account standing in startling contrast to the Socialist Realist twaddle of the extracts from the early novels and stories with which he had made his initial impact. Since coming to the West in 1981 Loest has written energetically and produced two novels, *Völkerschlachtdenkmal* [The monument], (1984) and *Zwiebelmuster* [Onion pattern], (1985) as well as the collection of travelogues *Saison in Key West. Reisebilder* [Season in Key West: travelogues], (1986).

57 **News from Soviet Germany.**
Fritz Löwenthal. London: Gollancz, 1950. 344p.

The author of this book was a Communist Party – Kommunistische Partei Deutschlands (KPD) – Reichstag deputy and then an emigrant in the Soviet Union. In 1946 he became head of the Control Department of the Central Legal Administration of the Soviet Zone. This gave him the opportunity to see how the situation was developing throughout the Zone. Disillusioned, he fled to the West in May 1947. The book is based 'partly on official documents, partly on personal knowledge and investigation on the spot, confirmed by reliable information from other sources . . . from all parts of the Eastern Zone'. In some ways similar to Wolfgang Leonhard's *Child of the revolution* (q.v.) this book deserves to be more widely known.

18

Travellers' Accounts. Accounts by émigrés from the GDR

58 **A trip to the GDR: conversations and notes.**
Bernd Rabehl, translated from the German by Brown University
Collective. *New German Critique*, no. 2 (spring 1974), p. 4–15.

A former citizen of the GDR returns after an absence of twelve years and 'now his conceptions of socialism come face to face with the concrete results of socialist construction'. The article presents the results of his discussions with two men in positions of responsibility – a Party Secretary and the Economic Director of a factory – and it is clear there is no meeting of minds, largely because the experiences of East and West Germany diverge so widely. The notes which accompany the conversations are notably abstract and theoretical in nature.

59 **Von drüben nach hüben. DDR-Bürger in Westen.** (From over there to over here: GDR citizens in the West.)
Volker Runge. Wuppertal, FRG: Verlag 84 Hartmann & Petit, 1985. 107p. bibliog.

In the spring of 1984 over 20,000 GDR citizens moved to West Germany within a period of only a few months. Why the GDR authorities should have allowed such unusually large numbers of people to move at this time cannot yet be satisfactorily explained, but Volker Runge's book does present a useful summary of the main findings made by West German social scientists who studied the phenomenon. In essence, the researchers looked for answers to three questions: what kind of people are the émigrés?; how successful is their integration in West German society?; and how can they help to provide us with elusive empirical data on the GDR? Not all the results were predictable. For instance, less than a fifth of West German citizens who were interviewed gave their full support to the process of welcoming émigrés from the GDR; and it was the older generation who, despite having once lived in a united Germany, were least inclined to welcome their 'brothers and sisters' from the East. This result alone must raise serious doubts about the depth of West Germany's continuing, official commitment to the idea of German reunification.

60 **The Bialek affair.**
Stewart Thomson in collaboration with Robert Bialek. London: Allan Wingate, 1955. 203p.

Robert Bialek was an idealistic young communist who held posts in the Free German Youth (FDJ), the People's Police and in industry before fleeing to West Berlin in 1953. In best ghostwriter tradition, Thomson tells his story in the first person with the result that the events unfold in a dramatic, highly readable way. In these early postwar years Bialek came into contact with, among others, Walter Ulbricht, Erich Honecker (unfortunately spelled with two 'n's throughout the text) and Erich Mielke, so that a first-hand picture is provided of their activities at the time. As with all similar publications, the difficulty with this account is in deciding whether it provides a reliable source of information. There seems no reason why it should not be used cautiously alongside other works to gain an impression of certain people and events.

19

61   **Two interviews with Wolf Biermann.**
     Translated from the German by Jack Zipes. *New German Critique*, 10 (winter 1977), p. 13–27.

The strong opinions which emerge in these two interviews given early in 1977 shortly after his expatriation indicate that Wolf Biermann will be as politically provocative in the West as he was in the GDR. He delivers trenchant comment on the Stalinist bureaucracy of the GDR and its pursuit of the 'false goals of commodity production' as well as on the patronizing, misguided conceptions of left-wing West Germans about the GDR. He sets great store by the developing Euro-Communism movement in Western Europe, which he sees as a hopeful alternative to the fossilized socialism of the East. He indicates that he has no intention of being a passive observer in his new home but will become politically involved.

Westerners' accounts

62   **'Und willst du nicht mein Bruder sein . . .' Die DDR heute.** ('And if you won't be my brother . . .' the GDR today.)
     Timothy Garton Ash, translated from the original unpublished English version into German by Yvonne Vesper-Badal.   Reinbek, FRG: Rowohlt, 1981. 208p.

A thoughtful and at times provocative account of his experiences in the GDR by the correspondent of the London *Times*.

63   **Along the edge of the forest: an Iron Curtain journey.**
     Anthony Bailey.   New York: Random House, 1983. 352p.
     2 maps.

This book, parts of which were originally published in the magazine *The New Yorker*, is an account by an English journalist/writer of a journey which he undertook in the early 1980s along the length of the Iron Curtain. Long on descriptive detail but short on analysis, Anthony Bailey's narrative is frankly anti-communist in tone. Much of the book concerns his experiences on the western side of the German-German border, with visits to East and West Berlin thrown in, and includes the minutes of his discussions with local officials, hoteliers, border guards, American soldiers, and even one-time escapees, or exiles, such as the writer Thomas Brasch. An undemanding read which will interest those looking for a travelogue with a pronounced pro-Western and 'human interest' slant.

64   **Cold War in Germany.**
     Wilfred G. Burchett.   South Yarra, Australia: World Unity Publications, 1950. 258p.

In January 1946 Burchett was a member of the first group of Western newspaper correspondents to visit the Soviet Zone after the war, and one chapter of his book is devoted to his observations on the positive effects of land reform at that time. In all, Burchett spent over three years in Germany at the end of the war, and a central aim of his book is to expose what he sees, on the basis of his experiences, as a plot by British and American intriguers to turn the world against the Soviet Union while setting up a neo-Nazi régime in West Germany. In his view, Germany will one day be reunified, but how this happens will depend on the choice made between 'the peaceful way offered by the East or the military solution favoured by the men of Bonn'. A fiercely polemical work which is itself clearly a product of the Cold War it condemns.

65   **Notizen aus der DDR. Erlebnisse, Erfahrungen, Erkenntnisse in der unbekannten deutschen Republik.** (Notes from the GDR: experiences and findings in the unknown German republic.) Hendrik Bussiek.   Frankfurt am Main, FRG: Fischer, 1979. 314p. bibliog.

This book grew out of Bussiek's experiences as a correspondent based in the GDR between 1977 and 1979. It offers a comprehensive picture of life in the GDR, particularly in the 1970s, as seen from the vantage point of a critical Westerner.

66   **Die real existierende DDR. Neue Notizen aus der unbekannten deutschen Republik.** (The real existing GDR: new notes from the unknown German republic.) Hendrik Bussiek.   Frankfurt am Main, FRG: Fischer, 1984. 270p.

A correspondent in the GDR since 1977, Bussiek sets out, as in his first book, *Notizen aus der DDR* (q.v.), to provide his West German contemporaries with background information about the other German state. In doing so, he steers a clear course between anticommunist propaganda and uncritical praise, producing a text which is both balanced and lively.

67   **Reise in ein fernes Land. Bericht über Kultur, Wirtschaft und Politik in der DDR.** (Journey to a distant country: report on culture, economy and politics in the GDR.) Marion Gräfin Dönhoff, Rudolf Walter Leonhardt, Theo Sommer.   Reinbek, FRG: Christian Wegner Verlag, 11th ed. 1971. 147p.

In March 1964, the year in which this book was first published, its three authors travelled the length and breadth of the GDR for ten hectic days and then returned to the Federal Republic to write a series of articles for their weekly newspaper, *Die Zeit*, outlining their impressions of the country and its people. The articles provoked wide and often heated discussion, and when they were rapidly turned into a book, this became, for a while, a bestseller. Taken as a whole, the book is of interest today not least for the way in which it calls for a more open and positive relationship between the two Germanies, thus anticipating the *Ostpolitik* (Eastern Policy) put into effect by Willy Brandt and the Social Democratic Party (SPD) in the late 1960s and early 1970s.

68   **The other Germany.**
John Dornberg.   Garden City, New York: Doubleday, 1968.
370p.

Dornberg, a German-born American journalist (emigrated 1939), has travelled extensively in the GDR since 1960, observing events and recording conversations with citizens from all stations and walks of life. This volume is the fruit of this activity and provides a sympathetic and interesting review of East Germany's history, economic performance and institutions: the emphasis is on the state of the nation since 1961. Walter Ulbricht is seen as the 'labial proctor', sly and ruthless but not merciless, and fascinating characterizations of personalities and events are provided with a journalist's eye for living detail which is absent in drier, more academic works. The conclusion is that the GDR is a state enjoying the not uncritical loyalty of its subjects and that it is a far more frank and open society than we would expect from its reputation in the West. An extremely worthwhile volume for its attempts to reach the people behind the events and institutions.

69   **Wo Deutschland liegt. Eine Ortsbestimmung.** (Where Germany
lies: an orientation.)
Günter Gaus.   Hamburg, FRG: Hoffman und Campe, 1983.
288p.

When relations between the two German states were normalized in 1972, they stopped short of full diplomatic relations and each state is represented in the other's capital not by an embassy but by a 'Permanent Mission'. Günter Gaus headed the negotiations which led to agreement on these missions. He was formally accredited as head of the Federal German mission in East Berlin on 20 June 1974 and remained in post until the autumn of 1982. Thus, the reflections contained in this book are based on an almost unique personal and professional experience. One chapter is devoted to German-German relations which, so the author states, must be qualitatively better than the relationship between Washington and Moscow for German interests to be satisfied. Gaus is well aware of the implications of this claim but goes on to argue that West German policy towards the GDR can play a major role in heading off confrontation between the blocs and thus make an important contribution to peace. As a Social Democratic Party – Sozialdemokratische Partei Deutschlands (SPD) – appointee, Gaus naturally pleads a case which is not entirely supported by the present (1986) government in Bonn, arguing both that the concept of nation is not important and for a greater 'inner' recognition of the GDR.

70   **Behind the curtain.**
John Gunther.   New York: Harper, 1949. 361p.

An American journalist recounts his impressions, experiences and on-the-spot analyses of post-war Europe. The work contains some fascinating eye-witness observations on the Berlin Air-Lift of 1948–49 and of the mood and tensions of the time. The author explores, in particular, the sense of confusion and perplexity which seemed to surround both US and Soviet policy at a time when permanent division of Germany was not quite yet a certainty.

71   **The muted revolution: East Germany's challenge to Russia and the**
      West.
      Welles Hangen.   London: Victor Gollancz, 1967. 234p. map.

This book is principally a collection of journalistic impressions gained whilst
the author was an American correspondent in Germany from 1955 onwards. Its
contents range from a portrait of Walter Ulbricht to a description of the GDR's
agriculture. Hangen's thesis was that during the late 1960s the GDR was gaining
in significance as a state and developing a distinct identity. Hence, he was critical
of the United States and the Federal Republic for ignoring these facts. He also
claimed that the East German régime was becoming less tied to the Soviet Union
and that a day might come when both German states decide that they have more
in common with each other than with their principal ally. Whilst international
recognition of the GDR has shown the first part of this argument to be largely
correct, the political division of Germany and Europe seems to be little changed
from the position two decades ago.

72   **The other Germans: report from an East German town.**
      Hans Axel Holm, translated from the Swedish by Thomas
      Teal.   London: Penguin, 1971. 314p.

This book's purpose is 'to try to give a picture of people living together in a small
East German town, of their individual and not purely political ambitions and
problems'. The town in question is Neustadt-Glewe, and Holm's approach was
reportedly to conduct about 100, often lengthy, interviews during two separate
visits, amounting to seven weeks in all, which he made to the town in 1967 and
1968 (an unspecified number of the interviews were in fact conducted outside of
the GDR with refugees). The material was not recorded, or even written down,
during the course of the interviews, apparently because of the interviewees' fear
of surveillance. Instead, the author wrote it out immediately after each interview.
Despite his assurance that this method involved as little reworking and
manipulation of the material as possible (he admits to some rearrangement where
identification of the speakers had to be prevented), it seems doubtful whether any
interviewer could have such great powers of detailed recall as to reassure us
completely on this score. Nevertheless, an interesting general impression is
provided of the wide variety of views (ranging from communist to neo-fascist) to
be found in a small GDR community in the late 1960s.

73   **Germany's other half: a journalist's appraisal of East Germany.**
      Franz von Nesselrode.   London, New York, Toronto: Abelard-
      Schuman, 1963. 207p. map.

Von Nesselrode, a German-born American journalist, presents his reader with a
digest of information largely generated during a ten-day trip to the GDR in
August 1961. During this trip he travelled 1,000 miles in a Tatra 603 put at his
disposal by the GDR authorities, seeing several towns and cities including Berlin,
Leipzig, Dresden, Stalinstadt, Schwarze Pumpe, Schwedt, Bautzen and Rostock.
His account is therefore necessarily rather impressionistic but is interesting for the
way it challenges the grossly distorted view of the GDR which, in his view,
prevails in the West. He insists that East Germans are well-fed (indeed, over-
fed), that excellent health and education provisions exist, that an ambitious
building programme is under way, and that the much-vilified Walter Ulbricht is

'rather a well-intentioned person . . . who has the preservation of peace very much at heart', but he also attacks the absence of true democracy, the lack of political freedom, and the censorship of all news and opinion. An interesting, if rather superficial, early attempt to correct the 'Cold War' perception of the GDR in the West.

74 The three Germanies.
Bernard Newman.   London: Robert Hale, 1957. 252p. maps.

This book deals principally with the two German states but also has a chapter on the Oder-Neisse territories, which are the third Germany referred to in the title. This chapter is primarily a discussion of the problem of the Oder-Neisse frontier, less a report from Germany of the type that forms the majority of the book. Newman devotes almost half of his work to the GDR, reporting – almost entirely negatively – impressions from visits and giving certain factual information, for instance the prices of consumer goods. He concludes with an expression of fear that constant propaganda might win over the next generation for communism.

75 Beyond the Berlin Wall.
Bernard Newman.   London: Robert Hale, 1964. 187p. maps.

Presents a series of impressions gained from visits to the GDR. Besides descriptions of many parts of the country – the majority of chapters are centred round a visit to a particular area – there are accounts of conversations together with a certain amount of historical, economic and political information. Newman writes from such an extreme anti-communist bias that one is forced to the view that his conclusions are as unreliable as his use of German; he has Marx writing *Das Capital* (sic) and coins a new verb, to *republikflucht* (flight the republic).

76 Encounters in democracy: a US journalist's view of the GDR.
Margrit Pittman.   New York: International Publishers, 1981. 229p. bibliog.

The author has had a long experience of the GDR and spent six years there (1974–79) as correspondent of the *Daily World*. The book takes an entirely positive view of the country's development which corresponds closely to the GDR's own official self-image. As a Jewess, Margrit Pittman was forced to flee Nazi Germany and find refuge in the United States. She now confesses it to be 'the profound satisfaction of my life to see a socialist state rise on German soil, free of exploitation and racism'. She frequently quotes from her many interviews with GDR citizens, none of whom have more than relatively minor complaints about socialism in the GDR. The problem of 'dissidence' is only briefly mentioned, and the expulsion of Wolf Biermann in 1976 is justified on the grounds that he 'had, for years, expressed negative views of the development of the GDR and reviled its working class'.

77 Germany beyond the wall: people, politics . . . and prosperity.
Jean Edward Smith.   Boston, Massachusetts; Toronto: Little, Brown, 1969. 338p. bibliog.

Smith describes his highly readable book as 'a first-hand account of life in East Germany' as he experienced it in the spring and summer of 1967 and the spring of

1968. A Canadian academic based at the Center of International Studies at Princeton University, the author manages to combine the sophistication of the professional political analyst with the tourist's ability to be interested in, and surprised by, the details of everyday life. In diary-like fashion he describes encounters with politicians, functionaries, academics and 'ordinary' citizens of the GDR in a variety of locations such as Berlin, Blankenburg and Dresden. His main, fully justified conclusion is that the Western view of the GDR in the late 1960s is 'distressingly out of date', particularly in the way it disregards the country's remarkable economic progress since the building of the Wall. Equally well-founded is his view that this progress was achieved by a population which at the same time chose deliberately to disregard politics and the régime, although success did subsequently lead to 'a growing national consensus' and thus increased acceptance of the political leadership. For this reason Smith pleads for more Western contacts with the GDR, failing which a continuation of present trends must mean that the people of East Germany will move even further from the West. This analysis bears a striking resemblance to the thinking which, in the late 1960s and 1970s, led to the eventual abandonment by the Federal Republic of Konrad Adenauer's bankrupt 'policy of strength' towards a GDR which refused to collapse under such pressure, and to the adoption of Willy Brandt's celebrated *Ostpolitik* with its emphasis on preserving and strengthening the links between the people of East and West Germany.

78 **Leben in der DDR.** (Life in the GDR.)
Eva Windmöller, Thomas Höpker. Hamburg, FRG: Goldmann, 1980. 223p.

The authors, a husband-and-wife team, lived for two years in the GDR as journalists working for the West German magazine *Stern*. Their aim in this book is to help open-minded readers to understand ordinary life in the other Germany. The text is written in a lively journalistic style, but the excellent photographs are equally important for the way in which they capture so much of the everyday reality of the GDR.

Flora and Fauna

79 **The Country Life guide to the birds of Britain and Europe.**
Bertel Bruun, illustrated by Arthur Singer, revised edition in
collaboration with Lars Svensson, Håkan Delin. Feltham,
Middlesex, England: Country Life Books, rev. ed. 1978. 320p.
maps. bibliog.

A compact guide which contains an abundance of information on 'the breeding
birds, the regular visitors, and the casual visitors which have been recorded at
least five times this century'. The text, a map and an illustration of each bird are
placed together, making it relatively easy to identify and learn about those birds
which may be found in East Germany.

80 **The Hamlyn guide to the seashore and shallow seas of Britain and
Europe.**
A. C. Campbell, illustrated by James Nicholls. London, New
York, Sydney, Toronto: Hamlyn, 1976. 320p. maps. bibliog.

Intended to provide both layman and student with a simple means of identifying
most of the common marine plants and animals in the field, this guide can be used
to glean information on the form and habitats of a number of common species to
be found on the GDR's Baltic seashore. The book is easy to use, has a valuable
glossary of technical terms, and contains excellent colour illustrations.

81 **A field guide to the butterflies of Britain and Europe.**
Lionel G. Higgins, Norman D. Riley. London: Collins, 1970.
380p. maps.

This compact guide book describes and illustrates all the butterflies of the western
palearctic region. By referring to the distribution maps (p. 341–64) the reader can
identify which butterflies may be found in East Germany. The book includes 760
excellent illustrations in colour by Brian Hargreaves.

26

82   **Mammals in colour.**
Leif Lyneborg, translated from the Danish by Gwynne Vevers,
Winwood Reade.   Poole, England: Blandford Press, 2nd ed. 1977.
247p. maps. bibliog.

The first section of this guide (p. 13–100) contains colour illustrations by Henning
Anthon of the mammals of Britain and Europe. The second section (p. 101–243)
contains a short introduction to each of the systematic groups and an account of
each species, including information on geographical range together with appropriate
distribution maps.

83   **A field guide to the birds of Britain and Europe.**
Roger Peterson, Guy Mountfort, P. A. D. Hollom. Revised edition
in collaboration with I. J. Ferguson-Lees, D. I. M. Wallace,
introduction by Sir Julian Huxley.   London: Collins, rev. ed. 1965.
344p. maps. bibliog.

An invaluable short guide to 583 distinct species, including distribution maps
which show each bird's breeding range as well as its winter range. The book
contains over 1,200 illustrations.

84   **Flowers of Europe.**
Oleg Polunin, with line drawings by Barbara Everard.   London,
New York, Toronto: Oxford University Press, 1969. 662p. map.
bibliog.

Describing itself as 'the first attempt of its kind to describe and illustrate in a
single volume the commoner and most attractive seed-bearing plants to be found
throughout Europe', this volume indicates the exact distribution of each of the
major species by using the international registration letters established in 1949. It
also notes the most important uses of European plants. A total of 192 pages of
colour photographs are included (between pages 626–27).

85   **Trees and bushes of Europe.**
Oleg Polunin, with drawings by Barbara Everard.   London, New
York, Toronto: Oxford University Press, 1976. 208p.

Superbly illustrated with colour photographs and drawings, the book enables the
reader to identify 'all the native trees and bushes that grow wild in Europe to over
two metres' as well as those which have been introduced to Europe. A system of
symbols provides the key as to which trees and bushes can be found in central
Europe, including East Germany. A section on the uses made by man of selected
trees and bushes is of additional interest.

86   **Flora europaea.** (European flora.)
Edited by T. G. Tutin (et al.).   Cambridge, England: Cambridge
University Press, 1964–80. 5 vols. maps.

A work of immense scholarship which contains a classified description of all the
major species of European flora and identifies the particular countries in which
each is found, the two Germanies being treated as a single territory. This work is

indispensable for anyone with more than a layman's interest in flora. In 1982 D. M. Moore published his *Flora europaea check-list and chromosome index* (Cambridge, England; London; New York; New Rochelle; New York; Melbourne; Sydney: Cambridge University Press, 423p.) in response both to 'requests by many users of *Flora europaea* . . . for information on the sources of the chromosome numbers cited in that work' and also to the need for a basic checklist for the taxa recognised in the flora.

87   **A field guide to the mammals of Britain and Europe.**
F. H. van den Brink, translated from the Dutch and edited by Hans Kruuk, H. N. Southern, foreword by Roger Tory Peterson.   London: Collins, 1967. 221p. maps. bibliog.

A total of 177 species of mammal are illustrated in this guide (the excellent colour illustrations are by Paul Barruel). By consulting the numerous distribution maps as well as the text the reader may identify those mammals to be found in Germany and in East Germany in particular.

History

88 **DDR Werden und Wachsen.** (The inception of the GDR and its
    growth.)
    Akademie der Wissenschaften der DDR. Zentralinstitut für
    Geschichte. (Academy of Sciences of the GDR, Central Institute
    for History.) Berlin (East): Dietz Verlag, 1974. 576p.

This history deals with the period up to the aftermath of the Eighth Party
Congress of the Socialist Unity Party (SED) in 1971, the year in which Walter
Ulbricht gave way to Erich Honecker. According to the preface, the book's aim is
less to give a comprehensive history of the GDR than to concentrate on
significant events, with particular emphasis being placed on the 'creative role of
the working people'. Thus two pages are devoted to the shining example set by a
worker, one Frida Hockauf whose 1953 promise to work more effectively is given
pride of place in the seventh chapter of the second edition. Predictably, the 1974
GDR view of the world predominates throughout; Nikita Khrushchev only
achieves one mention and that merely in a reference to the 1961 Vienna summit.
Given its compartmentalization, this book is perhaps best used for reference
purposes when a GDR view of a certain event is wanted.

89 **The GDR and the German nation.**
    Ronald Asmus. *International Affairs*, vol. 80, no. 3 (summer
    1984), p. 403–18.

Examines the Socialist Unity Party's (SED) strategy of tracing the GDR's roots
deep into the German historical past and presenting the GDR as the continuation
of all progressive German historical traditions. This policy, though perhaps not as
new as the author suggests, is identified here as an attempt by a 'chronically
insecure political leadership to legitimate its own existence'. Various historical
arguments are adduced to underline this thesis and there is also an interesting
section on the rewriting of history to fit the new mould. However, there are

29

dangers too. The 'new socialist national history' is not taken very seriously in the West and the East German Party leadership needs to be alert to the risk that it could backfire on the SED.

90 **Geschichte der Deutschen Demokratischen Republik.** (A history of the German Democratic Republic.)
Von einem Autorenkollektiv unter Leitung von Rolf Badstübner.
(By a collective of authors led by Rolf Badstübner.) Berlin (East): VEB Verlag der Wissenschaften, 1981. 402p. maps. bibliog.

This volume deals with the years from 1945 until the 9th Party Congress of the Socialist Unity Party (SED) in 1976. Its 'scientific starting point', as stated in the introduction, is the work of Karl Marx, Friedrich Engels and V. I. Lenin. Besides the text, there is also a documentary section giving such information as the dates of the congresses of the various parties and statistical data in the form of diagrams. That the group writing the book worked under the aegis of the Council for History in the Higher Education Ministry says something about the nature of GDR historiography. Given this, it is not surprising that the text reflects official viewpoints on such issues as the 'German question' and the events of June 1953.

91 **Uprising in East Germany: June 17, 1953.**
Arnulf M. Baring, translated from the German by Gerald Onn, with an introduction by David Schoenbaum and a foreword by Richard Löwenthal. Ithaca, New York: London: Cornell University Press, 1972. 194p. Reprint of 1965 ed. bibliographical essay.

Baring describes both the developments leading up to the 1953 rising and the June events themselves. His conclusion is that the conditions outlined by Lenin as encouraging a revolutionary situation applied in the GDR in June 1953. His other major point is that they are unlikely to recur as Western inactivity both in 1953, and subsequently, led most East Germans to come to an accommodation with the régime. That the West did not exploit the diplomatic opportunities that followed the death of Joseph Stalin is the thesis of Löwenthal's foreword, which links the rising with the wider setting of world politics. Schoenbaum, too, takes this view whilst also stressing the subsequent stability achieved by the GDR. Baring's objective and factual account along with the documentation he provides make his book invaluable for those who want more than propaganda in connection with the June rising.

92 **Modern Germany: society, economy and politics in the twentieth century.**
V. R. Berghahn. Cambridge, England; London; New York: Cambridge University Press, 1982. 314p. bibliog.

Includes a generalized informative review of mainly economic developments in Eastern Germany from 1945, although its claim for originality in the broad coverage of different aspects of German history (society, economy, domestic and foreign policy) and in the presentation of statistical material is not especially borne out with respect to the GDR.

93 An introduction to the social and economic history of Germany.
Helmut Böhme, translated by W. R. Lee.   Oxford, England:
Basil Blackwell, 1978. 171p. bibliog.

As part of a general study of the economic history of Germany in the 19th and
20th centuries, the conditions in East Germany immediately after the war are
described in the broadest terms along with the abolition of the private capitalist
system. The coverage is somewhat superficial for the GDR and does not consider
in much detail the social implications of the economic re-structuring or
developments into the 1950s and beyond. The author's immediate concerns are
Allied policy at the time of the division of Germany and the implications of the
American economic aid programme for the Federal Republic.

94 Zone of silence.
Landrum Bolling.   In: *This is Germany*. Edited by Arthur Settel.
Freeport, New York: William Sloane Associates, 1950. Reprinted
by arrangement with William Morrow, 1971, p. 370–413.

A foreign correspondent for Central Europe in 1946–48, Bolling describes the
contradiction between Soviet reparations policy and the aim of winning over the
Germans to communism. Thus Germany remained both a material and moral 'top
prize' for the Russians. Bolling details the process of extraction of war booty and
of dismantling, as well as the establishment of the SAGs (Soviet Joint-Stock
Companies, set up as a means of channelling reparations to the USSR) and
conditions in the uranium mines whose output assisted the Russian atomic
programme. The final extent of Soviet reparations remains unknown, although
they transformed the face of the economy. On the political side, the initial soft-
selling of Marxism, the role of the anti-fascist committees and the policy decisions
of the Antifascist Democratic Bloc (called into being in 1945 by the Soviet
authorities to coordinate political activities) are reviewed, alongside the formation
of the Socialist Unity Party (SED). The key role of the mass organizations in the
campaign to win over minds is also considered and attention is given to
educational policy. According to the author, East Germany at that time was a
police state of harsh proportions.

95 The East German Rising.
Stefan Brant, translated from the German by Charles Wheeler,
foreword by John Hynd.   London: Thames & Hudson, 1955.
202p.

This account of the events of June 1953 begins with a survey of the history of the
Soviet Zone/GDR until that point. There follow graphic descriptions of what
occurred in various parts of the country, before wider conclusions are drawn. The
account is marred by exaggeration – one chapter is entitled 'Eighteen Millions
make history' – and the general tone is marked by Cold War rhetoric. The
conclusion that presses for a united Germany within the frontiers of 1937 is also
wildly unrealistic, even at the time it was written.

96 **The German problem reconsidered: Germany and the world order
1870 to the present.**
David Calleo.   Cambridge, England: Cambridge University Press,
1978. 239p. bibliog.

A united Germany has always been a problem to itself and its neighbours and the
German problem dominated world history from the late 1860s until after World
War I. By the late 1970s, though, it was generally held that the settlements
following World War II and the resulting division of Germany had largely
resolved the traditional German problem. Calleo questions this assumption,
pointing out that Germany may not remain in its present divided condition, and
seeks to analyse past and present aspects of the German problem in this light.

97 **D.D.R.: Allemagne de l'Est.** (GDR: East Germany.)
Georges Castellan.   Paris: Editions du Seuil, 1955. 414p. bibliog.
maps.

This early survey aims to give a description of various aspects of the GDR. It has
five major divisions: foundations; economic and political structures; the new
social order; the churches; and the climate – three chapters on law and justice,
education and culture. Although the tone is critical on occasions, as when the
judicial system is seen as being subordinated to political considerations, this book
is not marked by one-sided Cold War positions. Castellan is also perceptive; it is
particularly noteworthy that in the conclusion the division of Germany is seen as a
lasting phenomenon, not just because of the disagreements of the superpowers,
but also because differing attitudes are developing within the populations of the
two German states.

98 **La République Démocratique Allemande.** (The German
Democratic Republic.)
Georges Castellan.   Paris: Presses universitaires de France, 1961.
128p. map. bibliog.

Castellan's aim is to provide objective information about the GDR of the early
1960s. Hence he eschews polemical criticism, limiting himself to contrasting on
occasions ideal and reality. His five chapters are entitled: 'The dictatorship of the
proletariat'; 'The construction of socialism'; 'Industry and the working class'; 'The
new order in the countryside'; and 'The third (capitalist) sector and the middle
classes'. He admits in his introduction that regretfully he has had to exclude the
cultural dimension. His conclusion is that the GDR will remain and grow, not just
through external Soviet support but also through its own progress. Although this
view has been proved largely correct, Castellan's tendency to play down the
significance of the human exodus from the GDR was misguided, as the measures
taken in the year of the book's appearance show.

99 **East Germany.**
David Childs.   London: Ernest Benn, 1969. 286p. map.

This pioneering work appeared at a time when interest in the GDR was beginning
to grow in Great Britain and the book provided refreshingly objective information
over a wide area. It consists of twelve chapters dealing with a range of political,
sociological, economic and educational topics with most space devoted to the

Socialist Unity Party (SED) and the ruling élite. Since it is primarily a factual rather than an analytical work, it is to some extent superseded by events and subsequent publications but is interesting in that, since it was written when the GDR was still establishing itself, speculation about the country's future inevitably played an important rôle in it. The author's hopes that the GDR might be accepted as a legitimate state, not just through external recognition but also through internal reforms, might not have been entirely fulfilled.

100 **East Germany.**
Melvin Croan. In: *The communist states in disarray 1965–1971.*
Edited by Adam Bromke, Teresa Rakowska-Harmstone.
Minneapolis, Minnesota: University of Minnesota Press, 1972.
363p. bibliog.
In this perceptive essay Melvin Croan highlights a central paradox of the GDR which emerged in the 1960s but which, it might be argued, obtains even today. On the one hand, the 1960s must be seen as a period of sociopolitical stabilization and 'phenomenal growth' when East Germany became a major economic power with the highest standard of living in the communist world, a fact which Croan believes furthered 'the process of reconciliation between the population and the régime'. In sum, the decade saw such a radical transformation in the country's situation that the GDR 'may perhaps now appear to be a paragon of progress and possibly even a model of communist political development'. On the other hand, Croan tempers this optimistic view by insisting on the paradox that, despite undoubted progress, the GDR remains politically one of the most reactionary communist states. Evidence of this he sees, for instance, in the GDR's obstructionist attitude towards détente and in its hardline attack on Alexander Dubček's Czechoslovakia. Moreover, he believes that the use of political terror towards society may have been de-emphasized but it is held ready in reserve.

101 **DDR Geschichte und Bestandsaufnahme.** (GDR history and review.)
Ernst Deuerlein. Munich: DTV, 1970. 3rd ed. 367p. map. bibliog. (DTV Paperback Series, no. 347).
This volume consists primarily of a collection of documents preceded by an introduction, in which Deuerlein examines the origins of the division of Germany, the attitude of the GDR population to its rulers and the difficulties involved in trying to make the GDR comprehensible to Western readers. The documents themselves are divided into five chapters which are arranged chronologically and which contain an historical introduction to the years in question. They are largely from official GDR sources, that is to say Party and government declarations, although there are some critical comments from former GDR citizens and West German sources.

102 **Kurze Geschichte der DDR.** (Short history of the GDR.)
Stefan Doernberg. Berlin (East): Dietz Verlag, 1964. 558p.
This history of the GDR, sometimes described as 'official', takes as its starting point the end of World War II and concludes in the first part of 1964 before the fall of Nikita Khrushchev. It is arranged chronologically in four sections, generally

in accordance with the normal periodization of GDR history. Thus the first part deals with the 'anti-fascist democratic transformation' and the foundation of the GDR. The general tone reflects GDR thinking at the time: there is polemical criticism of the Federal Republic but the concept of Germany as a whole and the prospect of unity remain present. There is also criticism of Joseph Stalin and the 'cult of personality'. Although the book is in no sense objective – the intellectual opposition associated with the name of Wolfgang Harich (a young philosopher at East Berlin's Humboldt University arrested in 1956 and imprisoned for alleged counter-revolutionary activities) is seen as being in close contact with the American secret service – it does contain insights into GDR history, not least through its chronological table of events, as well as into GDR historiography.

103   **German history in Marxist perspective: the East German approach.**
Andreas Dorpalen, foreword by Georg G. Iggers.   London:
Tauris, 1985. 543p. bibliog.

The product of fifteen years of intensive research, this book is a scholarly, balanced and highly readable analysis of the interpretation of German history proposed by GDR historians. Dorpalen begins with a consideration of the institutional framework (Party, academies, universities) and of the theoretical presuppositions (Marxism-Leninism) in relation to which the development of GDR historiography since it was founded in the early 1950s must be seen. He then turns to an investigation, chapter by chapter, of the predominant view of successive phases of German history which GDR historians project. He concludes that one of the most striking aspects of GDR historiography is its compactness and cohesion. Its picture of German history is 'one of notable simplicity in its basic outline'. Dorpalen is not uncritical of this picture (for example, he rejects the Marxist-Leninist 'law of history' which accords to the masses the decisive role in history) but he rightly points to aspects from which Western historians have much to learn. A biographical index presents details concerning leading GDR historians.

104   **Potsdamer Schlösser in Geschichte und Kunst.** (Potsdam's castles in history and art.)
Udo Dräger (et al.).   Erfurt, GDR: Edition Leipzig, 1984. 208p.

A superbly illustrated history of Potsdam and its castles from 1660 to the present.

105   **One Germany or two.**
Eleanor Lansing Dulles.   Stanford, California: Hoover Institution
Press, 1970. 315p. bibliog. (Hoover Institution Publications,
no. 86).

The 1969 elections in West Germany brought to an end twenty years of Christian Democrat rule. Though Willy Brandt had been Vice-Chancellor and an innovative Foreign Minister in the Grand Coalition from 1966, his scope for manoeuvre had been limited by the need to make compromises with the senior coalition partner, the Christian Democratic Union (CDU), and by external events such as the Warsaw Pact invasion of Czechoslovakia. Thus his election victory raised many questions for future developments in West German politics and foreign policy. Eleanor Dulles, a veteran commentator on German affairs, particularly on Berlin, has taken this opportunity to assess German post-war

34

history to this point and 'to indicate the likely future direction of policy'. The author interviewed many distinguished people for this study, including Willy Brandt, and has produced an informed and generally balanced view. The chapter on the history of the GDR includes a personal account of a short visit to the GDR in 1967, which possibly served to reinforce American prejudice against communist countries at the time, but still makes interesting reading nearly twenty years later.

106 **The German Democratic Republic.**
Arthur M. Hanhardt. Baltimore, Maryland: Johns Hopkins Press, 1968. 126p. bibliog. (Integration and Community Building in Eastern Europe).

As part of this series Hanhardt's book is concerned with the GDR's developing role within the socialist community as well as with historical events in the country itself. How far the GDR has become part of the Eastern Bloc is shown in part through a tabular presentation of the number of bilateral treaties entered into with other socialist countries. By 1962, there were 116 with the Soviet Union alone. The text itself is arranged chronologically and deals reasonably objectively with a variety of issues and areas under such general headings as 'belief system' and 'social system' which are then subdivided. 'Basic values and goals' and 'identification with other countries' are two subdivisions under the belief system heading. Hanhardt's conclusion that the future of the GDR was likely to be characterized by political stability and modest prosperity has not turned out to be far from the mark.

107 **German Democratic Republic.**
Arthur M. Hanhardt. In: *Communism in Eastern Europe.*
Edited by Teresa Rakowska-Harmstone, Andrew Gyorgy.
Bloomington: Indiana University Press, 1979, p. 137–61.

Although beginning with a review of the formative historical framework of the Soviet Zone and political developments 1949–71, Hanhardt pays particular attention to the new Erich Honecker leadership and the changes since the demise of Walter Ulbricht, including the return to the ideological basis and the programme of socialist rationalization. He assesses the provisions and prospects of the 1981–85 Five Year Plan alongside socioeconomic difficulties derived from consumer expectations. Recent cultural policy is also briefly considered. Finally, after an analysis of the current policy of 'demarcation' vis-à-vis West Germany, he refers to the internal stabilizing effects of minimal inflation and a comprehensive welfare state but asserts that no prospective leader exists to move the GDR from its present status alongside the USSR.

108 **Western approaches to East German history.**
Russell Hardin. *New German Critique*, no. 2 (spring 1974), p. 114–23.

Hardin surveys principally the first generation of books on the GDR, including those by Ernst Richert, Jean Edward Smith and David Childs (1969), that went beyond Cold War tracts. His initial complaint is that many of them do not make for interesting reading, whilst more seriously he complains of a lack of analysis and rigour. More generally, he notes that few Western observers mention the considerable movement of population to the East, preferring to stress the exodus from the GDR, which is rarely analysed sociologically. Hardin also points out that developments common to all industrialized countries, for instance the drop in cinema audiences, are attributed by some to political factors when they occur in the GDR. Although he does hand out some bouquets, Hardin remains, in general, critical of most Western scholarship on the GDR.

109 Bureaucracy and revolution in Eastern Europe.
Chris Harman.   London: Pluto Press, 1974. 296p.

In this critical survey of Eastern Europe from 1945 to 1970 Harman concentrates on the crises in Soviet-dominated societies and sees Stalinism as having reproduced all the problems that plague the capitalist West: in particular, the modern industrialist working class created in the East will prove to be monopolistic communism's own gravedigger. The workers' revolt of 1953 provides the main East German evidence for this theory. Harman describes the causes and course of the uprising, relaying at length eye-witness accounts by Robert Havemann and Heinz Brandt. The two main causes are seen as the miserable standard of living and open division within the Socialist Unity Party (SED) itself reflecting a Kremlin power struggle in the wake of Stalin's death.

110   GDR: an historical outline.
Heinz Heitzer.   Dresden, GDR: Verlag Zeit im Bild, 1981. 266p. bibliog.

Written by the deputy director of the Central Institute of History at the Academy of Sciences of the GDR, this volume may be regarded as the 'official' interpretation of the country's own history. It sees history as proof of socialism's superiority over capitalism and of its importance as a means of preserving peace. Blame for the division of Germany is placed firmly on the Western allies, the demonstrations of 17 March 1953 are seen as a 'counter-revolutionary putsch' instigated by agents provocateurs from the West, and the building of the Berlin Wall in August 1961 is described as a necessary security measure which 'saved peace in Europe'. The volume is illustrated by excellent photographs.

111   Illustrierte Geschichte der Deutschen Demokratischen Republik.
(Illustrated history of the German Democratic Republic.)
Heinz Heitzer, Günther Schmerbach.   Berlin (East): Dietz, 1984. 361p.

An excellent selection of photographs, many in colour, enliven this history of the GDR.

112   Back into power: a report on the new Germany.
Alistair Horne.   London: Max Parrish, 1955. 323p.

Alistair Horne, the *Daily Telegraph* correspondent in Germany in 1952–54, concentrates mainly on the role of Konrad Adenauer, whom he evidently much admires as the architect of West German recovery and integration into the West. East German affairs, however, figure prominently in his account of the USSR's resistance to the European Defence Community Treaty, the re-arming of the GDR and the 'phoney' peace conference in Berlin in 1954. Against a background of economic repression and the June 1953 Uprising, Horne concludes that there is no evidence that the Russians contemplated German reunification at all seriously, their prime aim being the wholesale imposition of communism and the isolation of the Federal Republic from its Western allies.

113 **Profile of East Germany.**
Edited by Lex Hornsby. London: Harrap, 1966. 120p.
Claiming to be the first comprehensive and objective work in English on East Germany to be published since 1949, this is a very favourable review of achievements in the GDR in the fields of the economy, agriculture, science, education, welfare and culture. The book avoids controversy but supplies much detailed information with diagrams and photographs.

114 **Der dritte Weg: Die antistalinistische Opposition gegen Ulbricht seit 1953.** (The third way: the anti-Stalinist opposition against Ulbricht since 1953.)
Martin Jänicke. Cologne, FRG: Neuer Deutscher Verlag, 1964. 267p.
In this highly detailed and well documented account Jänicke – along with the Socialist Unity Party (SED) itself – includes any anti-Stalinist (but pro-communist) expression of opposition as belonging to the 'Third Way'. Finding evidence of anti-Stalinism in most areas of activity in the GDR, he concludes that opposition first manifested itself in bourgeois circles directly after World War II, shifted to the workers around 1953 and, from 1956, focussed on the intelligentsia, who have been the most consistent critics of the régime despite improvements in general living standards. An oppositional element within the SED itself is emphasized, with the moral for the West lying in the need to abandon conservative notions of an undifferentiated and totalitarian Party membership.

115 **The Soviet Zone of Germany.**
Edited by Henry A. Kissinger, Carl J. Friedrich. New Haven, Connecticut: Human Relations Files, 1956. 646p. bibliog. maps.
This extensive survey of the GDR of the mid-1950s is a typed monograph produced at Harvard University. It covers sociological, political and economic aspects of the GDR and is the product of a team of researchers. There is a considerable amount of documentary material, including a list of newspapers and biographies of leading GDR personnel. The tone is generally critical – 'art is the mere handmaiden of politics' with individuality thrown 'into the garbage-bin' – but there is much useful information, not least in the sections on the economy.

116 **The terror machine.**
Gregory Klimov, translated from the German by H. C. Stevens, introduced by Edward Crankshaw, Ernst Reuter. London: Faber & Faber, [n.d.]. 400p.
This book is the memoir of a Soviet officer who served with the occupation forces in Germany and defected to the West. It is, therefore, the 'inside story' of aspects

37

of this occupation, confining itself largely to the author's personal experiences. These include contact with the Western allies in Berlin and Frankfurt and a meeting with an old acquaintance who has become a major in the security services. Through its direct and vivid style, the book provides an interesting insight into the mechanisms of the occupation and into the mentality of the people operating it.

117 **Crisis and revolt in a satellite: the East German case in retrospect.**
Wolfgang H. Kraus. In: *Eastern Europe in transition*. Edited by Kurt London. Baltimore, Maryland: Johns Hopkins Press, 1966, p. 41–65.

Kraus describes in detail the events leading up to, and surrounding, the East German uprising of the 17 June 1953. He concludes that, despite subsequent Soviet and Socialist Unity Party (SED) contentions, the uprising was completely spontaneous and virtually unorganized, with the dominant participants being workers, young people and even farmers. The revolt is compared with uprisings in Poland and Hungary, where, however, unlike the GDR, intellectuals played a major part. In all three countries revolutionary situations developed at a time of anticipated liberalization and out of a crisis of authority, which, in Ulbricht's case, was resolved in his favour in view of the popular threat to the Soviet system.

118 **German politics under Soviet occupation: the unification of the Communist and Social Democratic Parties in the Soviet Zone.**
Henry Krisch. New York: University of Columbia Press, 1974. 312p. bibliog.

Krisch concentrates on providing a detailed account of the process which culminated in the unification of the Kommunistische Partei Deutschlands (KPD) and Sozialdemokratische Partei Deutschlands (SPD) in 1946. He divides his work into three parts: background; the development of the two parties until autumn 1945; and the subsequent campaign for unification. From his study he draws general conclusions about the development of German left-wing politics, the nature of occupation politics and Soviet foreign policy. Krisch's view is that in general the SPD was not opposed to unification but disliked the methods used. On occupation policy, he believes that the success of the Soviet Union on this issue of unification in its own zone raised worries elsewhere and prevented the all-German dimension of its policy being realized. As for Soviet foreign policy, Krisch does not believe it was clearly defined but developed as a result of this kind of disappointment.

119 **The Germans in the Cold War.**
Richard Löwenthal. In: *This is Germany*. Edited by Arthur Settel. Freeport, New York: William Sloane Associates, 1950. Reprinted by arrangement with William Morrow, 1971. p. 40–73.

Löwenthal, former Reuters correspondent and London *Observer* journalist for German affairs from 1948, describes the rapid eclipse of communist popularity in the Eastern Zone after the end of World War II, which he attributes to the ferocity of the war with Russia. Only the unsentimental managerial classes and the officer corps, who have been deliberately wooed by the Russians as potential moral allies, looked favourably upon the prospect of an alliance between German efficiency and Soviet might. Also documented are the enforced fusion of the Social Democratic and Communist Parties, the role of the Social Democratic Party (SPD) 'revolt' in Berlin in 1946, and the implacable hostility of Kurt Schumacher, leader of the SPD in the Western zones of occupation, to proposals for 'national unity' with the communist régime. With the Berlin Blockade (1948–49), the Paris Conference of 1949 and the formation of the Western Bizone by joining together the American and British Zones of Occupation, the partitioning of Germany became complete and the Cold War a fact of life, with the Oder-Neisse line established as a permanent boundary and the East German government growing more narrowly communist than nationalistic.

120 **Eastern Europe in transition.**
Edited by Kurt London. Baltimore, Maryland: Johns Hopkins Press, 1966. 364p.

These proceedings from the Fifth International Conference on World Politics, which was held in 1965, include two major contributions specifically on the GDR. Wolfgang Kraus analyses the revolt of the 17 June 1953 and compares it with similar uprisings in other East European countries, while Karl Thalheim reviews the development of the East German economy in the framework of the Soviet Bloc, including the New Economic System of 1963. Thalheim argues that the system does not fundamentally alter the basis of the socialist economy, or its shortcomings, and that economic links with the USSR will intensify. In a third contribution, Boris Meissner looks at the Soviet-Eastern European pact and alliance system, into which the GDR, of course, is integrated. He itemizes the main provisions of treaties concluded in the early 1960s and presents them as a consolidation of Soviet hegemony.

121 **The German Democratic Republic from the sixties to the seventies: socio-political analysis.**
Peter Christian Ludz. Harvard, Massachusetts: Center for International Affairs Harvard University, 1970. 99p. bibliog. (Occasional Papers in International Affairs, no. 26).

Ludz's starting-point is the attempts made in the 1960s by the GDR authorities to modernize their country. He examines general social and political change in that decade, concluding that with economic progress a limited national consciousness has developed. Consideration is also given to changes within the Socialist Unity Party (SED) and the developing position of the GDR within the East European pact system. The author makes the point, however, that there has been no real political change, with the SED remaining in tight control. It is asserted that, despite the economic stability achieved, the problem of political instability remains so that consolidation is sought through gaining a position of importance within the Eastern bloc and through international recognition. Ludz's account provides a succinct summary of a particular period of the GDR's history.

History

122 East Germany.

Martin McCauley.   In: *Communist power in Europe*. Edited by
Martin McCauley. London: Macmillan, 1977, p. 58–72.

Details the Allied plans for Germany as discussed during the war and subsequent
political events in the Soviet Occupation Zone prior to the national division. The
emphasis is on the roles of the German parties and the Soviet promotion of the
Socialist Unity Party (SED). McCauley concludes that, without Soviet pressure, a
social-democratic German state would probably have emerged in the Russian
Zone since most political parties were in favour of socialism. The leaders of the
Christian Democratic Union (CDU) and the Liberal Democratic Party of
Germany (LDPD) realized their common interests too late in the day to influence
events, although the Soviets themselves might have gained more in the way of
economic development for the GDR and provoked less animosity if the SED's
ascent to power had been more gradual.

123 The German Democratic Republic since 1945.

Martin McCauley.   London: Macmillan, 1983. 282p. 3 maps.
bibliog.

In under 200 pages, McCauley undertakes an ambitiously comprehensive survey
of all the major features of the GDR's development from 1945 to mid-1982. To
this he adds a chronological table (70p.) which lists the most important events
which took place in that period. The author treats the GDR not in isolation but
within the context of East-West rivalries, offering especially useful insights into
the persistent 'tension between the German and Soviet traditions in the GDR'.
While stressing the country's successes in the economic and social spheres, the
author criticizes particularly its 'new ruling class', bureaucratic centralism, and the
powerful pressure to conform. He concludes with a gloomy economic prognosis
for the 1980s, the likely effect of which will be 'discontent but not enough to
threaten the stability of the state'.

124 Public opinion in semi-sovereign Germany.

Edited by Anna J. Merritt, Richard L. Merritt.   Urbana, Illinois;
Chicago; London: University of Illinois Press, 1980. 273p.

This report on public opinion surveys conducted for the American High
Commission for Germany includes surveys of GDR opinion which were taken in
West Berlin among GDR citizens visiting that part of the city. The period covered
is from 1949 to 1955. The acknowledged problem with these surveys is that there
is no way of knowing how representative they were of public opinion throughout
the GDR at that time. The picture that emerges is that in the early 1950s the
majority of the GDR population was alienated from its rulers, was distrustful of
the Soviet Union and wanted the West to take a tough line.

125 The return of Germany: a tale of two countries.

Norbert Muhlen.   London: Bodley Head, 1953. 310p.

This book, although dated, is of historical interest. It deals with the whole of
Germany with a number of chapters, or parts of chapters, devoted to the GDR.
The main thesis in the chapter 'East Germany's Red Reich' appears to be not
only that the GDR maintains a totalitarian form of government comparable to

National Socialism but also that former Nazis hold considerable power and influence. Another chapter 'Soviet Man of German Make' takes issue with what are seen as the heinous educational and cultural policies of the GDR. In the conclusion Muhlen sees Germany as the stage of the major confrontation between the world's leading ideologies. Although he sees failings in West Germany he believes it essential that the Western side prevails; what is more the United States should promise to 'liberate the oppressed' and back up these promises by 'actions'.

126 **The Eastern Zone and Soviet policy in Germany 1945–1950.**
     J. P. Nettl.   London: Oxford University Press, 1951. 324p. maps.
This impressively comprehensive survey of the immediate postwar years deals firstly with the collapse of the old order in Germany and with Allied plans for the country. The major part of the work is then devoted to developments in politics, administration and the economy in the Soviet Zone and the GDR. Nettl concludes that the Soviets were more interested in furthering national interests than applying Marxist-Leninist ideology, as the primacy given to reparations shows. Thus he sees certain paradoxes in the GDR of 1950, for instance the appeal to bourgeois nationalism in the Socialist Unity Party's (SED) campaign for national unity – something that would expand Soviet influence westwards – and the related fact that the GDR remains a middle-class society. Nevertheless, he does perceive tendencies towards what was to occur subsequently, the establishment of the typical East European pattern in the GDR.

127 **Germany divided.**
     Terence Prittie, introduction by Sir Ivone Kirkpatrick.   London:
     Hutchinson; Boston, Massachusetts: Little Brown, 1961. 381p.
     map. bibliog.
Written by one of Britain's leading journalists specializing in German affairs, this book reflects upon many aspects of German history and Germany's division. As a regular visitor to Germany since the 1930s, though not always a voluntary one (the author was a Prisoner of War), Prittie provides a perceptive analysis liberally sprinkled with personal anecdotes and reminiscences. His account of the position of students and young people in the GDR in the 1950s is one of the most readable that is available in English. Prittie also devotes a long section to the case of the alleged double defector, Dr Otto John, based partly on an interview with John and his wife. Prittie regards John's strange story as an example of the 'stress imposed on every thinking German by the unnatural division of his country'.

128 **Twenty-five years on: the two Germanies 1970.**
     Stanley Radcliffe.   London: Harrap, 1972. 254p. bibliog.
In this standard text book for students of both West and East Germany, Radcliffe describes both succinctly and comprehensively key aspects of the GDR at the very end of the Ulbricht era, including: its constitution and political structure; the basic organization of labour; natural resources and their exploitation; economic policy; welfare provision; education; and cultural policy. A concluding section 'taking stock' concentrates on the development of inter-German relations and the ramifications of a possible rapprochement at the moment when *Ostpolitik* was poised for its major breakthrough.

41

History

129 **Das zweite Deutschland. Ein Staat, der nicht sein darf.** (The second
   Germany: a state which should not be.)
   Ernst Richert.   Frankfurt am Main, Hamburg, FRG: Fischer,
   1966. 257p. bibliog.
Despite the second part of the title this book is anything but a Cold War tract
aimed at vilifying the GDR. Richert is merely concerned to stress the ideal of
German unity and the final part of the book postulates possible ways of
overcoming division, some of the suggestions prefiguring aspects of Brandt's
Ostpolitik. The major part of the text is a remarkably objective picture of the
GDR dealing with a wide variety of topics, including the role of the Party, the
attitudes of youth, and the system of economic planning. Richert is at pains to
stress that the GDR is not as Western propagandists imagine it; most people have
come to terms with their lot and the system functions reasonably well. This was
pioneering work in its time and remains well worth reading.

130 **Der 17. Juni.** (The 17th of June.)
   Curt Riess.   Berlin (West): Ullstein, 1954. 260p. map.
This book provides a dramatic reconstruction of the June 1953 Uprising, told
primarily in the present tense and relating the activities of individuals involved,
who range from participants in the uprising to Walter Ulbricht and Otto
Grotewohl. The result is interesting reading but with a feeling too that one is as
much in the world of Frederick Forsyth as in that of historical reality. In so far as
Riess analyses events, he exaggerates their significance, seeing in the June days
something akin to the beginning of the end of SED rule.

131 **Geschichte der SED. Abriss.** (History of the SED: a sketch.)
   Authors' collective led by Günter Rossmann.   Berlin (East):
   Dietz, 1978. 677p.
The official history of the Socialist Unity Party (SED).

132 **How communist states change their rulers.**
   Myron Rush.   Ithaca, London: Cornell University Press, 1974.
   346p.
The unsuccessful attempts to unseat Ulbricht in 1953 and 1956 and his eventual
replacement by Honecker are discussed in two of the book's twelve chapters.
Rush interprets Ulbricht's downfall as the result, above all, of the Soviet Union's
dissatisfaction with his policies (for instance, with his obstruction of Soviet foreign
policy) and, though to a lesser extent, of the manoeuvrings of a conspiratorial
group of Socialist Unity Party (SED) leaders – Erich Honecker, Willi Stoph and
Paul Verner.

133 **From Hitler to Ulbricht: the communist reconstruction of East
   Germany, 1945–46.**
   Gregory W. Sandford.   Princeton, New Jersey: Princeton
   University Press, 1983. 313p. bibliog.
This volume deals with the first year of Soviet occupation in Germany describing
such events as the land reform of 1946 and the expropriation of major industry.

Besides noting that similar events occurred in other European states within the orbit of Soviet influence, Sandford is concerned with the question whether the kind of 'people's democracy' created in the Soviet Zone was one brief stage on the inevitable road to communism, as it was perceived by the Western allies, or whether it was a model for a possible united Germany, as some historians claim. Although he is critical of Western occupation policy for being too defensive, Sandford is unwilling to endorse the second view. The 'democratic' elements introduced in the Soviet Zone were imposed from above and did not come from the people themselves. Hence the Western allies were justified in their suspicions.

134 **Russian Zone.**
Gordon Schaffer.   London: George Allen & Unwin, 1947.
2 maps.
Describing his book as 'a record of conditions I found in the Soviet-occupied zone of Germany during a stay of ten weeks', Schaffer presents the reader with a carefully documented account of his findings. Of particular interest are the numerous interviews (for example, with Fritz Selbmann, Minister of Economic Planning in Saxony) from which he quotes liberally. He finds in the zone a genuine sense of freedom following years of Nazi oppression but argues that the majority of Germans have learnt nothing from their experiences and would still follow any demagogue who knew how to manipulate them. Schaffer is very sympathetic towards Russian attempts to build a new Germany but does not play down the problems involved. Only very occasionally does he seem, with hindsight, too optimistic (he predicts, for instance, that widespread fraternization between Russians and Germans has and will continue to break down barriers between the two peoples). The book contains a wealth of useful detail on: the rebuilding of Dresden; the restructuring of the Zone's economy and industry (as well as agriculture); the process of denazification; the growth of political life; the role of trade unions and cooperatives; the reshaping of the education system; and the problem of rationing. An important contemporary source on the origins of the GDR.

135 **The wartime alliance and the zonal division of Germany.**
Tony Sharp.   Oxford: Clarendon Press, 1975. 220p. maps. bibliog.
How was Germany divided? It is easy to overlook the fact that protracted negotiations took place during the course of World War II in order to arrive at the map of Germany as it looks today. This volume examines these negotiations in detail and sets them in their military context. The author has made extensive use of British Foreign Office and Cabinet papers, and has conducted a number of interviews with officials and participants in the negotiations. One chapter deals with the Western withdrawal from the Soviet Zone and entry into Berlin and highlights, in particular, the different emphasis of British and American policy on this question.

136 **The German question 1945–1973; continuity in change.**
John K. Sowden. Bradford, England: Bradford University Press,
in association with Crosby Lockwood Staples (London), 1975.
404p. bibliog.

This most painstaking and thorough analysis of the situation in Germany since
World War II, succeeds in presenting a handy, if lengthy, reference book for the
newcomer to the study of modern Germany. Many will find this volume
particularly welcome for its clear exposition of the territorial, historical and
national factors involved in the German question, as a springboard for further
study. The last three chapters deal in detail with the treaties making up Willy
Brandt's *Ostpolitik*. A useful post-postscript takes account of Brandt's resignation
(following the revelation that his personal assistant had long been an East
German spy) and the 1974 amendments to the GDR constitution, which
effectively ended the constitutional endorsement of the idea of one German
nation.

137 **17. Juni 1953. Arbeiteraufstand in der DDR.** (17th June 1953: the
Workers' Uprising in the GDR.)
Edited by Ilse Spittmann, Karl Wilhelm Fricke. Cologne, FRG:
Edition Deutschland Archiv im Verlag Wissenschaft und Politik,
1982. 224p. bibliog.

This book is not simply an historical account of the events of June 1953. A section
entitled 'Analyses' includes essays on such subjects as Soviet policy towards
Germany immediately prior to the rising, the judicial consequences of the rising
and its portrayal in literature. There follows a section of reports and reflections by
people in, or near, the events themselves. These include eye-witness accounts by
strikers and comment from, among others, Robert Havemann and Alfred
Kantorowicz. The volume is rounded off by a varied documentation and a
chronicle of relevant events from June 1952 to September 1953. The documentation, besides containing newspaper texts of the time, embraces cultural policy and
the role of RIAS (Radio in the American Sector), often seen in the GDR as a
fermenter of the revolt.

138 **Sozialismus in einem halben Land.** (Socialism in half a land.)
Dietrich Staritz. Berlin (West): Wagenbach, 1976. 197p.

Analysing the transformation of the Soviet Zone into a people's democracy,
Staritz demonstrates how the Kommunistiche Partei Deutschlands (KPD) evolved
its strategies and rapidly harnessed the Sozialdemokratische Partei Deutschlands
(SPD) in a hegemony of socialist parties. Suggesting that the prevailing Western
view of an 'enforced' unification between the KPD and SPD underestimates the
support for merger at factory level, he argues that the conflict between mass
democracy and centralism afforded the Socialist Unity Party (SED) a dilemma in
its efforts to gain support from the workers while at the same time regarding itself
as a Leninist new-type party and the avant-garde of socialist transformation. The
sudden push towards people's democracies from 1948, however, was not – as is
often argued – so much a reaction to anti-Soviet US policies (which extended to
before the war) as a product of the internal dynamics of the socialist controlled
countries themselves. By 1952 the SED had attained its goal of centralist control
through economic planning, a bureaucratic apparatus, a cadre system and, perhaps,

most important of all, a functionalist trade union organization. The same author has also written an excellent history of the GDR entitled *Geschichte der DDR 1949-1985* [History of the GDR, 1949-85] (Frankfurt am Main, FRG: Suhrkamp, 1985. 278p. bibliog).

139 Socialism with a German face: the state that came in from the cold.

Jonathan Steele. London: Jonathan Cape, 1977. 256p.

The first half of this book is devoted to an account of the development of the GDR, beginning with the founding of the German Communist Party in the aftermath of World War I. In the second part the author investigates four themes: the realities of 'People's Democracy'; leisure, crime and private life; social services; and the self-image of the GDR. Steele praises the GDR's achievements in such fields as agriculture, education, medical care, and women's rights, but he is critical of other aspects. For example, the will of the Socialist Unity Party (SED) may not be challenged and the Berlin Wall is 'a humiliating admission of failure which to this day remains one of the ugliest sights in Europe'. He sees such faults as 'the products of special conditions and the continuing confrontation with West Germany', the implication being that, once these factors no longer obtain, so the defects will disappear. This is a somewhat surprising judgement even from an author who takes an unusually sympathetic view of the GDR.

140 Socialism in Germany: a short history of the German Democratic Republic.

Ernie Trory. Brighton, England: Crabtree, 1979. 80p.

The author's aim is to help 'to refute the lies that are constantly being circulated in this country (UK) by the mass media' about the GDR. His pamphlet covers the history of the GDR until 1978.

141 The GDR under Honecker 1971–1981.

Edited by Ian Wallace. Dundee, Scotland: GDR Monitor, 1981. 116p. (GDR Monitor Special Series, no. 1).

The nine papers collected here were originally delivered at an international conference on the GDR held at the University of Dundee in 1981. They deal with: social policy; the politics of leisure; cultural politics; Volker Braun's work of the 1970s; the dissident thinker Rudolf Bahro, the publication of whose book *Die Alternative* (*The Alternative in Eastern Europe*, translated from the German by David Fernbach, London: New Left Books, 1978) (q.v.) in the West for the first time in 1977 led to his imprisonment and subsequent emigration to West Germany [see also David Bathrick's 'The politics of culture' (q.v.) and 'Rudolf Bahro's *Neo Leninism* in context' (q.v.)]; the GDR's status as a 'nation'; the division of German literature; women and work; and women as social visionaries in the GDR literature of the 1970s.

142 The GDR in the 1980s.

Edited by Ian Wallace. Dundee, Scotland: GDR Monitor, 1984. 154p. (GDR Monitor Special Series, no. 4).

This volume contains the nine papers delivered at an international conference on the GDR held at the University of Dundee in 1983. Four of these are in English:

History

'The GDR and the German Question in the 1980s'; 'The GDR's established authors and the challenge of the 1980s'; 'The nature of dissidence in the GDR'; and 'The GDR and the states of Southern Africa in the 1980s'. The contributions in German deal with: Christa Wolf's prose-work *Kassandra* (Berlin (East): Aufbau, 1983); lyric poetry in the 1980s; Sarah Kirsch's volume of poetry *Erdreich* (Stuttgart, FRG: Deutsche Verlags-Anstalt, 1982); and the GDR's energy policy. A short story by Joachim Walther is also included.

143 **Kleine Geschichte der DDR.** (Short history of the GDR.)
Hermann Weber. Cologne, FRG: Edition Deutschland Archiv im Verlag Wissenschaft und Politik, 1980. 200p. bibliog.

Each of the seven chapters of this book is set out according to a fixed pattern. They commence with a précis of major developments followed by a chronicle of principal events before turning to a number of themes relevant to the years under discussion. Another feature is the incorporation of texts and documents, one example being Ulbricht's criticism of Stalin in 1956, another the words and music of Louis Fürnberg's 1949 anthem which claimed not only that the Party is always right but also that it gave 'sun and wind'! Towards the end of the book there are brief biographies of the major figures in the history of the GDR. This work provides a useful introduction to the history of the GDR, although the sceptical tone would not endear it in the GDR itself.

144 **DDR Grundriss der Geschichte 1945–81.** (An outline history of the GDR, 1945–81.)
Hermann Weber. Hanover, FRG: Fackelträger-Verlag, 1982. 3rd ed. 242p. bibliog.

The first two-thirds of Weber's work is an historical survey divided into six chapters more or less in line with the normal periodization of GDR history. Each chapter is sub-divided into two parts: the political system; and the social order. Within the second category, such topics as educational and cultural policy are discussed. The final third of the book consists of short biographies of approximately 100 major figures in GDR history and a chronology of events. Weber writes in a clear informative way so that his work provides an excellent introduction to the subject. At the same time, he does not hide his critical stance towards the GDR. Despite the stability provided by Soviet backing and Party rule, he sees the GDR haunted not only by economic crises but also by its inability to satisfy the needs of the population for greater freedom.

Population and Minorities

145 **Die Sorben. Wissenswertes aus Vergangenheit und Gegenwart der sorbischen nationalen Minderheit.** (The Sorbs: useful information from the past and present of the Sorb national minority.)
H. Brüchner (et al.). Bautzen, GDR: VEB Domowina Verlag, 5th ed., 1979. 279p. bibliog. map.
A useful introduction to the GDR's only ethnic (Slav) minority, the Sorbs. A history of the Sorbs until 1945 is followed by an account of their part in the GDR's own development, and a discussion of their schools, their language, their literature, and other achievements in the arts, as well as their costumes and customs. A chronological table of events in their history and a section of black-and-white photographs is also included.

146 **Lusatian in the German Democratic Republic today.**
W. B. Lockwood. *Slavonic and East European Review* (June 1957), p. 462–72.
An informative article on the Wendic (Lusatian) language of the GDR's Sorbian minority.

147 **The German Democratic Republic: the state and its population.**
Roy E. H. Mellor. In: *The two Germanies: a modern geography.*
Roy E. H. Mellor. London; New York; Hagerstown, Maryland; San Francisco; Sydney: Harper & Row, 1978, p. 353–67. maps. bibliog.
An excellent, compact discussion of the major factors affecting demographic trends, population densities, territorial planning, and territorial-administrative organization in the GDR. These are placed in the context of developments in the socialist bloc countries as a whole, but equally important is the explicit comparison drawn throughout with West Germany.

47

Population and Minorities

148 **La République Démocratique d'Allemagne: population et politique.**
(The German Democratic Republic: population and politics.)
Detlev B. Rein. *Documents* (France), vol. 34, no. 4 (1979),
p. 131–37.

Analyses the demographic situation in the GDR concentrating on a comparison
with that of the Federal Republic, and examining the political measures taken in
1972 and 1975–76 to promote the growth of families.

149 **Zwanzig Jahre demographische Entwicklung in der DDR.** (Twenty
years of demographic development in the GDR.)
Erich Strohback. *Jahrbuch für Wirtschaftsgeschichte*, no. 2
(1972), 289–311.

An article which follows the Party line and which describes and measures
demographic conditions, including population structure, dispersion, living and
health conditions, in 1946 after the 'wars and economic crisis of the capitalist era'.
The author shows how these inherited conditions continued to affect demographic
development in the 1950s-60s which was characterized by a high mortality rate
and a relatively low birth rate, resulting in a declining population and an
imbalance in regional distribution. It is claimed that, despite these disadvantages
from the past, socialist population policy has achieved success, especially in
women's participation in the economy, in marriage trends, in health care, and in
class structure.

Women

150　**Lesbians in the GDR: two women.**
Anonymous, translated from the German by Jeffrey Davis, Karl-
Ludwig Stenger. *New German Critique*, vol. 23 (1981), p. 83–96.
Two GDR women describe their experiences as lesbians in socialist society,
portraying the GDR as a male dominated, and sexually severely traditional,
society in which there is routine discrimination against homosexuals.

151　**Women in political leadership positions in the GDR.**
Michael Dennis. *GDR Monitor*, no. 3 (summer 1980), p. 25–31.
The author seeks to account for women's inadequate access to senior political
posts in the GDR and examines four significant causes: lack of systematic female
staff development programmes; prejudice against women executives; excessive
domestic burdens; and conventional sex-role stereotyping. A careful and useful
summary.

152　**Women and work in the GDR.**
Michael Dennis.　In: *The GDR under Honecker 1971–1981*.
Edited by Ian Wallace. Dundee, Scotland: GDR Monitor, 1981,
p. 97–106. (GDR Monitor Special Series, no. 1).
An excellent overview of the relationship between women and work in the GDR.
Dennis discusses female participation rates, the feminization of occupations and
relative male and female earnings. He also analyses attitudinal surveys regarding
combinations of work and home-making by women, the relation of material to
non-material motives in working, women's attitudes to part-time and shift work,
as well as the factors involved in women achieving managerial positions.

153 **Social and cultural changes in the lives of GDR women – changes in their self-conception.**
Irene Dölling. *Studies in GDR culture and society 6: selected papers from the eleventh New Hampshire Symposium on the German Democratic Republic.* Edited by Margy Gerber (et al.). Lanham, Maryland; New York; London: University of America Press, 1986, p. 81–92.

Described as a 'cultural theoretician' at the Humboldt University of East Berlin, Irene Dölling uses sociological data and literature emanating from the GDR to assess whether East German women have achieved 'emancipation through labor', whether they are experiencing a return to a 'new motherliness' in reaction to the double burden of work and family, and whether they remain subject to 'unbroken conservatism' in sex relations and social norms. Dölling concludes that work, even if not yet qualitatively equal to that of men, offers the only opportunity for female emancipation, despite the persistence of the 'double-burden' and a return to attitudes of motherhood reflecting a wish for a genuine totality of human personality. A useful and thoughtful article on a complex subject, if rather more discursive than empirical.

154 **Die politische Rolle der Frau in der DDR.** (The political role of women in the GDR.)
Gabriele Gast. Düsseldorf, FRG: Bertelsmann Universitätsverlag, 1973. 249p. bibliog.

This is the standard work on the political role of women in the GDR and it documents in great detail the fact of their relative exclusion from positions of power, both in the Marxist-Leninist party (SED) and in the state executive – very much in parallel to the overall situation in the Federal Republic. The first section considers aspects of the Marxist-Leninist theory of emancipation and the difficulties involved in their practical implementation. In the two following sections (which make up the bulk of the work) the analysis of female representation concentrates, first, on the women in the Marxist-Leninist party (SED) and, second, on their position in the state executive, bearing in mind the penetration of the second by the first. It leaves out of the account female participation in the 'bourgeois' parties and in the mass organizations, including the Women's League (DFD). The text is supported by fifty-two tables, copious annotations and an index of personalities mentioned.

155 **Zwischen Familie und Beruf. Die Stellung der Frau in beiden deutschen Staaten.** (Between family and career: the position of women in the two German states.)
Gisela Helwig. Cologne, FRG: Verlag Wissenschaft und Politik, 1974. 112p. bibliog.

This is the first of three comparative studies by this author which should be taken together (see item nos. 156 and 157). In a series of comparative chapters each dealing with both states the book describes and assesses the social context of sex stereotypes, sex equality in family law, girls and women in education, the distribution of women in work (women's share of different professions and of higher status posts, for example) including measures to support working women, and their motivation to take up work.

156 **Frau '75 Bundesrepublik Deutschland – DDR.** (Women '75 Federal Republic of Germany – GDR.)
Gisela Helwig. Cologne, FRG: Verlag Wissenschaft und Politik, 1975. 105p. bibliog.
Published for International Women's Year, this work presents comparisons in a more readily assimilable form than the author's 1974 (q.v.) publication (Federal Republic on even-, GDR on odd-numbered pages). It covers: marriage and family law; girls and women in education; the distribution of women in work, including measures to support working women; and women in politics and mass organizations. The volume contains useful comparative statistics and like her later book published in 1982 (q.v.) it is a very useful ready-reference work for the specialist and the layman.

157 **Frau und Familie in beiden deutschen Staaten.** (Women and family in the two German states.)
Gisela Helwig. Cologne, FRG: Verlag Wissenschaft und Politik, 1982. 149p. bibliog.
This work updates much of the material of the author's 1974 and 1975 books (q.v.) and adopts the same easy-reference layout as the 1975 publication. It covers: girls and women in education; the employment distribution of women; marriage and the family; measures to enable women to combine family and career responsibilities; and women in politics and mass organizations. There is a chapter of comparative statistics and an appendix reproducing parts of relevant documents. A useful work to all readers.

158 **Women under communism.**
Barbara Wolfe Jancar. Baltimore, Maryland; London: Johns Hopkins University Press, 1978. 291p. bibliog.
This volume analyses the position of women under communism with reference to all the Soviet communist countries of Europe as well as to Cuba and China. It does so not in a survey by country but in a comparative study under selected criteria. Important among these are the socioeconomic environment (including employment patterns and promotion), trends in family size, communist ideology and the persistence of traditional ways, the female proportion of the political élite, legislation concerning marriage and the family, officially sanctioned role stereotyping, and, finally, self-images of women as a group. The book contains useful appendixes, including 32 pages of tables, and a good index.

159 **Zur gesellschaftlichen Stellung der Frau in der DDR.** (The social position of women in the GDR.)
Herta Kuhrig, Wulfram Speigner. Leipzig, GDR: Verlag für die Frau, 1978. 369p. bibliog.
An official report on women's equality in the GDR. A theoretical introduction to the question of women in Marxist ideology and in socialist society precedes

Women

sections concerned with: social research and public policy in the fields of women and work; female education; marriage and the family; child-minding facilities; reduction of housework; and health care for women and (especially, working) mothers. A useful source of information.

160 **Social change and women's issues in the GDR: problems of women in leadership positions.**
Christiane Lemke.   In: *Studies in GDR culture and society 2: proceedings of the seventh International Symposium on the German Democratic Republic.* Edited by Margy Gerber (et al.).
Washington, DC: University Press of America, 1982, p. 251–59.
After discussing the causes and implications of the fact that women make up approximately half of the GDR's workforce but occupy only 30 per cent of the leadership positions, the author concludes that a re-evaluation of the social status of women is called for even though 'their situation is much better than in the early years of the GDR and much better than in other socialist and western countries'.

161 **Gretchens rote Schwestern. Frauen in der DDR.** (Gretchen's red sisters: women in the GDR.)
Jutta Menschik, Evelyn Leopold.   Frankfurt am Main, FRG: Fischer Taschenbuch Verlag, 1974. 194p. bibliog.
Describes the position of women in the GDR, outlines the legislation to support women from 1945 to 1973 and devotes considerable attention to women at work and to women's corresponding roles in private life in the family. The authors conclude with observations on the new image of women in GDR media and books. It is asserted that, whatever the current situation of GDR women compared with those in the West, the practical measures in the GDR to support women mean that East German women are more emancipated than their Western counterparts.

162 **Frauen in der Bundesrepublik und in der DDR: Anspruch und Wirklichkeit.** (Women in the Federal Republic and the GDR: claim and reality.)
Gertrud Pfister.   In: *Beiträge zur Deutschlandforschung.* Edited by Dieter Voigt, Manfred Messing. Bochum, FRG: Studienverlag Brockmeyer, 1982, p. 210–37. bibliog.
A short comparative discussion of women's position in law, politics and education, at work and in private life.

163 **Geschlechterstereotype in Systemvergleich – eine Analyse von Heiratsanzeigen.** (Sex stereotypes in a system comparison – an analysis of 'lonely hearts' columns.)
Gertrud Pfister, Dieter Voigt. In: *Beiträge zur Deutschlandforschung*. Edited by Dieter Voigt, Manfred Messing. Bochum, FRG: Studienverlag Brockmeyer, 1982, p. 238–85. bibliog.

The authors conclude that efforts in the East and West to give women equal status have not overcome traditional sex stereotypes and that these will continue to restrict men's and women's choices in life.

164 **Women in the two Germanies: a comparative study of a socialist and a non-socialist society.**
Harry G. Shaffer. New York: Pergamon, 1981. 235p. bibliog. (Pergamon Policy Studies on Social Policy).

Shaffer compares the situation of women in the two Germanies under a number of headings: the legal position; women at work; education and training; the home and family; and women's organizations. He rightly concludes that, although much remains to be done, the GDR has gone much further than its Western neighbour in promoting sex equality in all spheres of life. Forty tables and one figure are incorporated in the text.

165 **Women's careers: experience from East and West Germany.**
Ingrid Sommerkorn, R. Nave-Herz, Christine Kulke, with an introduction by Michael Fogarty. London: PEP, 1970. 132p. bibliog. (Vol. 36, Broadsheet no. 521).

Considers women in top jobs in East and West Germany and provides an excellent survey of the copious West German data and of the rather sparse information available from the GDR. A clear and concise guide, which is still useful today, especially in conjunction with the statistics presented in Gisela Helwig's *Frau und Familie in beiden deutschen Staaten* (q.v.) and her *Frau '75 Bundesrepublik Deutschland – DDR* (q.v.).

166 **Women in the GDR.**
Christel Sudau, translated from the German by Biddy Martin. *New German Critique*, issue no. 13 (winter 1978), p. 69–81.

A compactly informative article which demonstrates that the advent of 'real socialism' in the GDR has failed to bring any substantial emancipation for women. The author argues: that official government policy favours the nuclear family; that sexual stereotypes are perpetuated both in the home and in the education system; that women fill the traditionally low-paid jobs; and that they rarely achieve top positions in political or professional life. Furthermore, the necessity for the GDR economy that the majority of women work, leads to a double burden. Sudau quotes Irmtraud Morgner's observation that if the hours spent in household chores and at the workplace are totalled it emerges that

Women

women are responsible for working two-thirds of them. Given the lack of any independent women's movement in the GDR, Sudau is pessimistic about the chances of the situation improving.

Religion

167 Discretion and valour: religious conditions in Russia and Eastern Europe.

Trevor Beeson. Glasgow: Collins, 1974. 348p. map. bibliog.

Written with the advice and assistance of the International Affairs Department of the British Council of Churches, this book investigates religious conditions in European Russia and in eight East European countries including the GDR. In essence, Beeson challenges, quite correctly, the widespread impression in the West that the churches in the GDR are particularly oppressed: 'There are certainly severe social and political pressures but they are a far cry from the sort of persecution that has not been unknown in Eastern Europe.' Beeson's study of the GDR contains some useful observations, despite being written before the latest church-state accommodation (in 1978) and the peace movement of the late 1970s. The author provides: a brief historical sketch of church-state relations; some useful statistics; notes on the pastoral role of churches and on the training of clergy; information about church broadcasting and publishing as well as about church music. He outlines the churches' constitutional position and describes at some length the close restraints on Christian witness, in particular the discrimination suffered by young lay members of the churches.

168 The status of religion in the German Democratic Republic.

George H. Brand. In: *Religion and atheism in the U.S.S.R. and Eastern Europe.* Edited by Bogdan R. Bociurkiw, John W. Strong, assisted by Jean K. Laux. London; Basingstoke, England: Macmillan, 1975. 412p. bibliog.

Brand points to the paradox involved in the GDR's attempt to minimize the role of the Church in the upbringing of youth while maximizing its usefulness as a means of establishing and consolidating the state. He identifies three objectives in the state's policy towards the Church, all of which have been achieved: an erosion of the influence of religious education; the destruction of the Evangelische Kirche in Deutschland (EKD), an umbrella-organization which linked the Church in East and West Germany and thereby questioned the GDR's claim to be separate and autonomous; and the development of a core of 'progressive' clergy who would support state initiatives aimed at the socialist transformation of society. He likewise identifies three phases in Church-state relations: confrontation (essentially the 1950s); the search for a limited accommodation (1960s); and a mutual acceptance of each other's continued existence (early 1970s) which will shape the environment in which future debates will take place. This prediction has been fully borne out in recent years.

169 **Luther: 'One of the greatest sons of the German people'.**
Mark Brayne. *GDR Monitor*, no. 3 (summer 1980), p. 35–43.
An entertaining and perceptive analysis of the official rehabilitation of Luther in the GDR by a former BBC correspondent in that country, placing this development in the context of improved Church-state relations since 1978.

170 **Konfrontation oder Kooperation? Das Verhältnis von Staat und Kirche in der SBZ/DDR 1945–1980.** (Confrontation or cooperation?: the relationship between state and Church in the Soviet Zone/GDR 1945–80.)
Horst Dähn, foreword by Reinhard Henkys. Opladen, FRG: Westdeutscher Verlag, 1982. 295p. bibliog. (Studien zur Sozialwissenschaft Band 52).
A scholarly study which represents the first comprehensive analysis of the relationship between Church and state in the GDR. Dähn investigates the causes of the permanent conflict which, in varying degrees, has characterized that relationship, identifying both endogenous factors (the utter incompatability of the fundamental tenets of Christianity and Marxism-Leninism) and exogenous factors (for example, the Church's membership of an umbrella organization – the Evangelische Kirche in Deutschland (EKD) – which linked it with the Church in West Germany). He distinguishes three major phases: confrontation (1949–58); the gradual easing of confrontation (1958–68); and the development of a more relaxed relationship (1969 to the present). The author presents compelling evidence of a learning process which continues to affect how one side views the other, the most significant factor being the Church's acceptance of the reality of socialism in the GDR on the one hand and the state's acknowledgement of the Church as a negotiating partner on the other. He also takes the widely accepted view that the Church in the GDR has now become a minority Church, not because the atheistic philosophy of the state has proved more attractive but because of a general trend towards secularization which obtains equally in West Germany and elsewhere. Brief chapters are also devoted to, respectively, the Catholic Church, other religious communities, and certain groupings which the Socialist Unity Party (SED) attempts to use as a means of promoting its own policy towards the Church.

56

171 **The Luther anniversary in East Germany.**
Robert F. Goeckel. *World Politics*, vol. 37, no. 1 (Oct. 1984),
p. 112–33.

Traces the official GDR interpretation of Luther's historical role from initial condemnation to recent rehabilitation. Goeckel describes the official anniversary celebrations and discusses the Protestant churches' guarded reaction to these. He considers the influence of state policy and inter-German relations on the celebrations and emphasizes the short-term hard currency needs of the GDR as a major reason behind the 'intensive campaign to promote Luther Year tourism', one result of which, was an infusion of 140 to 200 million DM into the East German economy.

172 **The GDR: servant or subservient church?**
Peter Hebblethwaite. *Religion in Communist Lands*, vol. 6, no. 2
(summer 1978), p. 97–100.

In a Roman Catholic view of the churches in the GDR, the author discusses the moral limitations of the Protestant churches' policy of accommodation with the state. He also includes some remarks on the position of the Roman Catholic Church taken from an interview given by an unidentified Catholic priest.

173 **Die evangelischen Kirchen in der DDR: Beiträge zu einer
Bestandsaufnahme.** (The Protestant Churches in the GDR:
contributions to an assessment.)
Edited by Reinhard Henkys. Munich: Chr. Kaiser Verlag, 1982.
462p. bibliog.

Contains useful information on, and discussions of, the principal topics pertaining to the Protestant churches in the GDR. These include the theory and practice of the Socialist Unity Party (SED), the role of the Christian churches in socialism, the social and educational role of the churches, the churches' role in promoting peace, the internal life of the church, its theology and, finally, pointers to the future.

174 **Katholische Kirche in der DDR. Gemeinden in der Bewährung
1945–1980.** (The Catholic Church in the GDR: congregations in a
time of trial 1945–80.)
Wolfgang Knauft. Mainz, FRG: Matthias-Grünewald-Verlag,
1980. 240p.

A detailed history of the Roman Catholic Church in the GDR, written from the Catholic point of view. It uses a four-point chronology: a new beginning 1945–50; pastoral efforts 1950–56 in the face of anti-Church pressure from the state; the intensified struggle with the state 1957–61; and, finally, the period after 1961 which brought an eventual softening of state attitudes. The work contains a useful appendix of documents.

175 **Die Gegenwartslage der Evangelischen Kirche in der DDR: eine Einführung.** (The current situation of the Protestant Church in the GDR: an introduction.)
Otto Luchterhandt. Tübingen, FRG: JCB Mohr (Paul Siebeck), 1982. 106p.

The book is divided into three parts examining: the development of the relations between Church and state; the concept of the 'Church in socialism' and its concrete manifestation; and structural problems of the Church in a time of change, with a postscript on the danger of withdrawal of the Church into itself. An excellent basic source of information.

176 **Swords to plowshares: the Church, the state and the East German peace movement.**
Joyce Marie Mushaben. *Studies in Comparative Communism.* vol. 17, no. 2 (summer 1984), p. 123–35.

The author explores internal opposition in the GDR and points to the role of the churches and the attractiveness of the peace movement to GDR youth. She also examines the experiences of the East and West German peace movements linking them to the questions of national identity and reunification. Mushaben relates the movement's growth to the militarization of GDR society, the 'internal emigration' of young people and to neutralist all-German nationalism.

177 **Beyond the wall: the people communism can't conquer.**
Hank Paulson, with Don Richardson. Ventura, California: Regal Books, 1982. 173p.

The author, who is the Dutch founder of the East European Bible Mission, recounts some of his experiences as a smuggler of Bibles into the GDR and other East European states. He believes that, despite all the problems they face, 'committed Christians in Communist Eastern Europe far outnumber their counterparts in rich, carefree, professedly Christian Western Europe'. However, his book offers no more than a series of impressionistic vignettes in support of this contention.

178 **Church and peace in the GDR.**
Pedro Ramet. *Problems of Communism*, vol. 33, no. 4 (July-Aug. 1984), p. 44–57.

In a factually detailed survey, the author considers why the Protestant Church has supported the unofficial peace movement and criticized state policy openly, how the régime has reacted to this and what the short-term prospects are for an entente between Church and opposition in the GDR. He outlines the Church's policy of critical distance, its championing of 'internal peace' based on acknowledgement of pluralism and its opposition to the militarization of society. The article lists the four distinct bodies speaking for peace in the GDR: the official peace movement, known as the GDR's Peace Council (*Friedensrat*); the unofficial but régime-approved Christian Peace Conference; numerous so-called 'basic communities' and peace seminars organized within the Evangelical Church; and the 'independent peace movement' with 2,000 to 5,000 activists. Careful consideration is given to changing official attitudes to the 'swords into ploughshares' slogan and to the Church's partial withdrawal of support for protesting youth.

179 **Kirche als Lerngemeinschaft: Dokumente aus der Arbeit des Bundes der Evangelischen Kirchen in der DDR.** (The Church as a learning community: documents relating to the work of the Federation of Protestant Churches in the GDR.)
Edited by the Sekretariat des Bundes der Evangelischen Kirchen in der DDR. Berlin (East): Evangelische Verlagsanstalt, 1981. 275p.

This book is a collection of basic documents which together define the nature and role of the Protestant churches in the GDR. They are arranged in four sections: first, the community of Protestant Churches in the GDR (points of agreement in theology and tradition, for example); second, the Protestant churches as a learning community (including instruction, confirmation, training of lay persons); third, the place of the churches in society (Church-state relations, the churches' relation to socialism); and, fourth, the churches' responsibility towards the wider world (ecumenism, the churches' view of the struggle against racism in southern Africa and towards the Middle East). An essential source for all students of the subject.

180 **The Church in the German Democratic Republic.**
Roland Smith. In: *Honecker's Germany*. Edited by David Childs. London: Allen & Unwin, 1985, p. 66–81.

Over half this chapter is occupied by an history of the Protestant churches in the Soviet Zone and GDR from 1945, with a note on the Roman Catholic Church there. The rest concerns the present situation, which is characterized by the decline and imminent marginalization of the churches because of their stand over military service and defence studies in the schools, as well as their protection of the unofficial anti-nuclear movement.

181 **God and Caesar in East Germany: the conflicts of Church and state in East Germany since 1945.**
Richard W. Solberg, foreword by Bishop Otto Dibelius. New York: Macmillan, 1961. 294p.

Solberg describes in considerable detail what he calls 'the heroic struggle of Christian men and institutions in East Germany to maintain their integrity in the face of a totalitarian Communist state'. He emphasizes, justifiably, that the experience of Christians in the 1940s and 1950s hardly encouraged the view that communists might one day be committed to a policy of peaceful coexistence. Notwithstanding this, despite all the 'bitter persecution' and 'Communist terror', the Church in the GDR maintains, in his view, 'its integrity and its independence in contrast to both Catholic and Protestant Churches in Soviet Russia and in other Communist states of Eastern Europe'. On this basis it is reasonable to suppose that Solberg would today take a less sympathetic view of the Church's policy of 'critical solidarity' with the state than, for example, Trevor Beeson in his study entitled *Discretion and valour: religious conditions in Russia and Eastern Europe* (q.v.).

Religion

182 **Church and state in East Germany.**
Caroline Ward, postscript by Paul Oestreicher. *Religion in Communist Lands*, vol. 6, no. 2 (summer 1978), p. 89–96.

Outlines the structure and activities of (mainly) the Protestant churches in the GDR in the context of restriction by the state and concludes that Church and state have achieved mutual cooperation and tolerance. The postscript welcomes the results of the 1978 agreement between the Protestant churches and the state for it provided for the recognition of the rights of Christians by the atheistic state.

183 **East Germany: the federation of Protestant churches.**
Roger Williamson. *Religion in Communist Lands*, (spring 1981), p. 6–17.

Traces the post-1945 history of the Protestant churches in the GDR. The author outlines their persecution by, and eventual accommodation with, the state following the establishment of the BEK (Federation of Protestant Churches) and its recognition by the state. He also briefly considers their role as providers of social services and describes their attitude to abridgements of human rights by the state.

Society, Health and Welfare

184 **Grundlagen der marxistisch-leninistischen Soziologie.** (Foundations
of Marxist-Leninist sociology.)
Edited by Georg Assmann, Rudhard Stollberg.   Berlin (East):
Dietz Verlag, 1979. 404p.

A standard work for students and researchers, this is the first comprehensive
survey of the subject to appear in the GDR. It is in four parts and considers: the
aims and tasks of Marxist-Leninist sociology; the process of sociological research;
sociological analysis of particular features of developed socialist society; and a
survey and critique of non-Marxist sociology. Its aim appears to be to characterize
the practice of sociology in the GDR and consequently it contains no sociological
data on that country.

185 **U.S. research – a critical assessment of the social sciences.**
Thomas A. Baylis.   In: *Research and study of the German
Democratic Republic: a survey of work in the United States and the
Federal Republic of Germany*. Edited by R. G. Livingston.
Washington, DC: American Institute of Contemporary German
Studies, 1986, p. 1–13. bibliog.

Baylis argues that, while the quantity of English-language materials on the GDR
is satisfactory, the quality is often less so. He suggests that Americans should now
build on the acknowledged strength of US social sciences by taking a comparative
approach to the GDR, and that more studies of the GDR should be placed within
the context of contemporary social theory. Finally, he urges that American
scholars should undertake a more exacting evaluation of each other's work and be
prepared to engage in healthy controversy.

186 **Wenn ein Mensch stirbt . . . Ausgewählte Aspekte perimortaler Medizin.** (When a human being dies . . . selected aspects of perimortal medicine.)
Kay Blumenthal-Barby, introduced by Günther Baust. Berlin (East): VEB Verlag Volk und Gesundheit, 1986. 184p. bibliog.

A well-illustrated examination of death, its rituals, and care for the terminally ill, written by the GDR's leading expert on the subject. It provides its GDR readers with practical advice on what to do when someone dies.

187 **Null Bock auf DDR. Aussteigerjugend im anderen Deutschland.** (A bellyfull of the GDR: young drop-outs in the other Germany.)
Wolfgang Büscher, Peter Wensierski. Reinbek, FRG: Rowohlt Taschenbuch Verlag, 1984. 189p.

This lively, journalistic study by two *Der Spiegel* writers explores the possibilities – within the limitations imposed by strict state surveillance – of pursuing unorthodox, oppositional life styles in the GDR. In chapters dealing with punks, homosexuals, the literary and artistic fringe, unofficial ecological initiatives, the church and the peace movement and the development of a new consciousness among women, it detects the slow emergence, across a wide spectrum of activities and social groups, of an embryonic counter-culture.

188 **Society and democracy in Germany.**
Ralf Dahrendorf. London: Weidenfeld & Nicolson, 1967. 482p. bibliog.

Writing before détente and the dissident movement of the 1970s, Dahrendorf sees East Germany as the completion of the National Socialist version of the 'modern' social revolution where traditions of inherited privilege, family, class, property and regionalism have been annihilated to afford the theoretical possibility of true 'citizenship'. The public role of the 'co-ordinated man' now dominates and, while formal rights of citizenship for individuals have virtually disappeared, their social context is highly developed (with the reverse situation in West Germany). Steered discussion is highlighted as a decisive mechanism for the canalization of conflict in a totally planned society, with the pseudoworld of ideology dismissed as irrelevant to sociological reality – perhaps too readily in view of the way in which liberal communists have contrasted Marxian theory with dictatorial communism. A useful text for students of both West and East German sociology.

189 **Arbeiterklasse und Intelligenz in der DDR: soziale Annäherung von Produktionsarbeiterschaft und wissenschaftlich-technischer Intelligenz im Industriebetrieb?** (Working class and intelligentsia in the GDR: social rapprochement between production workers and technical intelligentsia in the factory?)
Günter Erbe. Opladen, FRG: Westdeutscher Verlag, 1982. 224p.

The standard work on the mutual approximation of social classes and strata under socialism in the GDR. In a systematic and detailed study the author concludes that, despite the fusion of particular sub-groups, production workers and technical staff still maintain their separate roles and functions in production.

190 **Social science research in the Federal Republic – methodological and conceptual problems.**
Gert-Joachim Glaessner.   In: *Research and study of the German Democratic Republic: a survey of work in the United States and the Federal Republic of Germany.* Edited by R. G. Livingston.
Washington, DC: American Institute for Contemporary German Studies, 1986, p. 48–67. bibliog.
Outlines a number of problems currently facing GDR studies in the Federal Republic of Germany. The author also argues the case for a greater integration of GDR studies with comparative communist studies in order to move them from the periphery into the mainstream of social science activity. Welcoming the move from the 'totalitarianism' to the 'modernization' paradigm in GDR studies in recent years, Glaessner points out that the consequent emphasis on scientific-technical developments has nevertheless meant that Party and state now receive less attention than they warrant, i.e., 'bluntly formulated, there is hardly any attempt at a political sociology of the Soviet type socialist countries'. This is an imbalance which, as the author cogently argues, must be corrected if the GDR is to be properly understood.

191 **Maternal and child health care in the German Democratic Republic.**
Robert A. Greenberg.   In: *Studies in GDR culture and society 2: proceedings of the seventh International Symposium on the German Democratic Republic.* Edited by Margy Gerber (et al.).
Washington, DC: University Press of America, 1982, p. 261–78.
A sober, factual account which concludes that the GDR has developed 'an impressive health and social services system, exemplified by the services provided for young parents and their children'. At the same time, the author does identify a number of relatively minor defects which require attention.

192 **The political direction of GDR health research and technology.**
Rainer Hohlfeld.   In: *Studies in GDR culture and society 3: selected papers from the eighth International Symposium on the German Democratic Republic.* Edited by Margy Gerber (et al.).
Lanham, Maryland; New York; London: University Press of America, 1983, p. 27–41.
The author discusses the GDR's health and health-care problems (arising, for example, from the 'chemicalization of life', pollution, bad nutrition, the hierarchical and impersonal patient-physician relationships) and the political issues involved. He identifies two clear tendencies in GDR health research: first, the 'scientification of health problems', favoured because of the Socialist Unity Party's (SED) belief that the solution of these problems depends on advances in science; and 'anti-reductionism', by which is meant the rejection of a purely biological understanding of health and disease.

Society, Health and Welfare

193 **Health care in the Soviet Union and Eastern Europe.**
Michael Kaser. London: Croom Helm, 1976. 252p. bibliog.

A comparative introductory survey of health care in all communist countries of Eastern Europe, which is prefaced by country-by-country accounts; the GDR occupies eighteen pages (p. 147–65). The author describes: legislation and policy; the age distribution within a stagnant population; the general health of the people; health service administration and facilities, including a substantial number of privately owned institutions, many of them in the hands of religious communities; and the financing of health care in an insurance-based system unique in Eastern Europe. This is the best work of its length on the subject and it contains useful tables; ten on the GDR and thirteen comparative tables which include the GDR.

194 **Living conditions in rural areas of the GDR.**
Ursula Koch. In: *Studies in GDR culture and society 2: proceedings of the seventh International Symposium on the German Democratic Republic*. Edited by Margy Gerber (et al.).
Washington, DC: University Press of America, 1982, p. 279–92.

Noting the GDR's success in improving living and working conditions in its rural areas, the author asks whether this has been accompanied by changes in people's consciousness and behaviour. She then adduces evidence [making particular use of Ursula Püschel's conversations with agricultural workers and others in her book *Unterwegs in meinen Dörfern*, Rostock, GDR: Hinstorff, 1980)] to show that this is indeed the case.

195 **Youth in East and West Germany.**
Edited by Eva Kolinsky. *Modern German Studies*, issue no. 1 (Aston University, Birmingham, England: Association for Modern German Studies, 1985), 108p.

The papers printed here were given at the Association for Modern German Studies Conference held in London in May 1984. They deal with various aspects of the life of young people in East and West Germany. Eva Kolinsky writes about youth and the political parties, examining political polarization and the effects of unemployment; Günther Kloss discusses the expanding educational possibilities for young people in the Federal Republic; Michael Dennis looks at youth in the GDR in terms of work, the family, sport and leisure pursuits and criminality; and Gisela Shaw examines the mirroring of the situation of young people in a selection of GDR short stories.

196 **Social structure in divided Germany.**
Jaroslav Krejci. London: Croom Helm, 1976. 219p. bibliog.

The author undertakes a comparison of social structure in the GDR and the Federal Republic of Germany. The criteria are income and wealth, stratification and mobility, and power and freedom. Most notably, he recalculates the relevant statistics to make the first detailed comparisons of the income of different strata in the respective populations. Differences between the two states are seen to arise from what Krejci calls their contrasting 'end-values': individual self-assertion in the West and collective striving in the East. The text is supported by forty-five tables and an appendix containing a further fifteen. Still essential reading for students of the GDR.

197 **Youth and youth policy in GDR society.**
Christiane Lemke. In: *Studies in GDR culture and society 3: selected papers from the eighth International Symposium on the German Democratic Republic*. Edited by Margy Gerber (et al.). Lanham, Maryland; New York; London: University Press of America, 1983, p. 101–10.

After outlining the major features of the GDR's youth policy, the author warns that its future success will depend in large measure on how far the younger generation's clear desire for independence and for the right to make decisions is respected.

198 **Studien und Materialien zur Soziologie der DDR.** (Studies and material related to a sociology of the GDR.)
Edited by Peter Christian Ludz. Cologne, FRG: Westdeutscher Verlag, 1964. 504p. bibliog.

This work, edited by a leading West German sociologist of the GDR, contains a number of sectorial analyses and assessments reflecting the state of research at the time. These are included under the general headings of: occupation and family; industry and factory; and school, university and research. There is also an account of sociology and philosophy in the GDR and a discussion of changes in the role of certain aspects of Marxist-Leninist ideology in that country. The whole is prefaced by the editor's tentative proposals for a sociological theory of totalitarian societies. The volume contains a very full bibliography.

199 **Experts and critical intellectuals in East Germany.**
Peter Christian Ludz. In: *Upheaval and continuity: a century of German history*. Edited by E. J. Feuchtwanger, preface by Klaus Schulz. London: Wolff, 1973, p. 166–82.

After outlining the difficulty of defining precisely what is meant by the 'intelligentsia' in East German society, Ludz develops the thesis that two groups can be identified, both of which have achieved a higher degree of societal integration than is evident in Western societies, where the intelligentsia occupies a relatively marginal position. The two groups are the experts, a product of the GDR's development towards an 'expertocratic career-orientated society', and the critical intellectuals, such as Wolf Biermann, Robert Havemann and Christa Wolf. Ludz lists the characteristics the two groups share: loyalty to socialism and the social reality of the GDR; criticism as well as appreciation of the West; their shared daily experiences of GDR life; a willingness to learn and change; and the belief that such values as personal responsibility, self-reliance, and responsible cooperation, should be given more scope in the GDR. Rather optimistically, Ludz believes that socioeconomic change in the GDR may eventually induce the Party leadership to listen seriously to the intelligentsia's proposals for alternative developments to Party policy.

200 **German Democratic Republic.**
Peter Christian Ludz. In: *Survey research and public attitudes in Eastern Europe and the Soviet Union.* Edited by William A. Welsh. New York: Pergamon, 1981, p. 242–97. bibliog.

The introduction contains an account of the GDR institutions pursuing survey research (interviews, questionnaires and sociological surveys). The author then proceeds to analyse such research considering its planning and financing, its functions, the subjects which have attracted attention, as well as techniques and methods of data analysis and presentation. The author concentrates on fields where GDR research results are accessible including media habits, family and women, education and youth, work and the workplace, leisure and life aspirations as well as social problems and social policy. Also included is a note on surveys of both attitudes to politics and ideology and of ethnicity and foreign cultures, of which very little indeed is published in the GDR. A very useful chapter, copiously annotated.

201 **Social policy under Honecker.**
Martin McCauley. In: *The GDR under Honecker, 1971–1981.* Edited by Ian Wallace. Dundee, Scotland: GDR Monitor, 1981, p. 3–20. bibliog. (GDR Monitor Special Series, no. 1).

In an informative summary, the author outlines the history of the notion of 'socialist social policy' as a set of measures to improve the position of particular groups in order, not so much to redistribute income, as to motivate them towards work. He discusses measures connected with housing and employment (especially female) as well as pensions.

202 **WANTED: theoretical framework for GDR studies. FOR SALE: a systems/functional approach.**
Anita M. Mallinckrodt. *GDR Monitor*, no. 10 (winter 1983–84), p. 12–27.

The authoress argues for a new model of GDR studies. Instead of the predominant 'totalitarian' theory, which is basically hostile to the GDR because it sees the system as incapable of evolution and concentrates on fragments rather than the whole, Mallinckrodt argues for a 'systems/functional' approach which looks at the GDR objectively as a functioning and dynamic political system with numerous interacting parts. As an example, the activities of peace and ecology groups and of socially critical artists are briefly reviewed and analysed from the viewpoint of the proposed framework. Such an approach throws up many questions and requires much research data but opens the way for a contextual understanding of social phenomena which current 'kneejerk' political reactions fail to offer.

203 **Sozialpolitik.** (Social policy.)
Edited by Günter Manz, Gunnar Winkler. Berlin (East): Verlag
Die Wirtschaft, 1985. 300p. bibliog.

A standard GDR work describing the scope and content of social policy in East
Germany. The concept is defined very broadly to include all action to improve the
level, and secure the uniformity of, living standards, as well as to improve
productivity and economic growth, especially through technical innovation.

204 **Personal and social consumption in Eastern Europe: Poland,
Czechoslovakia, Hungary and East Germany.**
Bogdan Mieczkowski. New York, Washington, London: Praeger,
1975. 343p. bibliog.

In the section of this study devoted to East Germany (p. 243–75), the author
shows how East German consumption patterns compare favourably with those of
other countries in Eastern Europe but unfavourably with those of West Germany.
In particular, the East German citizen has grown progressively worse off vis-à-vis
his Western counterpart since the building of the Berlin Wall. The author
concludes that the régime will ultimately be forced to accede more and more to
the demands of personal consumption.

205 **Möglichkeiten und Grenzen eines Vergleichs der Lebenshaltung in
beiden deutschen Staaten.** (The possibilities and limitations of a
comparison of the standard of living in the two German states.)
Ursula Nagel-Dolinga. Frankfurt am Main, FRG; Bern; New
York: Verlag Peter Lang, 1984. 243p. bibliog.

The author introduces this work with an extended discussion of the concepts
subsumed in the term 'standard of living' and of the divergences and similarities in
relevant conceptualization between the GDR and West Germany. She discusses
the selection of indicators in 'operationalizing' the theoretical notion before
presenting data under her chosen criteria: family and population; income; health;
nutrition; education; housing; work; leisure; crime; and transport and communications. In the final section she constructs an index of levels of life applicable to
both German states. This is an essential source for any serious student of the
subject, useful as much for its exhaustive conceptual and methodological
discussion as for its quantitative conclusions.

206 **Official policy and the attitudes of GDR youth towards marriage
and the opposite sex as reflected in the column 'Unter Vier Augen'.**
Rüdiger Pieper. In: *Studies in GDR culture and society 6: selected
papers from the eleventh New Hampshire Symposium on the
German Democratic Republic.* Edited by Margy Gerber (et al.).
Lanham, Maryland; New York; London: University of America
Press, 1986, p. 109–21.

Examines the East German equivalent of a weekly 'agony column' for adolescents
in order to formulate some tentative conclusions concerning both young people's
attitudes towards sexual relations and marriage and official policies as reflected in

the editorial reaction and advice given (other statistical sources for opinions and attitudes are also referred to). Homosexuality is also considered. The conclusion is that the way of life is traditional in the GDR, even with regard to the division of labour within the family, although women have grown more self-confident and demanding. Economic issues do not affect marriage and divorce, and the state strongly supports the institution of marriage. Alternative life-styles such as single parenthood and communes are not officially accepted. Homosexuality is seen as a problem to be treated sympathetically by the community and collective.

207 **Die Familie in der DDR.** (The family in the GDR.)
Wolfgang Plat. Frankfurt am Main, FRG: S. Fischer Verlag,
1972. 119p.

The author aims to confirm the thesis that the family continues to exist as an institution under socialism but that in the GDR it will eventually be radically different from the Western model. He outlines the new legal and social position of women in the GDR, presents material taken from interviews with families and provides chapters on housing policy, marriage partner selection, women in continuing education, divorce, and the historical relativity of models of the family. His conclusion (including an interview with a leading GDR sociologist) establishes that the GDR woman exercises a broader set of roles than her Western counterpart, a situation to which the socialist family will increasingly adjust.

208 **Gesundheitswesen in der DDR.** (Health services in the GDR.)
Maria Elisabeth Ruban. Berlin (West): Verlag Gebr. Holzapfel,
1981. 118p. bibliog.

Provides a concise outline of all aspects of health provision in the GDR. The volume embraces the origins and history of the system, medical institutions (including pharmaceutical production and distribution), all personnel connected with health care, health education and health-related behaviour among the population, the principal achievements and results of the system, as well as some remarks on the economics of health provision in the GDR. A useful introduction for all readers.

209 **Professional work and marriage: an East-West comparison.**
Marilyn Rueschemeyer. London; Basingstoke, England:
Macmillan, 1981. 197p. bibliog.

The author takes a comparative approach to the effects which work pressures have on personal relations outside of work in the United States, the USSR and the GDR. She presents a number of hypotheses based on original research, notably a series of intensive interviews with a limited number of people, but properly concedes that the conclusions she reaches in her pioneering study are necessarily tentative, and in need of further investigation.

210 **The use of time.**
Alexander Szalai. The Hague, Paris: Mouton, 1972. 868p.
bibliog.

A study of the daily activities – measured in terms of 'time-budgets' – of urban
and suburban populations in twelve countries with differing political and
socioeconomic systems. The statistical data alone comprizes almost half of the
book and represents several years' survey work. Two project-participants from
the Research Group on Living Standards from the Berlin-Karlshorst Institute of
Economics of the GDR, Günter Manz and Gerhard Lippold, contribute articles
analysing the use of time in the community of Hoyerswerda, which is in the
process of industrialization and which is seen as a prototype of the future GDR
city. They compare the time structure of inhabitants of the old and new town and
consider working and leisure time, and time spent on family obligations. On the
basis of this data they also attempt a prognosis of future living standards.

211 **Beiträge zur Deutschlandforschung.** (Contributions to research on
Germany.)
Edited by Dieter Voigt, Manfred Messing. Bochum, FRG:
Studienverlag Brockmeyer, 1982. 311p. bibliog.

A collection of sociological studies on aspects of GDR society (including
sociological research in the GDR; the sociology of sport; health care and higher
education) together with comparative studies of East and West Germany (the
position of women and sex-role stereotyping) and an account of the reception of
GDR sociology in West Germany.

Politics, Government and Ideology

212 **Un pays méconnu: la République Démocratique Allemande.** (A misunderstood country: the German Democratic Republic.) Gilbert Badia, Pierre Lefranc. Paris: Edition Leipzig, 1963. 316p. maps.

Despite its language and place of distribution, this is essentially a GDR publication, indeed, it was printed in the GDR. The message of the title is fully underlined by the text, even if concessions are made to French readers and the final section is labelled 'current problems'. The general premise is that the GDR is a peace-loving, socialist country. The subjects dealt with are principally economic life, political life and social institutions.

213 **The technical intelligentsia and the East German élite: legitimacy and social change in mature communism.** Thomas A. Baylis. Berkeley, California; Los Angeles; London: University of California Press, 1974. 314p. bibliog.

Argues that a technical intelligentsia has grown in the GDR which is characterized by a broad spectrum of political attitudes (perhaps the most widespread being a relative indifference to politics and ideology) but whose most basic urge is the accomplishment of professional tasks. This intelligentsia's expertise is consciously used by the Party and by ideologists to strengthen the régime's legitimacy. At the same time, the technological and consumer values which the régime encourages, and the constant use of material indices for measuring the GDR's achievements, guarantee that the political influence of the technical intelligentsia will be felt. This will keep alive, at least, the possibility that a form of élitist pluralism may legitimately replace the present autocratic political structure. This is a well-written, scholarly book which will appeal to the general reader as much as to the specialist.

214 **Policymaking in the German Democratic Republic.**
Edited by Klaus von Beyme, Hartmut Zimmermann, translated
from the German by Eileen Martin. Aldershot, England: Gower
for the German Political Science Association, 1984. 401p. bibliog.
(German Political Studies, vol. 5).

This volume consists of nine studies, each by a different West German political
scientist, and each devoted to an important aspect of GDR policymaking: the
distribution of power; economic policy; foreign trade; military policy; education;
cultural policy; social policy; intra-German relations; and the GDR's measurable
achievements as compared to those of other socialist countries. The whole is
rounded off with an extensive bibliography of almost entirely German sources
(80p.). Concentrating not on the officially ascribed functions of GDR institutions
but on the ways in which they actually function in practice, the authors present
the GDR's sociopolitical system as a dynamic process which is still only
inadequately understood. There is in many areas a simple lack of information,
and the 'wide and demanding programme of research' to which this gives rise is
still in its early stages. The quality of the translation is very uneven and
constitutes the book's major weakness.

215 **The theory of fascism in the German Democratic Republic.**
Bernhard Blanke, Reimut Reiche, Jürgen Werth. *International
Journal of Politics*, (winter 1972/3), p. 82–103.

This article undertakes a critique of an issue which has been considered unworthy
of serious attention in the West, viz. the Marxist theory that fascism is merely the
agent of monopoly capital in its most terroristic form as a last-ditch defence
against socialism. Using the German experience as a testing ground, the authors
point to the much more complex causes surrounding the fascist takeover than the
theory allows and to the fact that the financial barons – despite short-term profits
from re-armament – did not control Hitler, nor his conduct of the war. Moreover,
they indicate that not only did capitalist interests not shape the overall social
ideology of Nazism, but neither can their role explain the extreme 'bestiality' of
the régime (embarrassing, of course, is the communists' own contribution to
Hitler's rise to power). They further argue that recourse to 'mediaevalist'
analogies with the Federal Republic does grave injustice to enlightened elements
in the West.

216 **Contemporary Germany: politics and culture.**
Edited by Charles Burdick, Hans-Adolf Jacobsen, Winfried
Kudzus. Boulder, Colorado; London: Westview Press, 1984.
436p.

Contains contributions on different aspects of the GDR prior to the mid-1980s.
Hans-Adolf Jacobsen describes events leading up to the division of Germany
while Rüdiger Thomas portrays the country's development since 1949, from the
'formational phase', 1945–49, to the 'socialist revolution phase', 1949–61, and
'postrevolutionary consolidation' from 1961. The political/organizational system is
described, with concise reviews of economic development, the re-structuring of
society, social security and the issue of German reunification (see item no. 253).
Concerning literature and the restrictive cultural policy, Frank Trommler argues

Politics, Government and Ideology

that the general development has been disappointing, with writers first unable to come to grips adequately with the fascist past and more recently retreating into introspection because of their frustration with socialist reality. Looking at East German art, Karin Thomas sees a long farewell from traditional socialist realism since 1970, with one school portraying historical or contemporary social conflict, while another, more individualistic and expressive, experiments with Western abstract techniques.

217 **Régime, society, and nation: the GDR after thirty years.**
Melvin Croan. *East Central Europe*, vol. 2 (1979), p. 137–51.
An eminently readable and lucid review of the political climate in the GDR during the late 1970s, paying particular attention to the official dilemma over national identity and the impact of numerous areas of West German influence. Croan concludes that the Socialist Unity Party (SED) has now grudgingly come to acknowledge that a sense of ethnic nationhood persists within the GDR and predicts for the 1980s a continuation of the policy initiated under Erich Honecker of domestic consumerism, albeit with an overlay of strict authoritarian control and with the same team of functionaries that had served under Walter Ulbricht. The inter-German issue will continue, however, to ensure oscillation between accommodation and confrontation.

218 **Politik, Wirtschaft und Gesellschaft in der DDR.** (Politics, economy and society in the GDR.)
Günter Erbe (et al.). Opladen, FRG: Westdeutscher Verlag, 2nd. ed., 1980. 434p. bibliog.
This book was conceived as an introduction to the GDR to be used by political education students. It is not exhaustive, omitting, for example, references to historical developments, cultural and social policy and foreign affairs. The main topics covered are the political system, the legal system, the economy, agriculture, education and the social structure. The general tone is factual but criticism is not avoided.

219 **German Democratic Republic (East).**
Current World Leaders. Almanac Issue, vol. 29, no. 2 (March 1986), p. 155–56.
An up-to-date listing of state, government and political party leaders. The publication also includes a note of major cities, population, area, membership of international organizations, and political parties. Changes to this information are given in each issue of *Current World Leaders* (five per year), and a full listing is found in each *Almanac Issue* (three per year).

220 **Die Partei hat immer recht.** (The Party is always right.)
Ralph Giordano, preface by Wolfgang Leonhard. Berlin (West): Verlag europäische Ideen, 1980. 271p.
Giordano's description of his eleven years as a member of the West German Communist Party from 1946 to 1957 is, as Wolfgang Leonhard notes in his reprinted preface to the edition of 1961, 'not the biography of a disappointed

72

Communist but an anatomy of Stalinism'. In describing the path which led to his
eventual break with the Party (an act of self-liberation), Giordano provides vivid
insights into the beginnings of the Johannes R. Becher school for writers in
Leipzig and the tortuous mendacities of officially imposed literary policy in East
Germany.

221 **Bureaucratic rule: overcoming conflicts in the GDR.**
Gert-Joachim Glaessner. Cologne, FRG: INDEX e.V. 1986.
64p. bibliog. (Research Project: Crises in Soviet-type Systems,
Study no. 13, directed by Zdenek Mlynar (Vienna) and a Scientific
Council).

Arguing that the GDR has been more flexible and innovative than other socialist
states in dealing with crises, this pamphlet nevertheless sees the country as likely
to face very serious tests in the future, notably on the ecological and economic
fronts. In this situation, the Socialist Unity Party (SED) is confronted by a stark
and uncomfortable choice: either to resist the widespread desire for more power-
sharing and in this way make crisis and conflict unavoidable; or to acknowledge
and give ground to that desire but in so doing run the risk of losing control of the
dynamic forces which it has set free. An incisive analysis of 'the persisting
contradiction between the drive towards efficiency and the democratization of
existing structures', spoiled only by some stilted English.

222 **Geist und Macht in der DDR. Die Integration der kommunistischen
Ideologie.** (Thought and power in the GDR: the integration of
communist ideology.)
J. Wolfgang Görlich. Olten, Switzerland; Freiburg im Breisgau,
FRG: Walter Verlag, 1968. 219p. bibliog.

A volume for specialists which analyses the development of philosophy under the
aegis of Marxism-Leninism in the Eastern half of Germany between 1945 and
1966. The initial phase (1945–49) involved the mass emigration of the 'classical'
philosophers who were unwilling to subsume all to Soviet Marxism-Leninism, and
this era was followed by the reception of official Marxism-Leninism (1949–53) and
the conflicts between the Socialist Unity Party (SED) and the non-dogmatic
Marxist humanists, Ernst Bloch and György Lukács (1953–57). During the
subsequent period of the 'Construction of Socialism', GDR philosophers re-
assimilated and adapted bourgeois elements, especially from sociology, anthro-
pology, ethics and the sciences in order to develop theories of the socialist
personality, imperialism and aspects of metatheory. An underlying theme for
philosophy in the Marxist state, Görlich argues, is the tension between intellectual
analysis and the exigencies of Party policy.

Politics, Government and Ideology

223   **East Germany.**
Andrew Gyorgy.   In: *Eastern European government and politics.*
Edited by V. Benes, A. Gyorgy, G. Stambuk. New York;
Evanston, Illinois; London: Harper & Row, 1966, p. 100–39.
bibliog.

Reviews constitutional developments, problems of political leadership and the machinery of economic and social repression. The Berlin question, intrabloc relations and contacts with the West are also analysed. Despite the fiercely anti-communist stance, a very comprehensive picture with much information is transmitted, covering most aspects of the GDR. In conclusion, Gyorgy sees the GDR in the middle of economic depression (the 1959 Seven Year Plan had been re-revised), and labouring under a huge gap between a silently antagonistic populace and a Stalinist leadership. Despite this gloomy picture, industrial progress is seen as remarkable, with the country commanding an undeniable economic and cultural potency.

224   **East Germany: from goals to realities.**
Arthur M. Hanhardt.   In: *Political socialization in Eastern Europe: a comparative framework.* Edited by Ivan Volgyes. New York: Praeger, 1975, p. 66–91.

In the context of the important agencies of political socialization in the GDR (the family, the Church, youth groups, schools, trade unions, the army and the Party itself) the author considers the ideal of the 'socialist personality' which the state is attempting to nurture. Hanhardt assesses the degree to which individuals actually conform to this ideal in their attitudes and real patterns of social behaviour. Despite the problem of the lack of data and empirical research, the indications are that the GDR has achieved more in this respect than other East European countries and that the mutually supportive human relations of the collective are perceived positively by East Germans in many walks of life.

225   **The governments of Germany.**
Arnold J. Heidenheimer.   London: Methuen, 1961. 230p. bibliog.

Contains a mass of information on East Germany and its evolution, adopting a heavily critical stance towards the 'SED régime', which undoubtedly reflects the year of publication (i.e., that of the construction of the Berlin Wall). Areas covered comprise: the immediate post-war situation; the GDR as a camouflaged one-party state; the Socialist Unity Party's (SED) organizational structure; and the transmission-belt function of other parties and organizations. The strengths of this study lie in the detailed portrayal of government organs and the Party bureaucracy and of the economic planning mechanism (albeit before the 1963 reforms). The education system, judiciary and civil service continue to suffer, in the author's opinion, from a lack of professional standards in view of the programme to recruit from the working class. A most useful volume for those interested in the condition of the GDR in its first decade, even if the work is rather locked in the Cold War era.

226 **The government of Germany.**
John H. Herz. New York; Chicago; San Francisco; Atlanta,
Georgia: Harcourt, Brace & World, 1967. 172p. maps. bibliog.
One of the nine chapters of this book (p. 129–44) is devoted to 'Berlin and the
Soviet Zone'. Here Herz draws the picture of 'a thoroughly manipulated society'
which is 'neither really German nor democratic' (it was imposed on the East
Germans by the Soviet Union). Nevertheless, he comes to the conclusion that
more and more of its citizens are coming to see the GDR as theirs and not merely
as something transitory. In view of this, Herz points to the urgent need for
reunification, but this is a solution to the German problem which today seems
increasingly less realistic. Rather it is the growing contacts between East and West
which resulted from the Federal Republic's new *Ostpolitik* (Eastern Policy) of the
late 1960s and early 1970s which offers the best hope for keeping alive the sense
of a single German identity.

227 **From my life.**
Erich Honecker, preface by Robert Maxwell. Oxford; New
York; Toronto: Pergamon, 1981. 515p.
The lavishly-produced English translation of Honecker's autobiography in the
'Leaders of the World' biographical series edited by Robert Maxwell. Honecker
traces his life and career from his childhood in the Saarland, through his
involvement in the pre- and postwar communist youth organizations, to his
leadership of the GDR since 1971.

228 **The government of East Germany.**
Otto Kirchheimer. In: *Germany and the future of Europe.* Edited
by Hans J. Morgenthau. Chicago: University of Chicago Press,
1951, p. 131–41.
Disregarding the Constitution of the GDR as irrelevant to sociopolitical reality,
Kirchheimer describes: controls on basic industries and agriculture; the
relationship between ministries and the Socialist Unity Party (SED); and recent
purges associated with the rise of Walter Ulbricht. The mass organizations and
the bloc Party system are seen as ancillaries to the Party, with the Trade Union
Federation experiencing problems in motivating workers for official policies.
Party control is described as repressive rather than terroristic. As for the future,
the author concludes by asking whether East Germany would be permitted to
develop higher living standards and whether a reunited Germany would preserve
present (i.e. 1950–51) East German patterns? A useful and in some ways
farseeing view of the GDR published at a very early stage of the country's
development.

229 **Nation building and régime stability in the DDR.**
Henry Krisch. *East Central Europe*, vol. 3, no. 1 (1976),
p. 15–29.
Examines the steps taken by the GDR leadership to establish a GDR nationhood
separate from that of the Federal Republic and relates these steps to various
theories of nationalism. The central part of the article consists of a review of the
policy of delimitation (*Abgrenzung*) as reflected in various statements by leading

GDR figures, and in the 1974 constitutional amendments. Additionally, Krisch stresses that close ties with the Soviet Union are part of the national identity sought by the GDR leadership. The author does not come to any clearcut conclusions about whether the leadership's view of a distinct GDR nationhood will prevail, or whether traditional all-German linguistic and cultural ties will retain their significance.

230 **Political legitimation in the German Democratic Republic.**
Henry Krisch. In: *Political legitimation in communist states.*
Edited by T. H. Rigby, Ferenc Fehér. London: Macmillan, 1982,
p. 111–25.

Krisch sees the GDR as seeking legitimacy through the attainment of economic success, close ties with the Soviet Union and through the authority of the Party. Its major difficulty is in the national area, as the territory of the GDR does not correspond with that of a traditional nation. Although the régime faces a variety of problems in this and other areas – it is difficult to achieve economic influence, for instance, given the present state of the world economy – the author does not believe that the GDR is faced with an immediate crisis of legitimacy. There is a good deal of stability within the Party and educational and professional opportunities exist for many citizens. Krisch believes that the attainment of legitimacy is important to the GDR régime, even if it could survive without much popular consent given the Soviet presence. Consent, he claims, is needed to achieve economic and social objectives.

231 **Honecker and the new politics of Europe.**
Heinz Lippmann, translated from the German by Helen Sebba.
New York: Macmillan, 1972. 272p. bibliog.

Written within a few months of Erich Honecker's accession to power in 1971 as successor to Walter Ulbricht, this biography adopts a balanced, fair-minded approach, and the picture of Honecker which it paints can be regarded as fundamentally sound even today. The author had the opportunity to observe his subject at close quarters between 1946 and 1953, when he himself worked as a Party functionary in the GDR before moving West, but he properly admits that parts of his account are based only on published sources and therefore cannot claim to be definitive. The book is divided into three parts: 'Childhood and Youth' (the period up to 1945, by which time Honecker was in fact thirty-three); 'A Partner in Power' (1945–55); and 'A Functionary in the Apparatus' (1955–71), the most detailed of these being the second which makes up half the book. Honecker finally emerges as 'living proof that a worker who had little opportunity for education in his youth is quite capable of carrying great responsibility, even in a completely industrialized society'.

32 **German Democratic Republic.**
    Richard F. Staar. In: *Communist régimes in Eastern Europe.*
    Edited by Richard F. Staar. Stanford, California: Hoover
    Institution Press, 1982. 4th ed. p. 100–29. bibliog.

The topics covered in this chapter include: the constitutions of 1949 and 1968; the
governmental structure; the electoral system; agriculture; dissent; the Socialist
Unity Party (SED); and domestic and foreign policies. The author argues that,
provided that the GDR can continue to meet the rising expectations of its
citizens, the country should remain stable and 'play a vital role in the Soviet bloc
as well as in the world arena'.

33 **The changing Party élite in East Germany.**
    Peter Christian Ludz, translated from the German by the Israel
    Program for Scientific Translations, foreword by Zbigniew
    Brzeziński. Cambridge, Massachusetts; London: MIT Press,
    1972. 509p. bibliog.

In this 'classic study' (Brzezinski), the GDR is seen as having evolved from a
totalitarian to an authoritarian system by the beginning of the 1960s. Unlike
totalitarian élites, the political decision-makers in the GDR are compelled, in
Ludz's view, by the conditions of a modern, technological society to consult
technical experts in a process which is characterized as 'consultative authoritarianism'. In effect, decisions can no longer be taken on purely political grounds
and without reference to social and economic considerations. Investigating the
Socialist Unity Party's (SED) organizational system, its social structure, and its
ideology, Ludz argues that the older, more dogmatic generation of leaders has
given ground to younger, more highly qualified functionaries, with a corresponding increase in professional mobility but without any real liberalization of the
political system.

34 **Legitimacy in a divided nation: the case of the German Democratic
    Republic.**
    Peter Christian Ludz. In: *Legitimation of régimes: international
    frameworks for analysis.* Edited by Bogdan Denitch. London:
    Sage, 1979, p. 161–75. (Sage Studies in International Sociology,
    vol. 17).

Ludz's contribution, like the others in the volume, arises from a 1977 New York
conference. He points to the difficulty of applying the concept of legitimacy to a
communist society and makes the point that the Socialist Unity Party (SED) does
not make the achievement of legitimacy a major priority compared with the
maintenance of power. Whilst Ludz acknowledges that it is also important to look
at the concept of legitimacy from the viewpoint of the ruler, he concludes that the
GDR as a state lacks legitimacy, not least because of the lack of national identity.
The level of material prosperity achieved by the GDR has been insufficient to
compensate for division and the lack of opportunities for political participation.

235 **Marxism-Leninism in the German Democratic Republic: the Socialist Unity Party (SED).**
Martin McCauley. London; Basingstoke, England: Macmillan, 1979. 267p. 3 maps. bibliog. (Studies in Russian and East European History Series).

Discusses the evolution of the SED, paying particular attention to the Soviet connection. Since the GDR has developed her own economic system and the Party's standing depends on the degree of success of its economic policy, McCauley examines this factor in some depth. On the other hand, culture, education and religious affairs 'have not been accorded the space they merit'. Short biographies of leading political figures are included in an appendix.

236 **Official and unofficial nationalism in the GDR.**
Martin McCauley. *GDR Monitor*, no. 5 (summer 1981), p. 13–20.

By official nationalism, McCauley means the Party line on the national question, which the article traces from the post-war period until Erich Honecker's confusing and subsequently forgotten 1974 doctrine which distinguished two distinct German nations living in their separate states but yet spoke of the two sharing a common nationality. By contrast, unofficial nationalism ranges from traditional identification with Germany as a whole, to the view of Party members who are less than enamoured with a slavish imitation of the Soviet model. McCauley concludes that the Socialist Unity Party (SED) is faced with a hard task if it is to overcome unofficial nationalism, not least because to do so it will have to master an increasingly difficult economic situation in order to gain increased popular support.

237 **Legitimation in the German Democratic Republic.**
Martin McCauley. In: *Eastern Europe: political crisis and legitimation*. Edited by Paul G. Lewis. London; Sydney: Croom Helm, 1984, p. 42–67.

Reviews chronologically the Socialist Unity Party's (SED) progress on the path to legitimation, which is understood to mean primarily support for the régime by the internal population. The conceptions of nation and statehood in the light of changing Soviet policy, the continual presence of West Germany and – more recently – international détente and diplomatic recognition are examined. McCauley further contrasts Marxist and Leninist notions of the legitimacy of Party rule and assesses the degree to which different social classes have reacted to the SED's claim for political legitimation. The author concludes that, despite majority conformism at present, economic problems confronting the GDR in the 1980s could produce lower living standards for most citizens with social achievement being reserved for only a minority élite. These developments could seriously endanger the SED's claim to rightful power, despite the newly-won international sovereignty.

238 **DDR – Vor und hinter der Mauer.** (GDR – before and behind the
Wall.)
Günter Minnerup.   Frankfurt am Main, FRG: isp-Verlag, 1982.
107p.

Contains two essays, the first of which is a re-working of an article originally
published in English in the *New Left Review* [under the title 'East Germany's
frozen revolution' (q.v.)]. The second essay consists of eight 'theses' on the
German national question, which argue that the division of Germany and its
incorporation into respective superpower blocs is a hindrance to the development
of socialism in both German states. Not until the working classes of the FRG and
GDR are freed from the East-West ideological confrontation and its exploiters
will they re-discover a true sense of common nationhood and social consciousness.
A lively collection of thoughts and propositions requiring acceptance of simple
class categories, social labels and collective motives.

239 **East Germany's frozen revolution.**
Günter Minnerup.   *New Left Review*, issue no. 132 (March/Apr.,
1982), p. 5–32.

In a comprehensive and informative article covering many aspects of the
development and bureaucratic apparatus of the GDR, Minnerup argues that,
through its petrification in the Stalinist mould, East Germany has failed to
become a pole of attraction for world socialism and has lost the socialist potential
of its advanced economy. The GDR is seen as a stable and economically viable
state, but one which lacks the national identity and internal pressures of other
East European countries which are necessary if Soviet hegemony is to be seriously
challenged. East Germany, it is argued, is therefore vulnerable to reformist
movements through its proximity to West Germany, and its ability to provide
permanent socialist dimensions for the future is also threatened.

240 **Is it true what they're saying about East Germany?**
Norman M. Naimark.   *Orbis*, no. 3 (fall 1979), p. 549–77.

In a combative article, Naimark challenges the much more positive image of the
GDR which, since the mid-1960s, has replaced the Cold War view of that country
as a totalitarian state. In essence, Naimark rejects the 'new emphasis on
quantifiable aspects of GDR life' and the importance attached to 'the statistical
accomplishments of modernization strategies' (in essence, the evidence of
economic, social and educational growth in the GDR) because this approach is
too one-sided, and loses sight of the fact that 'the political system was, and
continues to be, imposed on East German society . . . fear and resentment among
the East German population is not mentioned. The Berlin Wall is defended by
even more involuted arguments than those preferred by East German ideologues.
The most deadly border in the history of the modern world is totally left out of
the picture, as is the resulting apathy and hopelessness pervading the East
German population.' In such sweeping generalizations Naimark is guilty of
overstating his case, which is thereby seriously undermined.

241 **Die DDR-Elite oder Unsere Partner von morgen?** (The GDR élite, or our partners of tomorrow?)
Ernst Richert. Reinbek, FRG: Rowohlt, 1968. 122p.

This is a complex volume for 'East Berlin gazers' which analyses, not events so much as the known backgrounds, personalities and formative influences of the GDR 'élite' in the late 1960s, ranging from individuals like Walter Ulbricht, Erich Honecker and Willi Stoph, to leading first secretaries of the 'Bezirke' and the emerging classes of managers, technologists, social scientists and academic ideologists. Some attention is also given to the army and to those who 'never made it' for whatever reason, as well as to the tensions between the old guard of veteran communists and the younger functionaries. The new type of young leader in the GDR is seen as being aged between thirty-three and forty-four, a graduate, a manager with a technical background (not a lawyer) and emerging from central government rather than the local Party organization. A highly informative dossier which gives flesh, bone and character to otherwise abstract figures.

242 **Freedom, democracy, human rights – for whom and for what?**
Tord Riemann, Ernst-Otto Schwabe. Berlin (East): Panorama DDR, 1976. 63p.

An East German view of the definitions of freedom (for both the individual and the media) and human rights, reflecting the sensitivity of this issue for the GDR in the wake of the Helsinki Agreements and rising internal dissidence. This volume is useful for it shows how liberty is linked to economic security and provides a strong critique of Western indignation over human rights in communist countries.

243 **Other governments of Europe: Sweden, Spain, Italy, Yugoslavia and East Germany.**
Michael Roskin. Englewood Cliffs, New Jersey: Prentice-Hall, 1977. 182p. bibliog.

Includes an excellent short review of aspects of East Germany, written in a relaxed style. Roskin concludes that, compared to other European governmental models, the GDR is 'a perfection of the Soviet system', largely owing to its Prussian traditions and technological base. A brief but informative historical review of the country's development is supported by descriptions of the major institutions, including the Socialist Unity Party (SED). Quite novel for such a wide-ranging article is the attention given to such issues as national pride and history, with an engaging mix of objective facts and impression. Apposite comparisons are drawn with West Germany and the overall conclusion is that the GDR is governed through 'control without terror' by a party which has delivered economic stability but remains unsure of popular loyalty.

244 **Politics and change in East Germany: an evaluation of socialist democracy.**
C. Bradley Scharf.   Boulder, Colorado: Westview Press; London: Frances Pinter, 1984. 221p. map. bibliog.

The aim of this volume is to provide an introduction to East German politics and society which is 'readily comprehensible to English-speaking audiences'. Its recurrent central theme is the GDR's search for a sense of national identity. The author points to four major factors which are at play here: the influence of German cultural tradition; the extent of Soviet penetration; the attempt to plan the economy on socialist principles; and the development of an advanced urban-industrial society which has given rise to new ecological problems.

245 **National consciousness in divided Germany.**
Gebhard Ludwig Schweigler, introduction by Karl W. Deutsch.
London; Beverly Hills, California: Sage, 1975. 287p. bibliog. (Sage Library of Social Research, vol. 15).

The so-called 'German Question', which arose with the dismemberment of the Reich at the end of World War II, may be formulated in simple terms: can the division of what remained of Germany in 1945 into two separate states – the Federal Republic and the Democratic Republic (both founded in 1949) – be regarded as more than a temporary arrangement? The importance of Schweigler's challenging book is that he answers this question with an unequivocal 'yes'. He does so on the basis of a study of public opinion, which demonstrates that the citizens of each state have developed a separate national consciousness which has replaced the single 'German' national consciousness they might once have shared. More controversially: 'A way back toward a politically effective all-German national consciousness just does not appear to be possible.' In direct contradiction to those who say that peace in Europe will be secure only when German reunification is achieved, Schweigler argues that the two stable states which have actually become established are the best guarantee of that peace. He adduces a wealth of evidence from public opinion surveys which support his case, although the preponderance of his material inevitably relates to the Federal Republic. Indeed, 'the unavailability of hard data directly from the GDR makes any attempt to gauge East German national consciousness a hazardous intellectual enterprise', and this is undoubtedly the point on which Schweigler's thesis is most open to question.

246 **The government and politics of East Germany.**
Kurt Sontheimer, Wilhelm Bleek.   London: Hutchinson, 1975. 205p. bibliog.

This study by two West German political scientists constitutes a model of analysis, balancing the critical approach of outsiders with an objective presentation of the GDR as perceived from within. Although rather modestly not claiming to present new research findings, it tries to present the first total picture of the political, social and economic system of the GDR together with its foreign policy. There are sections on: the division of Germany and the birth of the GDR; the role of ideology compared with social reality; the Socialist Unity Party (SED) and the National Front; the structure and administration of the state; the legal and educational systems; the economy; foreign relations; and defence. The volume concludes with a thoughtful consideration of both West and East German perceptions of nationhood and the concept that a supranational 'European peace' may supersede the traditional preoccupation with state frontiers. A useful annotated and thematically arranged bibliography is appended.

247 **Untertänigkeit: heritage and tradition.**
Dietrich Staritz, translated from the German by Margy Gerber.
In: *Studies in GDR culture and society 6: selected papers from the eleventh New Hampshire Symposium on the German Democratic Republic*. Edited by Margy Gerber (et al.). Lanham, Maryland; New York; London: University of America Press, 1986, p. 37–48.

Analyses the perpetuation of the historical German penchant towards authoritarianism which, in the immediate post-war period, remained strong in both the Western and Soviet Zones. Whereas the Western powers relied on the long-term persuasive effects of democratic institutions and procedures to counteract these attitudes, the communists trusted in socio-economic changes and even exploited subservience in the short term to establish Party authority, especially among the older generation. Not until the 1970s has this GDR-specific authoritarianism shown signs of being questioned by a younger generation. The need for greater consultation with various sections of society is likely to compel the Socialist Unity Party (SED) to compromise its bureaucratic-authoritarian style of administration.

248 **Nationalism in the German Democratic Republic.**
John Starrels. *Canadian Review of Studies in Nationalism*, vol. 2, no. 1 (fall 1974), p. 24–37.

Examines the phenomenon of East German nationalism from a sociological angle. Principally, this article reviews official attempts to stress a separate East German identity from the end of World War II up to Honecker's doctrine of demarcation (*Abgrenzung*) in the early 1970s. His view is that generational change and the growing acceptance of a set of norms and values have led to the formation of a separate GDR nationalism, although he believes that it is a largely non-emotional phenomenon.

249 **Politics in the German Democratic Republic.**
John M. Starrels, Anita M. Mallinckrodt. New York; Washington, DC; London: Praeger, 1975. 396p. (Praeger Special Studies Series).

Discounting the traditional totalitarian model, this work offers a 'systems-function' approach to the GDR which looks at what the homogeneous political system consists of from within, and how it actually functions (not how we think it ought to be). The system comprises 'input' and 'output' functions such as 'leadership selection' (= 'elections'), 'rule application' or 'enforcement' (= 'the bureaucracy' and 'judiciary'): the traditional terms are avoided as external prejudgments. Semantics notwithstanding, many traditional 'loaded' terms do crop up to describe what 'is', but this volume contains a welter of objectively presented data and analysis on political culture, ideology, communication, Party leadership, and the decision-making processes within the GDR. Neither are external relations and future prospects neglected, for the GDR has finally been accepted as an 'arrived' nation with a population passively accepting the requirements of public life. A textbook for students of the GDR's political system.

250 **Two Germanies and the transformation of Europe.**
John M. Starrels. In: *Innovation in communist systems.* Edited by Andrew Gyorgy, James A. Kuhlmann. Boulder, Colorado: Westview Press, 1978, p. 105–14.

Looks initially at the impact which Eurocommunism has had on the two Germanies. The author argues that while confirming the FRG's own long-standing anti-SED stance, a liberal communist movement willing to function within Western parliamentary systems not only challenges the Socialist Unity Party's (SED) authority as such, but also its claim to unique historical legitimacy (was this the only road to socialism after all?). The human rights declarations of Helsinki, intra-German détente and the competitive proximity of West Germany have, it is asserted, also stimulated a latent popular dissatisfaction. Finally, Starrels makes some general and somewhat abstract observations on the reunification question, which is seen as a function of how Europe as a whole might eventually evolve. If a Western communist power should attain power, then the SED would become an inevitable point of contrast.

251 **Ulbricht: a political biography.**
Carola Stern, translated from the German by Abe Farbstein.
London: Pall Mall Press, 1965. 231p. bibliog.

Stern justifies her biography of a man she calls a 'dull' dictator by asserting that there is a need to counteract both the widespread ignorance about Walter Ulbricht himself, and also the 'falsifications' of the history of German communism being produced in the GDR. Interestingly, she also defends Ulbricht against some of the charges often levelled against him in the West, such as his alleged guilt for the imprisonment of Ernst Thälmann, but she also unearths material which Ulbricht would have preferred to leave buried, for example his praise of Stalin's purges. Stern admits she finds it impossible to write dispassionately about the 'politically dangerous and spiritually warped German petty-bourgeois' who was then (and remained until 1971) the most powerful man in the GDR. Notwithstanding this, her account is both readable and informative and remains, even today, a valuable introduction to this important figure.

252 **The People's Republics of Eastern Europe.**
Jürgen Tampke. London; Canberra: Croom Helm, 1983. 178p.

Looking at Eastern Europe as a whole, Tampke rejects the prevailing Western view that the Soviet Union merely set up through force of arms a ring of unpopular puppet régimes, and that communist parties had acquired a considerable power base through consistent anti-fascism and German barbarities. In a chapter entitled 'The German Democratic Republic: Economic Miracle?' (p. 68–82), Tampke affords a well-argued, sympathetic study of its development, praising economic and social attainments, even finding that the Berlin Wall 'did not imprison the people of the GDR, as is so often claimed in the West'. He considers in detail the long-term educative aims of socialism in industry and is fiercely critical of GDR coverage by Western media. Western convergence theories predicting the end of socialism are reviewed and there is also a short section on recreation and entertainment (including nightlife and horse-racing). An informative view of the GDR from a clear sympathizer.

253   **The other German system: a look at the German Democratic Republic.**
Rüdiger Thomas.   In: *Contemporary Germany: politics and culture*. Edited by Charles Burdick, Hans-Adolf Jacobsen, Winfried Kudszus. Boulder, Colorado; London: Westview Press, 1984, p. 203–32. map. bibliog.

Thomas's essay begins with a discussion of the history of the GDR, which he divides into three main phases: the 'formational phase' (1945–49); the 'socialist revolution stage' (1949–61); and the 'post-revolutionary consolidation phase' (since 1961). He then considers the fundamental features of the GDR's political system as well as economic development, social mobility, and the question of social security. In his final section, he turns to the perennial problem of German reunification, which he sees as highly unlikely; rather, Germany faces a 'double future'. However, 'political unity is not a necessary condition for national identity', and Germans in both states will continue to have a special relationship to each other provided that channels of communication are kept open. A valuable contribution, occasionally spoiled by some leaden English.

254   **Political culture and the nation in the GDR.**
Werner Volkmer.   *GDR Monitor*, no. 11 (summer 1984), p. 13–23.

The question to which Volkmer addresses himself is whether there are separate political cultures in the two German states. He begins by tracing the changing attitude in the GDR to various aspects of German history, noting, for example, the rehabilitation of Martin Luther, before looking at official GDR views of the German nation. He notes in particular recent statements which again admit the possibility of reunification under socialism. To answer his major question, Volkmer discusses Günter Gaus' book *Wo Deutschland liegt. Eine Ortsbestimmung* (q.v.) in which it is claimed there is a distinct East German consciousness, a view Volkmer is unable to share. Volkmer sees the division of Germany emanating from continuing power politics much more than from a separate political culture.

255   **Walter Ulbricht. Biographischer Abriss.** (Walter Ulbricht: a biographical sketch.)
Heinz Vosske.   Berlin (East): Dietz, 1983. 422p.

The only biography published in the GDR to cover the whole span of Ulbricht's career. Earlier biographies include Johannes R. Becher, *Walter Ulbricht. Ein deutscher Arbeitersohn* [Walter Ulbricht: a German worker's son] (1967) and Lieselotte Thoms, Hans Vieillard and Wolfgang Berger, *Walter Ulbricht. Arbeiter, Revolutionär, Staatsmann. Eine biographische Skizze* [Walter Ulbricht: worker, revolutionary, statesman: a biographical sketch] (1968). Heinz Vosske is well qualified to write this biographical sketch: not only is he Professor of the

History of the German Labour Movement of the Central Committee's Institute for Marxism-Leninism and Director of the Socialist Unity Party's (SED) Central Party Archive, but he has also written biographies of two other GDR leaders, Wilhelm Pieck and (with Gerhard Nitzsche) Otto Grotewohl. Although the Ulbricht volume provides considerable biographical detail, it makes no attempt to discuss important and sensitive issues such as the internal opposition to Ulbricht in 1953 and between 1956 and 1957, the Ulbricht cult in the 1960s, the New Economic System after 1963, and Ulbricht's enforced resignation in 1971.

Dissent, Opposition and the Unofficial Peace Movement

Dissent and opposition

256 **The limits of the Leninist opposition: reply to David Bathrick.**
Andrew Arato, Mihaly Vajda. *New German Critique*, issue
no. 19, (winter 1980), p. 167–75.

Attacks the uncritical reception in the West of Rudolf Bahro and his book *Die
Alternative* [Stuttgart, FRG: Europäische Verlagsanstalt, 1977; translated into
English by David Fernbach as *The Alternative in Eastern Europe* (q.v.)] in the
West by Marxists such as David Bathrick [see 'The politics of culture', (q.v.) and
'Rudolf Bahro's *Neo Leninism* in context', (q.v.)]. The latter welcome Bahro
because he reaffirms certain assumptions which the authors believe can no longer
be taken for granted, i.e., the utopia of the end of political alienation in 'real
existing socialism', the progressive nature of so-called socialist societies given
certain reforms, and the traditional hostility of classical Marxist theory to the
institutions of civil society in its capitalist form.

257 **DDR-konkret. Geschichten und Berichte aus einem real
existierenden Land.** (GDR – in concrete terms: stories and reports
from a really existing country.)
Thomas Auerbach (et al.). Berlin (West): Olle & Wolter, 1981.
137p.

A collection of prose pieces and poems by six young writers, all of whom left, or
were expelled from, the GDR in the wake of the controversial expulsion of Wolf
Biermann in November 1976. The whole volume depicts life in the GDR in a
highly critical light. The title is an ironic reference to the motto adopted in the
early 1970s by the officially sponsored 'Bewegung schreibender Arbeiter'
(movement of worker-writers).

Dissent, Opposition and the Unofficial Peace Movement. Dissent and opposition

258 **The Alternative in Eastern Europe.**
Rudolf Bahro, translated from the German by David
Fernbach. London: New Left Books, 1978. 463p.

The point of departure for Bahro's book is that 'really existing socialism' has not improved the lot of the working masses but has merely reproduced their alienation and subordinate mentality in a different form. The significance of his radical critique is that it is mounted by someone who comes from within the Party ranks. Bahro sees the Stalinist bureaucratic-political structure of socialist societies as serving its own, rather than the interests of the community. He identifies as the main causes of economic inefficiency and stagnation: centralized planning; an obsessive approach to the fulfilment of production plans; and a distortion of information from the base to the peak of the hierarchical administrative pyramid which subordinates real productivity to meeting the expectations of the apparatus. He sketches an imaginative communist alternative which would entail: an abolition of subordinate mentality and behaviour; the elimination of bureaucratic corruption and privilege and the ending of what he calls 'the vertical division of labour'; a more equal wage structure; wider educational possibilities; and, above all, a much greater general involvement in genuinely democratic processes of decision-making and government.

259 **Introductory lecture to the *Alternative*.**
Rudolf Bahro, translated from the German by Karl Reyman. In:
Communism and Eastern Europe. Edited by Frantisek Silnitsky,
Larisa Silnitsky, Karl Reyman. New York: Karz, 1979, p. 186–232.

The oppositional book *The Alternative* (q.v.), prepared in secret for over five years by the lifelong Socialist Unity Party (SED) *apparatchik*, Rudolf Bahro, came from nowhere and with maximum publicity, to transform a hitherto unknown figure from obscurity to fame as possibly the GDR's most powerful dissident. Bahro prepared his own summary of his book in the form of six lectures which are reprinted here. He dissects the Soviet system as realized in the GDR in terms of the worker's 'subalternity' – his subordination to a state authority with a complex and brazenly exercised monopoly of economic resources. As a solution Bahro advocates a Marxist utopia which places social equality and equitable allocation over individual freedom. A new socialist party will achieve this and effect a restructuring of human needs. His avoidance of 'liberalism' in favour of a controlled levelling which will ultimately liberate mankind makes him unique among dissidents.

260 **The politics of culture: Rudolf Bahro and opposition in the GDR.**
David Bathrick. *New German Critique*, issue no. 15 (fall, 1978),
p. 3–24.

Bathrick explores the historical contingencies which led Rudolf Bahro to write his radical critique of 'real existing socialism' in the GDR. He sees Bahro as the first major voice of opposition from within the ranks of the Party apparatus. He is viewed as part of a minority, dissident intelligentsia which – unlike similar movements in other parts of Eastern Europe – has no links with a broad popular cultural base from which to draw support. Bahro's views are discussed in the context of literary dissenters such as Christa Wolf and Wolf Biermann whose, respectively, subjectivistic experimental techniques and raucous anarchistic tone

Dissent, Opposition and the Unofficial Peace Movement. Dissent and opposition

are seen as a threat to official modes of discourse. Bathrick's article also discusses the contribution made by Robert Havemann to the discussion about Marxism in practice: it takes a somewhat sanguine view of the possible influence which Havemann and Bahro, in his *The Alternative* (q.v.), may have on government policy in the GDR.

261 **Rudolf Bahro's 'Neo-Leninism' in context: reply to Andrew Arato and Mihaly Vajda.**
David Bathrick. *New German Critique*, issue no. 21 (fall 1980), p. 147–53.

In this reply to his critics Arato and Vajda (see 'The limits of Leninist opposition: reply to David Bathrick' q.v.), Bathrick, while agreeing in part with some of their reservations about his enthusiasm for Bahro's *The Alternative*, accuses them of 'abstraction' in their searching out of 'areas of theoretical failure'. He also accuses them of disregarding the context in which Bahro wrote the book – that of 'the most monitored social order in the Soviet bloc'. Bathrick reminds his critics that Bahro had paid the price of publicly presenting his theses in the forum of the factory where he worked with arrest and imprisonment.

262 **Opposition und Widerstand in der DDR. Ein politischer Report.**
(Opposition and resistance in the GDR: a political report.)
Karl Wilhelm Fricke. Cologne, FRG: Verlag Wissenschaft und Politik, 1984. 254p. bibliog.

Fricke's thesis is that, since the very beginnings of the GDR, the state has managed to 'criminalize' all forms of political opposition. By claiming that it alone represents the interests and will of the people, it is able to argue that any hint of criticism must be against the people themselves. Against this background, Fricke traces the systematic elimination over the years of all opposition. He describes the ruthless merging of the Sozialdemokratische Partei Deutschlands (SPD) and the Kommunistiche Partei Deutschlands (KPD) and the removal of all effective alternatives. He documents the resistance to the land reform programme and the origins and repercussions of the abortive Uprising of 17 June 1953. The author also follows the fortunes of individual dissidents of religious persuasion as well as those of rebels from within the Party itself: the Harich/Janka group in the 1950s, and later Robert Havemann and Rudolf Bahro. Finally, Fricke provides an account of the role of the 'Church in Socialism' and of the limited efforts of the unofficial peace and ecology movements. For an account of the author's own experience as a 'dissident' in the GDR, see item no. 269.

263 **Vernehmungsprotokolle. November '76 bis September '77.** (Notes of an interrogation: November 1976 to September 1977.)
Jürgen Fuchs. Reinbek, FRG: Rowohlt Taschenbuch Verlag, 1978. 134p.

In November 1976 the twenty-six year old GDR writer Jürgen Fuchs was pulled from Robert Havemann's car in East Berlin, arrested, and imprisoned until August 1977 when he was released to West Berlin. He was never officially charged for his vague crimes of 'slandering the state' or brought to trial. This book is an account of Fuchs' interrogation by the East German secret service and of the methods of psychological terror which they use to break those who fall into their hands. It is also a documentation of how Fuchs survived. At one point he says to his interrogators: 'the analysis of your machinations is my therapy'. His resistance, the maintenance of his sanity, were the result of his confronting his questioners with a detailed breakdown of the methods they were using against him.

264 **Gedächtnisprotokolle.** (Reports from memory.)
   Jürgen Fuchs, with an introduction by Wolf Biermann and songs
   by Gerulf Pannach. Reinbek, FRG: Rowohlt, 1977. 120p.

As Wolf Biermann notes in his foreword, both Fuchs and Pannach were in prison at the time this book was being prepared for publication. Fuchs's text is an attempt to reconstruct from memory the story of his developing conflict with authority, beginning in March 1975.

265 **A Christian in East Germany.**
   Johannes Hamel, translated from the German by Ruth West,
   Charles C. West, introduction by Charles C. West. London:
   SCM Press, 1960. 126p.

This book presents a selection from the writings of Johannes Hamel, pastor to the University of Halle and, from 1955 (apart from five months' imprisonment for his Christian beliefs), lecturer in practical theology in Naumburg. Its ten chapters include 'Pastor in the East Zone' and 'Conversations with Marxists' (both 1951).

266 **Interview with Robert Havemann.**
   Conducted by Pierre Hammer, translated from the French and
   with an introduction by Jack Zipes. *New German Critique*, issue
   no. 15 (fall 1978), p. 37–46.

This interview, secured with great difficulty while Robert Havemann was under strict house arrest in East Berlin in December 1977, is preceded by an account of his difficulties under the Nazis and subsequently at the hands of the East German régime. Havemann graphically details the harassment and surveillance – massive almost to the point of absurdity – which followed his involvement in the protest against the expatriation of Wolf Biermann. His comments broaden into a severe indictment of the GDR. He describes the almost total lack of trust by the people of their government and its official organs, low productivity and work morale, and widespread economic malaise (extortionate prices for consumer and luxury goods being used to subsidize low rents and basic food prices – a mechanism which favours the wealthy and privileged). Moreover, Havemann proceeds with statistics on the high suicide rate, thieving from the place of work, and comments on the inappropriateness of the Soviet model and on power struggles within the upper reaches of the Party. His gloomy account concludes with an attack on the pursuit of the false goals of Western consumerism and the retreat by large sections of the population into private, petty bourgeois idyll.

267 **An alienated man.**
Robert Havemann, translated from the German by Derek Masters. London: Davis-Poynter, 1973. 214p.

This translation of Robert Havemann's *Fragen Antworten Fragen* (Munich: R. Piper, 1970) combines autobiography with a Marxist critique of both Western capitalism and the distortions of socialism as it is currently practised in the GDR and elsewhere in Eastern Europe. Accounts of his treatment at the hands of the Gestapo in 1943–45, and of his interrogation by the East German secret service in 1966 and 1968, are intercut with reflections on the June 1953 Uprising in East Berlin, the Prague Spring of 1968 and, above all, on the reaction of totalitarian régimes to criticism from within. The book is a passionate argument for a humane socialism. Havemann believes this can only come about when the legacy of Stalinism has been eradicated and when Marxism ceases to be what the authorities, for their own convenience, wish it to be.

268 **The socialism of tomorrow.**
Robert Havemann, translated from the German by Karl Reyman. In: *Communism and Eastern Europe.* Edited by Frantisek Silnitsky, Larisa Silnitsky, Karl Reyman. New York: Karz, 1979, p. 173–85.

This essay, originally published on 10 October 1969 in the Hamburg liberal weekly, *Die Zeit*, is perhaps most representative of Robert Havemann's thinking with regard to the Dubček reform era in Czechoslovakia during 1968. Beginning by challenging the Marxist-Leninist view that the capitalist chain would inevitably break, Havemann asserts that socialist revolution has been typical, not of advanced, but industrially and politically backward countries like the Soviet Union, which has imposed a false set of untenable economic values (especially the denial of the law of value) in the heads of Party economists. Economic reform cannot, however, occur without political change, as was attempted by Dubček, from within the Party itself. In other socialist countries, however, such reform has never proceeded from the ruling party which is alienated from the socialist base. True socialism, Havemann argues, still lies in the future.

269 **The accused: seven East Germans on trial.**
Erika von Hornstein, translated from the German by Irene R. Gibbons. London: Wolff, 1965. 224p.

Recounts the story of seven 'representative' East Germans – Eva Fischer, Günter Zehm, Karl Wilhelm Fricke, Hans Beitz, Fritz Drescher, Wilhelm Rode and Werner Dirksen – who served prison sentences in East Germany 'because they were unwilling to submit to force'. The stories are presented as support for the author's contention that in the GDR 'the idea of justice has been destroyed' and that the country itself is 'one vast prison'. All seven prisoners moved to West Germany after either serving their sentences or being released as part of a general amnesty.

270 **Letter from Berlin: a young man in opposition.**
Nico Huebner. *Encounter* (July 1978), p. 84–88.

From the age of sixteen Nico Huebner, the son of influential members of the Socialist Unity Party (SED), refused to conform to the image of youth assiduously

90

promoted by the Party. He withdrew from the Free German Youth (FDJ) organization, protested against lack of freedom in the GDR, and applied for permission to leave the country for West Germany. This short article was sent to the West just before his arrest for refusing to do his military service. In it, he describes how young people like himself soon become painfully conscious of the disparity between Party ideology and actual experience, finding some relief only in the 'Youth Clubs' of the churches, Eurocommunism, the ideals of Robert Havemann and Wolf Biermann, or the West German media. He himself studied the philosophy of Arthur Schopenhauer (1788–1860) 'as a defence against external chicanery and as a relief from the burden of isolation and insecurity'. Nico Huebner now lives in West Germany.

271 **Ein Marxist in der DDR. Für Robert Havemann.** (A Marxist in the GDR: for Robert Havemann.)
Foreword by Hartmut Jäckel. Munich; Zurich, Switzerland: R. Piper, 1980. 208p.

Contains fourteen contributions, some literary (Wolf Biermann, Sarah Kirsch), some theoretical, and some reminiscences, on the theme of the democratic oppositional movement in the GDR, as recently embodied by the stand of the dissident scientist Robert Havemann whose 'Ten Theses' are also reproduced in this volume. Of historical interest are the recollections of the former Socialist Unity Party (SED) functionary, Wolfgang Leonhard, who was with the Ulbricht group in 1945 but left for Yugoslavia after Tito's break with Moscow in 1948 (see item no. 53). Whereas Heinz Brandt exhorts Havemann to come to the West, where and only where true socialism can evolve, Richard Löwenthal documents the origins of Havemann's disillusionment with Stalinism and his attempts to democratize dictatorial communism from within. Further contributions analyse Marxist-Leninist categories of freedom and dialectical materialism, as well as fundamental misconceptions about the proletariat, capitalism and history itself. Finally, Hermann Weber reviews bureaucratic-dictatorial, revolutionary and democratic varieties of communism.

272 **East European dissent. Volume 1: 1953–1964.**
Edited by Vojtech Mastny. New York: Facts on File, 1972. 291p. (Interim History Series).

This is a basic documentation of public dissent and oppositional manifestations in the Eastern Bloc between 1953 and 1964. Within a general review of the nature of East European dissent Mastny points out the requirements for ideologically based régimes to tolerate only orthodox thought, even in areas considered politically unimportant in the West. The volume documents the 1953 Uprising in the GDR and the state's reaction to it, the American food relief programme, and, in some detail, official reactions to the revolt by leading US figures. Leadership purges in 1954 are then considered and this is followed by the Harich Trial of 1957 and Ulbricht's final crushing of opposition within his own Party in 1958. Prominence is given to the building of the Berlin Wall of 1961 and thereafter to the annual tally of escapes to the West, especially those attracting media attention. A useful volume for quick, year-by-year reference to headline-catching political events.

Dissent, Opposition and the Unofficial Peace Movement. Dissent and opposition

273 **East European dissent. Volume 2: 1965–1970.**
Edited by Vojtech Mastny. New York: Facts on File, 1972. 255p.
(Interim History Series).

The starting-point of this volume is the death of the GDR's Deputy Premier Erich Apel in 1965 and the dismissal of Professor Robert Havemann. Also reviewed are Ulbricht's visit to Czechoslovakia in 1968, the crackdown on dissenting students (including Havemann's sons who protested against the Soviet invasion of the CSSR) and the efforts to establish greater control over the universities and remove the traditional academic domination of the humanities through a programme of close links with industry. The more dramatic escapes to the West are documented individually.

274 **In search of the forbidden nation: opposition by the young generation in the GDR.**
Wolfgang Mleczkowski. *Government and Opposition*, no. 2 (spring 1983), p. 175–93.

Argues that the GDR's attempts to win over its young people have been a failure. Even in the early post-war years many of those who moved to the West were young, although no specific opposition groupings developed among young people. It is the Berlin Wall which lies at 'the root of all the subsequent opposition arising in the younger generation'. Mleczkowski divides youth 'after the Wall' into four types: achievers (who use the goals of the régime to achieve their own aims); conformists; those who pursue their own ideas detached from, and parallel to, the state; and small numbers of outright opponents. The distinction between the latter two groups is seen as fluid. Their involvement in the autonomous peace movement and in the All-German orientation which is currently (1986) the subject of much discussion in the GDR – what the author calls that 'search for the forbidden nation' which contradicts the GDR's efforts to present itself as the true fatherland – is considered in some detail.

275 **The new communist opposition: Rudolf Bahro's critique of the 'really existing socialism'.**
Hugh Mosley. *New German Critique*, issue no. 15 (fall 1978), p. 25–36.

A succinct account of Rudolf Bahro's political and professional career, of how, in the wake of the Soviet invasion of Czechoslovakia, he came to write *The Alternative*, and of the circumstances which led to his arrest and imprisonment for treason. The bulk of the article is devoted to an analytical summary of Bahro's radical critique of official Marxism-Leninism, of socialism in practice and of his suggested strategy for a real communist alternative which would involve the dismantling of the 'vertical division of labour', the elimination of bureaucratic privilege and corruption, and the release of greater democratic and educational energies. Mosley sees the achievement of Bahro's book as being 'the creative revitalization of Marx's critique to question both Marx and his socialist post-history'.

276 **Gleichheit, Gleichheit über alles. Alltag zwischen Elbe und Oder.**
(Equality, equality above all else: everyday life between the Elbe and the Oder.)
Tina Österreich. Stuttgart, FRG: Seewald, 1978. 283p.

Having written in her first book *Ich war RF. Ein Bericht* (I fled the Republic: a report) an account of the imprisonment of herself and her family for planning to flee from the GDR to the West in the mid-1970s, Tina Österreich here turns to everyday life in the country, seeking an explanation for why so many citizens wish to leave East Germany. She begins with events from her own life before turning to examples from the lives of friends and relatives. Written in a simple, anecdotal style, the book amounts to a severe indictment of the 'system' as it operates at a local, daily level.

277 **Preface: the special case of East Germany.**
Karl Reyman. In: *Communism and Eastern Europe.* Edited by Frantisek Silnitsky, Larisa Silnitsky, Karl Reyman. New York: Karz, 1979, p. 159–72.

Introducing translated excerpts of writings by Robert Havemann and Rudolf Bahro, Reyman provides an informative review of the lives, activities and influence of these leading Marxist dissidents. Whereas Wolfgang Harich has modified his 1956 liberal views in favour of an immediate proletarian revolution providing 'communism now', Havemann envisages a communist utopia of total freedom and material well-being, while Bahro – in a new vision of Marxism – urges a totally controlled but balanced system in which the state no longer abuses its economic power. Finally, the controversial 'Manifesto' purporting to be a statement of opposition by middle and upper level Socialist Unity Party (SED) functionaries (see item no. 278) is analysed, despite the doubts about its authenticity. Reyman emphasizes the unique nature of East German dissident thinking, which, like the self-styled ideological purity of the SED itself, tends to be heavily 'systemic' and 'perfectionist' in character, seeing only 'either-or' propositions.

278 **Manifesto.**
BDKD (League of Democratic Communists), translated from the German by Karl Reyman. In: *Communism and Eastern Europe.* Edited by Frantisek Silnitsky, Larisa Silnitsky, Karl Reyman. New York: Karz, 1979, p. 233–42.

In 1978 the West German magazine *Der Spiegel* published a 'Manifesto of the First Organized Opposition in the GDR', which purported to originate from middle and senior level Socialist Unity Party (SED) functionaries. The authenticity of the document has been doubted, but it is reprinted here in excerpt form for the fuel it added to the concurrent Havemann-Bahro debate, and for the official concern it aroused on both sides of the Iron Curtain within the context of West German efforts to improve relations with the GDR. The document is fiercely critical of the country's subservience to the USSR and emphasizes the importance of German unity. The authorship is allegedly the illegal 'League of Democratic Communists' (BDKD), which asks for support to organize a unity of communist-democratic forces in East and West Germany.

Dissent, Opposition and the Unofficial Peace Movement. Dissent and opposition

279 **Communism and Eastern Europe.**
Edited by Frantisek Silnitsky, Larisa Silnitsky, Karl Reyman.
New York: Karz, 1979. 242p.

For those interested in the issue of Marxist dissidence within the GDR, this volume contains – in a section on the GDR (p. 159–242) – translated writings by Robert Havemann and Rudolf Bahro, as well as excerpts from the controversial 'Manifesto' of the League of Democratic Communists (BDKD) (see item no. 278) which was published in the West German magazine, *Der Spiegel*, in 1978 and purported to originate from critics within the Socialist Unity Party (SED) apparatus itself. Karl Reyman prefaces the collection with a brief review of the history of opposition to the SED (see item no. 277) and provides an informative introduction to the lives and activities of Wolfgang Harich, Robert Havemann and Rudolf Bahro.

280 **Limits to dissent in the GDR: fragmentation, cooptation and repression.**
Michael J. Sodaro. In: *Dissent in Eastern Europe*. Edited by Jane Leftwich Curry. New York: Praeger, 1983, p. 82–116.

Argues that the isolated forms of dissent which do exist in the GDR have had none of the serious repercussions on the stability of the régime which are manifest elsewhere in Eastern Europe. The author attributes this to: the homogeneity of the Socialist Unity Party (SED) and the unified front it presents to the world; the successful cooption of the technical intelligentsia; the ruthless suppression of dissent (especially since 1976); the lack of any mass support for dissident writers and intellectuals; and (contrary to the situation in Poland) the success of the régime in keeping the role of the Church – as well as that of the unofficial peace movement – within manageable bounds. Finally, and crucially, the East German government has fulfilled its social contract with the people by providing them with the highest standard of living in Eastern Europe.

281 **Rudolf Bahro: dissident in East and West: from *apparatchik* to environmentalist.**
Jürgen Thomaneck. In: *The GDR under Honecker 1971–1981*. Edited by Ian Wallace. Dundee, Scotland: GDR Monitor, 1981, p. 63–81. (GDR Monitor Special Series, no. 1).

An appraisal of Bahro's contribution as a dissident theoretician which sees Bahro's rejection of Marx's notion of the historic mission of the working classes as the focal point of his dissidence. Thomaneck reviews all of Bahro's writing, not just *The Alternative*. He asserts that prior to 1979 and his arrival in the Federal Republic Bahro was primarily concerned with a critique of existing socialism, but thereafter he became a supporter of the ecology movement within his own concept of socialism. Central to Bahro's critique of socialism is his view that the distribution of income is the biggest problem. As an ecologist he has attempted to re-define the notion of progress. Seeing the North-South divide, and not the class struggle, as the vital issue, he maintains that to encourage the developing societies along the road of consumer-orientated expansion can lead only to economic and ecological disaster. Thomaneck is at points very critical of Bahro, accusing him of 'West European cultural hubris, ethnocentricity, and . . . cultural neo-colonialism' and of being 'non-Marxist, non-Leninist, anti-Soviet and downright anti-Eastern Europe'.

Dissent, Opposition and the Unofficial Peace Movement. Dissent and opposition

282 **East Germany: dissenting views during the last decade.**
Werner Volkmer. In: *Opposition in Eastern Europe.* Edited by Rudolf L. Tökés. Baltimore, Maryland; London: Johns Hopkins University Press, 1979, p. 113–41.

The fact that the GDR has, as its neighbour, a country which shares the same history, culture and language distinguishes it, and the form which dissidence takes there, from other countries in the Soviet bloc. Volkmer identifies three kinds of dissidence: that expressed by workers in the form of protests and strikes over economic grumbles; the disaffection of intellectuals such as Wolfgang Harich, Robert Havemann and Rudolf Bahro with their different forms of challenge to existing socialism in the 1950s, 1960s and 1970s; and finally the dissent formulated by writers and artists in their creative work. He discusses here the Wolf Biermann expatriation and provides brief comments on the writing of authors such as Jurek Becker, Sarah Kirsch, Stefan Heym, Volker Braun and Reiner Kunze, whose activities have proved awkward for the GDR authorities.

283 **The nature of dissidence in the GDR.**
Wilfried van der Will. In: *The GDR in the 1980s.* Edited by Ian Wallace. Dundee, Scotland: GDR Monitor, 1984, p. 31–44. (GDR Monitor Special Series, no. 4).

Examines the critical dissent of the literary-artistic intelligentsia in the GDR as the product of an attempt to measure existing socialism with the yardstick of utopian communism. Dissidence in the GDR is seen as 'non-violent, individual or small group protest'. It is linked with the problem of modernism and also with the debate about two German literatures. Drawing on the model provided by György Konrad and Ivan Szelenyi in *The intellectuals on the road to class power* (Brighton, England: Harvester, 1979) it sees some brands of dissidence as manipulated and stage-managed by the authorities. The author discusses individual literary works by Stefan Heym, Rolf Schneider, Heiner Müller and Karl-Heinz Jakobs.

284 **Rudolf Bahro: critical responses.**
Edited by Ulf Wolter. White Plains, New York: M. E. Sharpe, 1980. 237p.

This collection of essays by a broad spectrum of European intellectuals of the left is the result of an 'International congress on and for Rudolf Bahro' held in West Berlin in November 1978 to discuss Bahro's book *The Alternative* (q.v.) and to call for his release from prison in the GDR. Discussing, inter alia, Bahro's place in the tradition of anti-Stalinist opposition, his contribution to the philosophy of Socialism, his critique of the Asiatic mode of production and State Socialism as well as his ideas on change in Eastern Europe, these essays reflect the lively controversy sparked off by Bahro's writing.

Dissent, Opposition and the Unofficial Peace Movement. The unofficial peace movement

285 **Opposition in the GDR under Honecker, 1971–85: an introduction and documentation.**
Roger Woods, with translations from the German by Christopher Upward. London: Macmillan, 1986. 257p. bibliog.

This book sets itself two major tasks: to help its readers towards 'a realistic view of just how widespread opposition is and whether it is a significant force in the GDR', and to ask how far opposition in the GDR is 'the product of a clash between traditional and new political values' and to what extent it derives from conflicts generated by the GDR's own particular brand of socialism. In his comprehensive introductory essay, Roger Woods perceptively discusses what is meant by 'opposition' in the GDR context and skilfully outlines the events and personalities associated with this concept since 1971, with particular attention being paid to dissident intellectuals (Rudolf Bahro, Robert Havemann, Stefan Heym), those 'ordinary' citizens who totally reject the GDR, and the unofficial peace movement. His comments are carefully linked to an excellent selection of well-translated documents. A useful chronology of events and an index are also included. Readers who wish to make up their own minds about the sensitive issue of opposition will be well served by this dispassionate and informative account.

The unofficial peace movement

286 **Is there a peace movement in the GDR?**
Ronald D. Asmus. *Orbis*, vol. 27 (summer 1983), p. 301–41.

Describes the genesis and activities of unofficial peace groups in the GDR under the aegis of the Protestant Church, seeing in these groups the largest such movement in Eastern Europe. The author discusses their call for a 'social-peace service' as an alternative to the draft and examines the repressive response by the authorities to this in their endeavour to restore conformity. Asmus relates the groups' reaction to Soviet foreign policy in the early 1980s and discusses the mediating role of the Church, the European political context affecting the peace movement, and the latter's prospects after 1983.

287 **Schwerter zu Pflugscharen, Friedensbewegung in der DDR.**
(Swords into ploughshares, the peace movement in the GDR.)
Klaus Ehring, Martin Dallwitz. Reinbek, FRG: Rowohlt Taschenbuch Verlag, 1982. 268p. bibliog.

Describes the recent history of the unofficial peace movement in the GDR against the background of the militarization of society through, for example, compulsory paramilitary training and defence studies in schools. These descriptions and accounts are interspersed with extended quotations from GDR sources and with the first-hand reports of the personal experiences of objectors in the GDR. A very useful source for the general reader.

Dissent, Opposition and the Unofficial Peace Movement. The unofficial peace movement

288 **The peace movement enters its second year.**
Gus Fagan. *Labour Focus on Eastern Europe*, vol. 6, nos. 1–2 (summer 1983), p. 19–21.

This report contains an account of the independent movement in the GDR against nuclear weapons in the context of inter-bloc tension, the militarization of everyday life in East Germany and the uneasy relationship between the state and the Christian churches which provide the forum for independent assembly and expression.

289 **The sword and the ploughshare: autonomous peace initiatives in East Germany.**
John Sandford. London: Merlin Press/European Nuclear Disarmament, 1983. 111p. bibliog.

In this succinct and balanced study, Sandford describes the autonomous peace movement which first came to attention in the GDR early in 1982 as 'above all a spontaneous movement of anonymous young people'. While carefully distinguishing it from the official Peace Council of the GDR, Sandford correctly warns against the temptation to see too pronounced a division between the two, pointing out that they themselves are keen to avoid an overt polarization. He makes the further valuable point that the word 'movement' should not be taken to imply a degree of cohesion and organization that is not possible within the context of the GDR. Indeed, were it not for the Church, which Sandford aptly terms 'the sole officially recognised "space" for the articulation of "unofficial" ideas' in the GDR, independent peace initiatives, even of a non-organized kind, would hardly be possible. Through discreet pressure rather than Western-style popular campaigns, the movement has focused attention on the issues which concern it most: military service, and possible alternatives; the militarization of daily life, notably of education (it was the 1978 decree on Defence Studies as a compulsory school subject which, 'more than anything else, was the factor that really awakened the new autonomous peace movement in the GDR'); the extent to which the GDR can make unilateral gestures to help lower both tension and the level of armaments; and human rights and civil liberties. Thus, as Sandford correctly emphasizes, there is none of the almost exclusive concentration on nuclear weapons which is so typical of peace campaigning in the West. The volume contains sixteen pages of documents in English translation.

Constitution

290   **Verfassung der Deutschen Demokratischen Republik.**
      Dokumente/Kommentar. (The constitution of the German
      Democratic Republic: documents/commentary.)
      Edited by Reiner Arlt (et al.).   Berlin (East): Staatsverlag der
      Deutschen Demokratischen Republik, 1969, 2nd ed., 2 vols.
      bibliog.

This official GDR presentation of the 1968 constitution begins with a series of
documents, including parliamentary speeches by Walter Ulbricht on the new
constitution. There follow the individual paragraphs of the constitution, each of
which is commented on. In this way, the reader learns that citizens' rights are not
connected with the 'protection of the supposed private sphere of isolated
individuals' but are designed to ensure that citizens play their part in socialist
society. This publication provides a valuable insight into constitutional thinking in
a communist country.

291   **The written constitution – the basic law of a socialist state?**
      Inge Christopher.   In: *Honecker's Germany*. Edited by David
      Childs. London: Allen & Unwin, 1985, p. 15–31.

Surveys the various constitutions of the GDR, pointing out that constitutional
changes are seen in the country itself as reflecting the historical development of a
socialist society. Hence the present constitution retains few vestiges of the 1949
constitution, which contained many features appropriate to a liberal democratic
state. Christopher draws attention to the major areas of change, including the
different interpretation of the national question. She pays particular attention to
the role of the judiciary, emphasizing that the GDR's constitution rejects the
Western idea of the division of power, that is, the separate powers of the
legislature, the executive and the judiciary as elaborated by Montesquieu in 1748.
She also deals with the question of human rights, which allegedly only exist within
the parameters of the socialist state. Although the author concedes that the

constitution omits reference to major elements of the political process, that it lacks the authority which an independent constitutional court would provide, and that much of it is propagandistic, Christopher does conclude that it is a true 'basic law of the GDR'.

292 **A constitutional history of Germany in the nineteenth and twentieth centuries.**
H. W. Koch. London; New York: Longman, 1984. 400p. maps. bibliog.

As the title implies, only a small portion of this book relates to the GDR, in fact just a part of the final chapter. This deals at most length with the events leading to the division of Germany and to the establishment of two German states. A brief section on the GDR is largely devoted to the constitution but does not lay enough stress on the different constitutions the GDR has lived under.

293 **Die Verfassung der Sowjetischen Besatzungszone Deutschlands. Text und Kommentar.** (The constitution of the Soviet Zone of Occupation in Germany. Text and commentary.)
Siegfried Mampel. Frankfurt am Main, FRG: Alfred Metzner Verlag, 1966. 2nd ed. 514p.

This book is so arranged that each paragraph of the 1949 GDR constitution is accompanied by a commentary. In his preface, Mampel points out that there are major discrepancies between the text of the constitution and the reality of the GDR. Thus, in the section on basic rights he refers to the discussion within the GDR about how the rights referred to in the constitution have developed subsequently, during the transition to socialism. Whilst in the nature of things this book cannot provide up-to-date information, it remains useful to those interested in the constitutional history of the GDR.

294 **Die sozialistische Verfassung der DDR. Text und Kommentar.** (The socialist constitution of the GDR: text and commentary.)
Siegfried Mampel. Frankfurt am Main, FRG: Alfred Metzner Verlag, 1972. 1,174p. bibliog.

As its length shows, this book is an exhaustive exegesis of the 1968 constitution, with about thirty pages reproducing the text of the constitution and the remainder devoted to comment and explanation. In his commentary, Mampel seeks to take into account the constitutional reality (*Verfassungswirklichkeit*) of the GDR, although he stresses that he is writing from a legal rather than a socio-political standpoint. This is clearly a book for the specialist.

295 **Die neue Verfassung der DDR.** (The new constitution of the GDR.)
Introductory commentary by Dietrich Müller-Römer. Cologne, FRG: Verlag Wissenschaft und Politik, 1974. 112p.

This volume contains the text of the GDR constitution following the 1974 amendments, the text of the law that provided for the 1974 revision and the commentary by Müller-Römer who begins by summarizing the changes made in

Constitution

1974, which he describes as creating a totally new constitution. He then provides a historical survey of the GDR constitutions, pointing to the impermanent nature of constitutional provisions in socialist societies. The final sections of the commentary deal with the provisions of the 1974 constitution with sections on the economic system, basic rights, administration and the law. Müller-Römer stresses the differences between the GDR constitution and that of a Western society, seeing in the GDR constitution a reflection of the 'totalitarian character of the SED-régime'.

296 **Die Verfassung der DDR. Entstehung, Analyse, Vergleich, Text.**
(The constitution of the GDR: inception, analysis, comparison, text.)
Herwig Roggermann. Opladen, FRG: Leske Verlag, 1970. 248p. bibliog.

Roggermann attempts to place the 1968 constitution, whose text forms an appendix to the book, in a variety of contexts. One interesting departure, which forms the other appendix, is to juxtapose the provisions of the GDR constitution with those of the Federal Republic's Basic Law in the areas of basic rights and duties and institutional and protective guarantees. Additionally, Roggermann seeks to explain the GDR constitution in terms of German and socialist constitutional developments and against the background of Marxist-Leninist ideology. A further major part of the work is an explanation of the provisions of the two constitutions. One interesting thesis is that, faced with problems common to all industrial states, the constitutions of both German states come up with comparable solutions behind the different ideological façades.

297 **Die Verfassung der 'Deutschen Demokratischen Republik'. Entstehung, Inhalt und Entwicklung.** (The constitution of the 'German Democratic Republic': origins, content and development.)
Werner Schulz. Frankfurt am Main; Herrenalb, FRG: Ikulta, 1959. 102p. bibliog.

In addition to the text of the 1949 constitution, this volume contains the historical background leading up to the establishment of the GDR under its first constitution. Approximately one third of the text is given over to a critical commentary on the constitution, which points out discrepancies between theory and practice. A summary postulates the thesis that in the GDR there is no possibility of preventing a single group from exercising uncontrolled power; not only is the constitution itself flawed – there is no separation of powers and no constitutional court – but also the Socialist Unity Party (SED) has usurped any constitutional rights theoretically enjoyed by the people.

Berlin (East), the Wall and Escapes

298 **Agreement on Berlin.**
Dennis L. Bark.   Washington, DC: American Enterprise Institute
for Public Policy Research; Stanford, California: Hoover
Institution on War, Revolution and Peace, 1974. 131p. map. (AEI-
Hoover Policy Study, no. 10).

This study of the negotiations leading to the Quadripartite Agreement on Berlin
in September 1971 attempts to 'adopt to some extent a West Berliner's point of
view'. The division of Berlin had always implied hardship and uncertainty for the
city's inhabitants and the building of the Berlin Wall closed the escape route to
the East Germans while increasing the isolation and vulnerability of the West
Berliners. However, the solution, or partial solution, of the Berlin problem lay
not with the Berliners, nor with the Germans, but with the Four Powers whose
desire for negotiations was tempered by an unwillingness to surrender positions.
The historical background to the negotiations is outlined in an introductory
chapter and the text of the agreement and some supporting documents are
included in the appendix. While seeing the agreement as a major contribution to
the improvement of East-West relations, the author is concerned that many issues
still remain to be resolved and is critical of the West for its failure to adopt a
tougher line on the question of the Soviet Consulate-General in West Berlin.

299 **Berlin East and West in pictures.**
David Binder, introduction by Charles B. Anderson.   London;
Melbourne, Australia; Johannesburg: Oak Tree Press, rev. ed.,
1965. 64p. map.

First published shortly after the construction of the Berlin Wall, this book remains
worth consulting today for its numerous photographs of Berlin in the late 1940s
and the 1950s. The accompanying text is generally factual in nature, an anti-
communist undertone being held largely in check, and is divided into six sections:
the area; history; the Wall; the people; the economy; and the future.

300 **The diplomacy of the Quadripartite Agreement on Berlin.**
Honore M. Catudal Jr., foreword by Kenneth Rush. Berlin
(West): Berlin Verlag, 1978. 335p. bibliog.

The Quadripartite Agreement on Berlin (1971), the major legal instrument
guaranteeing the status and future of West Berlin, was the outcome of delicate
and lengthy negotiations between the Four Powers (Britain, the United States,
the USSR and France). Set against the background of Berlin's history after the
building of the Wall, this book presents a detailed picture from 'behind the
scenes'. The exhaustive analysis of the negotiations themselves is based both on
the official record publicly available and extensive interviews with Western Allied
(but not with Soviet) and German officials. In particular, Catudal shows how both
sides were willing to make compromises to ensure a successful outcome. In a
lengthy foreword, Ambassador Kenneth Rush, who led the negotiations from the
American side, describes this account as 'essentially sound and authoritative',
while stressing that some information is of necessity classified and therefore
unavailable. *Ad interim*, this will probably remain the most useful reference work
on this subject.

301 **Bridge across the sky: the Berlin blockade and airlift, 1948–49.**
Richard Collier. London: Macmillan; New York: McGraw, 1978,
239p. map.

The dramatic story of the Soviet blockade of Berlin between June 1948 and May
1949 is here retold in the best traditions of 'fly-on-the-wall' journalism. Collier's
highly readable narrative benefits from his interviews with many of the pilots,
officials, and others who participated in the successful struggle to break the
blockade. Eight pages of photographs and a chronology of events are also
included. See also item no. 70.

302 **Living in Berlin.**
Barbara Einhorn. London; Sydney: Macdonald, 1986. 45p. map.

A lucid and attractively illustrated introduction to life in East and West Berlin
aimed at readers aged between nine and thirteen years. The text provides a
balanced impression of life on both sides of the Wall and the choice and layout of
photographs is excellent.

303 **The Berlin Wall.**
Norman Gelb. London: Michael Joseph, 1986. 291p. bibliog.

This is a competent book, made more interesting because the author was an eye-
witness to the events he describes. It takes us from the events leading to the
capture of Berlin in 1945 up to the present time. Its main focus of attention is
1961, when the Wall was built. An earlier and very thorough treatment of the
same subject can be found in Curtis Cate's *The Ides of August. The Berlin Wall
crisis, 1961* (New York: M. Evans, 1978. 534p. map. bibliog.).

304   **Berlin: success of a mission?**
      Geoffrey McDermott, foreword by Anthony Greenwood.
      London: André Deutsch, 1963. 147p. map.

The McDermott case and the McDermott plan for Berlin were headline news in the summer of 1962. Geoffrey McDermott, the senior British diplomatic representative in Berlin with the rank of Minister since July of 1961, was 'abruptly and mysteriously recalled by the Foreign Office', as the former Labour MP, Anthony Greenwood, writes in the foreword. The official reason for the subsequent enforced retirement was partly personal (McDermott's wife had been unwell) and partly the limited promotion prospects for those of his grade in the service. However, it was widely believed that the real reason was that McDermott's ideas and proposals for the future of Berlin had been a source of embarrassment, and had caused strain in relations between Britain and the Federal Republic at a time when Konrad Adenauer's support for British entry into the European Economic Community (EEC) was being sought. This book tells the story from McDermott's point of view and spells out his plan. In summary, this foresaw not only the recognition of existing German frontiers, but also of the GDR and of Berlin as a separate entity, as well as the admission of the *three* German states to the United Nations. Above all, though, it called for Four Power agreement that their common long-term aim was the reunification of Germany and a review of agreements in twenty years. In the wake of Western reaction to the building of the Berlin Wall, such a plan was bound to be controversial.

305   **Der Sowjetsektor von Berlin. Eine Analyse seines äusseren und**
      inneren Status. (The Soviet Sector of Berlin: an analysis of its
      external and internal status.)
      Siegfried Mampel.   Frankfurt am Main, FRG; Berlin (West):
      Alfred Metzner Verlag, 1963. 496p.

Despite the general relaxation of tension in recent years, the legal status of Berlin remains a point of contention. For the West, Berlin continues to be a single city under four power control and the Berlin Wall does not represent an international frontier. By contrast, in the East, even the roadsigns underline the view that (East) Berlin is the capital of the GDR. It is impossible to deny that *de facto* East Berlin (the Soviet Sector) has become more and more integrated into the GDR and Mampel's book traces the legislative history of this process prior to the early 1960s. A documentary section contains the decrees enacted shortly after the building of the Wall regarding the government of East Berlin. In conclusion, Mampel correctly forecasts that the integration will continue; the possibility of the greater tension he refers to, however, if the GDR were also to attempt to undermine the Allied legal position as part of this process, has thankfully not occurred.

306   **Living with the Wall: West Berlin, 1961–1985.**
      Edited by Richard L. Merritt, Anna J. Merritt.   Durham, North
      Carolina: Duke University Press, 1985. 242p. bibliog.

Although the emphasis in this collection of papers (delivered in their original form at a conference organized by the Aspen Institute, Berlin, and the Science Centre, Berlin, in 1981) is clearly on the Western part of the city, East Berlin and the GDR equally obviously play a central part in the discussion, notably in Richard L. Merritt's useful consideration of 'interpersonal transactions across the wall' (p. 166–83). Merritt shows that personal contacts between East and West Berliners have declined ever since the founding of the GDR and the Federal Republic. Hence, his conclusion: 'Every indicator available for the past three decades – for the 1950s, when the border was fully open, for the 1960s, when it was closed, and for the 1970s, when it was partially open again – shows a pattern of decreasing communication . . . In the place of community, estrangement is growing.'

307   **Comrade who went to the Wall for peace.**
      Paul Oestreicher.   *Guardian* (11 August 1986), p. 18.
Written to mark the twenty-fifth anniversary of the building of the Berlin Wall, this article by the International Affairs Secretary of the British Council of Churches argues that, far from being the threat to peace so often portrayed in the Western press, the Wall in fact saved the GDR from collapse and thereby removed the very real threat of war between East and West. This was the proudest claim of the GDR leader, Walter Ulbricht, although he admitted to Paul Oestreicher that the building of the Wall was paradoxically also the moment of his greatest humiliation.

308   **With the wind to the West: the great balloon escape.**
      Jürgen Petschull, translated from the German by C. Searls.
      London, Sydney, Auckland, Toronto: Hodder & Stoughton, 1980
      (English edition 1981). 181p.
The thrilling account of how, in 1979, two families made a daring escape from East Germany at night in a colossal home-made hot-air balloon. Although the focus is upon the tension surrounding the escapees' long preparations, and on the drama of the flight itself, the account provides a thought-provoking insight into the families' perception of life inside the GDR and of the conditions which made them risk so much.

309   **13. August 1961. Die Mauer von Berlin.** (13th August 1961: the
      Berlin Wall.)
      Jürgen Rühle, Günter Holzweissig.   Cologne, FRG: Verlag
      Wissenschaft und Politik (Edition Deutschlandarchiv), 1981. 176p.
      bibliog.
This volume consists of a general introductory historical essay by Rühle and a much lengthier documentary section edited by Holzweissig which deals with the period from ca. 1958 up to the Four Power Agreement on Berlin in 1971. Holzweissig divides this period chronologically into five chapters and in each case introduces a selection of documents. The final ones relate to the 1971 agreement. There follows a chapter on technical aspects of the Wall and one that consists largely of reprinted GDR statements which seek to justify its existence.

310   **The Berlin crisis 1958–62.**
Jack M. Schick.   Philadelphia: University of Pennsylvania Press,
1971. 266p. bibliog. map.
Published coincidentally at the time of the Quadripartite Agreement on Berlin
which sought to remove much uncertainty about Berlin's status and future, this
book analyses in depth the second Berlin crisis, which led to the building of the
Berlin Wall. It is the author's thesis that 'Berlin crises are Moscow's way of
opposing Bonn's policies: in 1958 it feared nuclear weapons acquisition'. This
was, of course, a central concern as the Cuban missile crisis was to underline a
year later, but not the only one. The book takes an historical approach but seeks
always to place the Berlin crisis in its wider international perspective. The author
has had the benefit of many interviews with diplomats, journalists and academics
and has assembled this study from a wide range of sources.

311   **The yellow pimpernels: escape stories of the Berlin Wall.**
Alan Shadrake.   London: Robert Hale, 1974. 160p.
This book contains a limited amount of historical background but concentrates, as
the second part of the title implies, on the efforts of numerous individuals to cross
into the West following the events of 1961 (see also items nos. 272 and 273). The
first part of the title refers to the people, many not motivated by high ideals, who
sought to make such crossings possible. The tone of the book is totally anti-
communist. However much one must sympathize with the plight of those
desperate to enjoy the human right of freedom of movement, it is a simplification
to present a picture of almost the whole population of the GDR as being eager to
leave. In any discussion of this issue, two other factors must be borne in mind:
that people do move in the other direction; and that many former GDR citizens
do not settle down satisfactorily in the West.

312   **The ugly frontier.**
David Shears.   London: Chatto & Windus, 1970. 231p.
Shears concentrates on the physical barrier between the two German states. After
describing how the process of separation culminating in the erection of the Berlin
Wall occurred, he turns his attention to the frontier as it was in the late 1960s. His
main concern is with how the frontier affected people's lives at this time, be they
travellers, or inhabitants of the border regions. He also devotes two chapters to
Berlin. Although he recounts some of the ways people have escaped from the
East, the tone never lapses into sensationalism. The overall political conclusion is
equally objective: the division of Germany is a lasting factor that politicians and
others will have to live with.

313   **Bedrohung und Bewährung.** (Standing firm against the threat.)
Kurt Shell.   Cologne; Opladen, FRG: Westdeutscher Verlag,
1965. 480p.
This study of the Berlin Crisis as it affected both the population and their political
leaders is a classic. Taking the events leading up to the building of the Wall as his
starting point, Shell examines the way in which the crisis developed, the attitudes
of the Four Powers, the two German states, and the non-aligned, in foreign policy
terms, and then goes on to discuss public opinion and public discussion of the

Berlin problem. The analysis of these last two areas, in particular, is as exhaustive as it is revealing. There was an obvious contradiction between West Berlin's symbolic role as guardian of freedom and democracy and the need, in view of the delicacy of the new political situation, for the political leadership to be more guarded in public pronouncements. Other areas covered by this study are concerned with Berlin's relations with the outside world and the effect of the Wall on East Berliners. This includes a discussion of the atmosphere and events in Berlin at the time of the death of Peter Fechter, a would-be refugee shot by East German border guards, who was left bleeding to death of his wounds at the border for nearly an hour with Western police and medical staff helplessly looking on. Fechter's death, just a few days after the first anniversary of the building of the Wall, had a profound influence on the thinking of Willy Brandt, then governing mayor, and the political leadership. An excellent book.

314 **Berlin Crisis of 1961: Soviet-American relations and the struggle for power in the Kremlin, June-November 1961.**
Robert M. Slusser. Baltimore, Maryland; London: Johns Hopkins University Press, 1973. 509p. bibliog.
As the title indicates, the author examines the Berlin Crisis in terms of the superpower dimension. Nevertheless, there is considerable reference to the role of the GDR in the Crisis and to that of its leader, Walter Ulbricht.

315 **Two Berlins – a generation apart.**
Prit Vesilind. *National Geographic*, (Jan. 1982), p. 3–51.
Describes the history of Berlin and its division into two cities. The section dealing with East Berlin emphasizes the contrast with the city's more wealthy Western half – doubly ironic given that East Berlin is itself one of the most prosperous cities in Eastern Europe. An informative, if slightly sanitized account, covering many aspects and containing some contradictions: for example, information on the new building programme in Berlin-Marzahn features alongside photographs of the war-scarred Prenzlauer Berg district. The text is accompanied by excellent photographs.

316 **750 Jahre Berlin. Das Buch zum Fest.** (750 years of Berlin: the Festival catalogue.)
Berlin (East); Leipzig: VEB Tourist Verlag, 1986. 368p. maps.
This book (printed on high quality paper) sets out the impressive programme of events devised by the GDR to celebrate the 750 years of Berlin's history. The events, planned to take place throughout 1987, include a rich succession of concerts, exhibitions, plays, operas and ballets. Of particular note, is the unusually high number of foreign companies and artists invited to take part in the festival. The catalogue also contains useful hints for visitors (addresses, telephone numbers, opening times).

Foreign Relations

General

317 **The dialectics of détente and discord: the Moscow-East Berlin-Bonn triangle.**
Ronald D. Asmus. *Orbis*, no. 4 (winter 1985), p. 743–74.

Presents a detailed and balanced interpretation of the serious strains which became evident in USSR-GDR relations in the course of 1984. At a time when the Soviet leadership was old and weak and lacking positive direction, a 'saga of discord' developed over the question of the GDR's desire to pursue good relations with West Germany, and in particular to go ahead with Erich Honecker's planned state visit to Bonn. Eventually the visit was postponed by the GDR, ostensibly because of some hostile posturing by conservative politicians in West Germany but more probably because of intense Soviet pressure. More generally, these events in the period immediately before Mikhail Gorbachev's accession to power are significant because they show 'the traditionally loyal and orthodox East German régime daring to challenge an old, decrepit, and divided Soviet leadership on an issue vital to Moscow's interests in Central Europe: East-West German relations'.

318 **Deutschland nach dem Grundvertrag.** (Germany after the Basic Treaty.)
Dettmar Cramer. Stuttgart, FRG: Verlag Bonn aktuell, 1973.
174p. bibliog.

It is often overlooked that the conclusion of the *Ostpolitik* raised the international status of both German states, not just the GDR. Indeed, one of the most important consequences of the bilateral Basic Treaty signed in 1972 was their admission to the United Nations in September the following year. Cramer takes this opportunity to retrace the steps leading to this point and to assess future developments. The author considers many aspects: the GDR's attitude to

Foreign Relations. General

Germany and the German nation; the relationship between the GDR and Eastern Europe; West German-Soviet relations under the changed circumstances; the stand adopted by some parts of the Christian Democratic Union (CDU)/Christian Socialist Union (CSU); and the question of reunification. This he sees as dependent on very substantial progress in East-West relations, so substantial indeed that the German question as we know it today would have paled into insignificance.

319 **Wer macht die Aussenpolitik der DDR?** (Who makes the foreign policy of the GDR?)
Anita Dasbach-Mallinckrodt. Düsseldorf, FRG: Droste, 1972. 364p. bibliog.

The simple title of this book is deceptive, for it is a closely researched study of an area about which very little information was available at the time. Who makes the foreign policy of the GDR and how? To provide an answer, the author focusses on four central areas: the decision-makers; the organizational structures; the decision-making process; and the decisions themselves. The method chosen combines social and political science theory with historical analysis and a study of official publications. The main conclusion is that, even as a junior partner of the Soviet Union, the GDR has enjoyed considerable freedom to manoeuvre and has been able to identify clear GDR foreign policy interests. In a lengthy case study of the meeting between Willy Brandt and Willi Stoph at Erfurt in March 1970, the phases characterizing the thinking of the GDR leadership are established and the main outcome of the meeting, from the GDR point of view, is described as the realization that earlier positions would have to be modified.

320 **Zweimal deutsche Aussenpolitik.** (German foreign policy times two.)
Heinrich End. Cologne, FRG: Verlag Wissenschaft und Politik, 1973. 216p. bibliog.

This two-part study provides both an historicopolitical and a systematic analysis of non-recognition. In the first part End analyses the events leading to the diplomatic isolation of the GDR by the West, and the policies and instruments employed to maintain the Western position. He shows how the GDR went some way towards undermining that position in the 1960s by developing relations with some Third World states, and how, finally, changes in international and domestic German politics helped to create the climate in which modifications to a previously rigid non-recognition policy could become a useful tactic. The second part focusses on a number of theoretical issues, in particular a comparison of the foreign policy potential, instruments and activities of the two German states which seeks to demonstrate the superiority of the FRG in the non-recognition area. In conclusion, End proposes a policy of 'co-operative non-intervention' as the optimum peace strategy for Germany.

108

321 **East Germany between Moscow and Bonn.**
Robert G. Livingston. *Foreign Affairs*, vol. 50, no. 2 (Jan. 1972),
p. 297–309.

The Quadripartite Agreement on Berlin was signed in September 1971. Couched
in general terms and skirting many issues, it placed the onus on the two German
states to come to agreement on the details by direct negotiation between
themselves. For the GDR, this was an historic development and Livingston takes
this opportunity to assess the internal political situation of this new arrival as a
'full fledged actor in the politics of European security' and what is more, an actor
with a new director, for Erich Honecker had only taken over from Walter
Ulbricht in May 1971. Livingston describes the GDR as a 'model of technocratic
conservatism' but emphasizes also that the Soviet Union remains the guarantor of
the GDR's 'durability and stability'. However, given the right conditions, the
author firmly believes that there is a specifically East German role to be played in
Europe.

322 **East Germany: the dilemmas of division.**
Martin McCauley. *Conflict Studies*, no. 119 (June 1980). 19p.
bibliog.

In the author's view the GDR – generally regarded as one of the most stable
states in Eastern Europe – has to contend with numerous sources of conflict. The
tensions arising from East-West German relations in general, and the situation of
Berlin in particular, provide the starting-point for this analysis. Eight sources of
conflict arising from the Quadripartite Agreement on Berlin are discussed; the
author argues that Soviet and East German interests have 'ensured that the
Agreement has proved workable' so far, but there are circumstances under which
the Berlin problem could be reactivated. Likewise, there are tensions arising from
the East-West German relationship which are played out in Africa and the Middle
East. As McCauley rightly points out, the GDR has already chalked up 'victory
after victory' here and the West Germans may find it difficult to rally African
support for their view of the German question as a result. Internal conflicts are
also discussed; cultural, economic, social and political, though the presence of
Soviet divisions, among other factors, has meant that instances of actual unrest
have been infrequent. Is all gloom and doom for the average East German? The
author thinks not: the East Germans know they are better off than their socialist
neighbours and the GDR is likely to survive because of this as well as 'the lack of
a real alternative'.

323 **Foreign policy making in the German Democratic Republic.**
P. Marsh. In: *Foreign policy making in communist countries*.
Edited by Hannes Adomeit, Robert Boardman. Farnborough,
England: Saxon House, Teakfield, 1979, p. 79–111.

It has often been taken as read that GDR foreign policy has no separate identity
of its own, apparently a curious assumption given the GDR's economic growth
into an advanced industrialized society. Marsh shows how Ulbricht exploited the
GDR's economic strength to acquire some foreign policy independence from the
Soviet Union, but then overstepped the mark. This, coupled with a decline in
GDR exports to the Soviet Union during 1970, encouraged the Soviets to search
for a new leader 'who understood correctly the need for GDR policies to fall into

line with those of the Soviet Union'. With the change to Erich Honecker, GDR politics and foreign policy have come full circle, back to its former 'position of loyal Soviet dependent and model of economic and political orthodoxy'. However, this loyalty has paid off; Honecker's reward comes in the form of Soviet support for *Abgrenzung* (demarcation). The author concludes that the GDR's economic strength could give it some freedom of foreign policy manoeuvre but its political dependence on Moscow will curtail it.

324 **Über Schwerter und Pflugschare. Die DDR-Friedensbewegung.**
(About swords and ploughshares: the GDR peace movement.)
Fritz Noll. Neuss, FRG: Verlag Planbeck, [n.d.]. 141p. (UZ Aktuell Series).

This book is in two parts: the first presents interviews with selected GDR citizens in support of official GDR foreign policy: which is presented in toto as a policy for peace (the unofficial peace movement being largely ignored); and the second contains a brief history and analysis of East-West tensions and of the arms race in which US and NATO policies are condemned.

325 **Die Aussenpolitik der DDR. Im Spannungsfeld zwischen Moskau und Bonn.** (The foreign policy of the GDR: caught between Moscow and Bonn.)
Walter Osten. Opladen, FRG: Leske, 1969. 125p. bibliog.

This excellent short book acts as a most useful guide to all the problem areas besetting GDR foreign policy before the launch of *Ostpolitik*. It covers such questions as the scope for an independent foreign policy, the issue of recognition, Berlin, the GDR and the Soviet Union, the GDR and the Warsaw Pact and, of course, ideological and national questions. There is also a short section on the East German Foreign Ministry and the training of diplomats. Though this ground has been trodden more thoroughly by other authors, this volume is invaluable as a handy reference work for this subject area.

326 **Der diplomatische Dienst der DDR. Namen und Daten.** (The diplomatic service of the GDR. Names and dates.)
Jürgen Radde. Cologne, FRG: Verlag Wissenschaft und Politik, 1977. 212p.

Contains 147 individual entries giving biographical details of GDR diplomats, including, where appropriate, information on their careers before 1945. Of the twelve tables in the book, nos. 1–4 identify personnel in the GDR's Foreign Ministry, and nos. 5–12 provide a chronological listing of the diplomatic relations set up with other countries between 1949 and 1975.

327 **New developments in intra-bloc relations in historical perspective.**
Eberhard Schulz. In: *Soviet-East European dilemmas: coercion,
competition and consent*. Edited by Karen Dawisha, Philip
Hanson. London: Heinemann for the Royal Institute of
International Affairs, 1981, p. 41–66.

There are many references in this excellent collection to East German-Soviet
relations and GDR foreign policy (see, for example, the chapter (p. 172–94) by
Edwina Moreton entitled 'Foreign policy perspectives in Eastern Europe') but
this contribution is the only one in the volume to offer a West German view.
Taking the situation in 1980 where 'the maintenance of East-West contacts was
left to the medium-rank powers in Europe' as his starting point, the author
attempts to place this distinctly new situation in historical perspective: one main
conclusion is that Western policies have often had a strong impact on intra-bloc
relationships in Eastern Central Europe. He outlines six partially overlapping
phases characterizing the period 1944–79, and examines in detail some conflicting
national interests during these phases. Schulz concludes that, though Moscow will
be concerned not to lose control, 'the experience, unprecedented since World
War II, of serious talks between the Central European powers across the
European dividing line, will leave behind a slightly changed atmosphere'.

328 **GDR foreign policy.**
Edited by Eberhard Schulz, Hans-Adolf Jacobsen, Gert Leptin,
Ulrich Scheuner, with a foreword by Arthur A. Stahnke,
translated from the German by Michael Vale. Armonk, New
York; London: M. E. Sharpe, 1982. 348p. bibliog.

This volume assembles ten scholarly essays on GDR foreign policy, each by a
different author (nine West Germans and one American). Six of the essays deal
with particular 'problems and conditions' which affect policy, such as the troubled
relationship with West Germany, the controversial status of East Berlin as the
GDR's capital, the country's economic situation, foreign trade and cultural policy
abroad. The final four chapters deal with the GDR's difficult position as a country
caught in a political and economic 'tug-of-war' between West Germany and the
Soviet Union.

329 **External influences on régime stability in the GDR: a linkage
analysis.**
Michael J. Sodaro. In: *Foreign and domestic policy in Eastern
Europe in the 1980s*. Edited by Michael J. Sodaro, Sharon L.
Wolchik. London: Macmillan, 1983, p. 81–110.

Sodaro's starting point is the high degree of influence on events in the GDR from
countries outside, including the Federal Republic and the Soviet Union. He then
examines the nature of the influence in both the economic and political spheres.
Economically, the Federal Republic causes difficulties by providing the citizenry
with a model of higher prosperity; at the same time, the GDR benefits from trade
arrangements and other forms of economic support. The Soviet Union's high
prices for energy in the 1970s have not helped the GDR. Politically, the GDR is
under pressure *inter alia* from inter-German contacts and the Helsinki process. In
conclusion, Sodaro maps out possible scenarios for the 1980s. The one he deems

most likely seems to have held good, namely that, despite all the difficulties, the GDR will remain stable and achieve modest progress.

330　**East Germany.**
John Starrels.　In: *The communist states in the era of détente 1971–1977.* Edited by Adam Bromke, Derry Novak. Oakville, Canada: Mosaic Press, 1978, p. 111–124.

This paper, from the proceedings of a conference originally held at McMaster University in 1975, provides a thoughtful and wide-ranging analysis of the effects and implications of détente for the most orthodox of Communist parties, the Socialist Unity Party (SED). Being in the front-line of socialist countries bordering the West, and practising a 'slab-like solidity' with the Communist Party of the Soviet Union (CPSU), the SED is caught in the dilemma of pursuing policies of internal relaxation and engagement with the West, while also maintaining utmost vigilance and circumspection – especially after decades of isolation and rejection and in view of the dangers posed by internal dissent. Relations with Poland and Czechoslovakia are examined, alongside the SED's strategy of appealing to 'positive neutral' countries in the West. The SED is seen as a potential troublemaker for the future of détente but also as capable of tolerating a degree of pluralism under pressure.

331　**East German foreign policy.**
J. M. Starrels, A. M. Mallinckrodt.　In: *The foreign policies of Eastern Europe: domestic and international determinants.* Edited by James A. Kuhlmann. Leiden, The Netherlands: A. W. Sijthoff, 1978. 302p. (East West Perspectives, no. 4).

A systematic and informative summary of the influences on GDR foreign policy covering four major areas: historical-cultural determinants; socioeconomic factors; institutional factors; and élites in the policy process. Taken together, a picture is presented which emphasizes 'the degree to which the GDR's foreign policy concept simultaneously involves external and internal concerns'. In the final section, the authors attempt a 'pre-theory of GDR foreign policy', which leaves the reader in no doubt that the 'external (Soviet) domination within the East German foreign policy-making process should continue over the foreseeable future'.

332　**East Germany.**
Karl C. Thalheim.　In: *East Central Europe and the world.* Edited by Stephen D. Kertesz. Notre Dame, Indiana: University of Notre Dame Press, 1962. 386p. map. (International Studies of the Committee on International Relations).

This chapter makes a contribution to a section in the book entitled 'Internal developments and foreign relations'. Where East Germany was concerned, the timing for the twin focus of such a study was not to be so appropriate again until Walter Ulbricht's intransigence on *Ostpolitik* eventually forced his resignation in 1971. This chapter takes as its background the ill-fated Seven Year Plan of 1958, the enforced collectivization of agriculture in 1960, rising numbers of refugees and the building of the Berlin Wall in August 1961 – all of which had helped to spread a very negative picture of the GDR internationally. These and other aspects are covered in comprehensive detail here; the author's exposition of the Soviet/GDR position on Berlin and German reunification at that time provides an excellent insight, and the section following offers a close analysis of the events surrounding the building of the Wall.

333 German reunification.
Philip Windsor. London: Elek Books, 1969. 140p. (International Relations Series).

The author's definition of reunification goes beyond the purely territorial and political. He is concerned here to identify 'a working European system within which the individual European states can conduct their relations and adjust their differences'. However, this will not be possible unless, or until, the division of Germany is overcome. In analysing the German problem, an appraisal of post-war German history is presented which focuses on the process of division and the development of the two German states in the 1950s. One chapter deals with Stalinist policy and East Germany; the inconsistencies and contradictions inherent in Soviet policy are examined but there is criticism of Western policy towards the GDR at this time too. The author charges the West with missing opportunities for reunification and, by its insistence on West German rearmament, with increasing Walter Ulbricht's importance for Soviet security and therefore, inevitably, with increasing Soviet control. Written after the Warsaw Pact invasion of Czechoslovakia but before the launch of Willy Brandt's *Ostpolitik*, the book concludes on a pessimistic note, indicating that 'the whole complex of problems is resolving itself into a clash of time scales between the two German states'.

Détente, *Ostpolitik* and relations with the FRG

334 East and West Germany: continuity and change.
Ronald D. Asmus. *World Today*, vol. 40 (Apr. 1984), p. 142–51.

The aim of this article is to assess the *Deutschlandpolitik* of the Helmut Kohl government at the half-term stage. As observers have commonly noted, in this regard, there are many similarities with Helmut Schmidt's government's policy and even a few improvements, at a time when East-West relations generally have been in decline, though – as the author warns – this uncoupling may not continue. Asmus also provides an excellent review of GDR attitudes to the new government; these can be described as initially apprehensive, but gradually relaxing, as Kohl's determination to tread his predecessor's path in relations with the GDR became clear. Though the author is generally positive in his assessment, he is critical of the 'advance concession' tactic, referring specifically to the 1 billion DM credit granted to the GDR and negotiated by Franz-Josef Strauss with practically no strings attached, which he sees as a clear signal that Bonn wished to make concessions in advance of INF (intermediate-range nuclear forces) deployment. The problem with this, in the author's view, is that Bonn virtually leaves it up to East Berlin to set the pace for reciprocal gestures.

335 **Neue *Ostpolitik*.** (New *Ostpolitik*.)
Peter Bender.   Munich: dtv, 1986. 290p. bibliog. (Deutsche Geschichte der neuesten Zeit – German history in the modern period – Series).

A most useful book which summarizes the development of the German question from the building of the Berlin Wall in 1961 to the conclusion of the Eastern Treaties in 1972. A final chapter analyses the implications of these treaties for European security, specifically the European Security Conference and MBFR (mutual and balanced force reductions) negotiations. Konrad Adenauer's Western-oriented policy had been conditioned by anti-communist Cold War attitudes but the main theme of this book is to underline the changes in West German attitudes to the division of Germany and communism which took place in the 1960s, without which a shift in policy would not have been possible. Appropriately, Bender starts with a look back to the 1950s in order to show that from the beginning West German *Ostpolitik* was doubly constrained: by fear of communism and by fear of the country's own past. A collection of important documents, a chronology and some statistical summaries are included in the appendix.

336 **East and West Germany: a modus vivendi.**
Karl E. Birnbaum.   Farnborough, England: Saxon House, D.C. Heath; Lexington, Massachusetts: Lexington Books, 1973. 157p. bibliog.

Birnbaum's book is essential reading for an understanding of the effects of the détente process on relations between the two German states. The interplay of forces leading to the negotiation and successful conclusion of Willy Brandt's *Ostpolitik* provides the starting point for this analysis. The author then concentrates on the official policies of the main actors, Moscow, Bonn and East Berlin, believing these to be 'the most dynamic and closely interrelated areas of policy immediately affecting conditions in the heart of Europe'. The future of East-West relations under these changed conditions is assessed. Birnbaum stresses the European interest in improved relations between the two German states. The texts of the treaties and relevant papers, notes and correspondence are included in extensive appendixes.

337 **The ordeal of coexistence.**
Willy Brandt.   Cambridge, Massachusetts: Harvard University Press; London: Oxford University Press, 1963. 112p.

As governing mayor of West Berlin during the Berlin Crisis which led to the building of the Berlin Wall, Willy Brandt is better placed than most to write a book on coexistence. As he says himself, Berlin is the city where 'in the years since 1945, coexistence has been a living experience'. This book contains the extended and revised text of two lectures delivered at Harvard University in October 1962. Revised, not because the author wished to make any alterations to the substance of the original, but to amplify certain aspects in the light of the

Cuban Missile Crisis soon after. The third chapter is devoted to the question of coexistence in, and with, Germany, and many ideas here were to become key elements in Brandt's *Ostpolitik* at the end of the 1960s. In particular, he states categorically: 'we must constantly re-examine what we can do . . . both to lighten the burden of daily life for our fellow countrymen in the Soviet Zone, and to keep alive the spirit of community between the people of my divided country'.

338   **Deutsch-deutsche Beziehungen.** (German-German relations.)
      Wilhelm Bruns.   Opladen, FRG: Leske, 1984, 4th rev. ed. 212p.
      bibliog.
The change of government in Bonn in October 1982, and the deployment of American intermediate-range nuclear missiles in West Germany in the autumn of 1983, placed many question marks over the future of relations between the two German states. Bruns reviews the development of German-German relations since the conclusion of the *Ostpolitik* in 1969. The result is a comprehensive survey of the most important developments, including Erich Honecker's Gera speech (October 1980). In this speech Honecker underscored his requirements for the future conduct of relations between the two German states, in particular, the recognition by West Germany of East German citizenship and the upgrading of the permanent missions of the two German states to full embassy level, including an exchange of ambassadors 'in accordance with international law'. As a staff member of the SPD-linked Friedrich Ebert Foundation, Bruns is necessarily tentative in his prognosis for the management of these relations under Chancellor Kohl. Though perceiving more continuity than change, he takes some Christian Democrat politicians to task for understating the importance of the Basic Treaty. A selection of relevant documents from both German states is included in the appendixes.

339   **The *Ostpolitik* and domestic politics in East Germany.**
      David Childs.   In: *The 'Ostpolitik' and political change in
      Germany*. Edited by Roger Tilford. Farnborough, England: Saxon
      House, D. C. Heath; Lexington, Massachusetts: Lexington Books,
      1975, 59–75.
Walter Ulbricht's resignation as first secretary of the Socialist Unity Party (SED) in May 1971 is widely regarded as the price he had to pay to the Soviet Union for seeking to thwart Moscow's *Ostpolitik* ambitions. Here, David Childs analyses this and other instances of the effect of *Ostpolitik* on the internal political scene in the GDR. Further changes took place 'at the top', reflecting Honecker's preference for the all-rounder rather than the narrow specialist. In addition to *Abgrenzung* (demarcation from the Federal Republic), other aspects of the SED's ideological response to this new challenge were, an ever closer relationship with Moscow, and what Childs terms 'ideological rearmament'. The cultural thaw of the early 1970s is seen as a deliberate attempt to win the support of writers in meeting this challenge. Childs concludes by outlining the reaction of East Germans themselves to the sudden influx of Western visitors and sees some possibility of serious discussion between the two Germanies with consequent benefits for both East and West.

340 **The GDR – a German nation or a socialist nation?**
Inge Christopher. In: *The GDR under Honecker 1971–1981.*
Edited by Ian Wallace. Dundee, Scotland: GDR Monitor, 1981,
p. 83–89.

There can be no doubt that West Germany's insistence on the 'special nature' of its relationship with the GDR at the time of the *Ostpolitik* put the GDR on the ideological defensive. Walter Ulbricht's perception of 'two states but one nation' was revised in favour of a theory propounding a socialist nation in the GDR and a capitalist one in the West. Between these two, so GDR theorists claim, an objective process of demarcation (*Abgrenzung*) is taking place. Inge Christopher has provided an extremely useful summary of the origins of the GDR's new thinking on this question and points to the major developments in the second half of the 1970s. These include questions of nationality (German) and citizenship (GDR) and reunification from the GDR point of view.

341 **Die Abgrenzungspolitik und die Entwicklung eines
Alleinvertretungsanspruches der DDR.** (The policy of demarcation
and the development of an East German claim to sole
representation.)
Ernst Deuerlein. *Politische Studien*, no. 23 (March/Apr. 1972),
p. 125–32.

This article was one of the first to deal with the then new policy of *Abgrenzung* (demarcation) and it remains one of the most important. The author, one of the most distinguished West German experts on the GDR, reviews the origins and nature of the demarcation policy, identifying it clearly as the political response to Willy Brandt's statement that relations between the two German states could only be of a special nature and examining some of the inconsistencies in the GDR position. He then goes on to propose the thesis that the origins of *Abgrenzung* can, in fact, be traced further back; indeed he puts forward a convincing case for discerning a long-standing East German claim to be the sole legitimate representative of the German working class.

342 **Bonn's eastern policy 1964–71.**
Laszlo C. Görgey. Hamden, Connecticut: Shoe String Press as an
Archon book, 1972. 191p. bibliog. (International Relations Series,
no. 3, published on behalf of the Institute of International Studies,
University of South Carolina).

This book covers two broad areas: the political influences at home and abroad which were eventually to lead to Willy Brandt's *Ostpolitik*; and the responses of the states of Eastern Europe, particularly of East Germany, to this new policy. Apart from using official documents and a wide range of published sources, the author, himself a former refugee from Hungary, has conducted many interviews with senior politicians and government officials. The focus is the Grand Coalition period (1966–69) when Willy Brandt as Foreign Minister and Chancellor Kurt Georg Kiesinger started to implement 'the most imaginative and realistic (policy) formulated by any West German government since the establishment of the Federal Republic', a policy which was brought to an untimely standstill by the Warsaw Pact invasion of Czechoslovakia in 1968 and which, though successful in other areas, had made no headway at all where the GDR was concerned. Görgey's analysis of Walter Ulbricht's response to the wind of change from Bonn and of Eastern European attitudes to the Czechoslovak crisis is excellent.

343 **The *Ostpolitik* of the Federal Republic of Germany.**
W. E. Griffith. Cambridge, Massachusetts; London: MIT Press, 1978. 325p.

The focus of this book is Willy Brandt's *Ostpolitik* which is analysed in some detail in the penultimate chapter. However, the bulk of the book is devoted to Bonn's attitudes to the German question before Brandt became chancellor in 1969. Though the coverage is comprehensive, there are also some unconsidered judgements, and the critical reader will look elsewhere for a more discerning view.

344 **Die Ost- und Deutschlandpolitik der CDU/CSU.** (The policy of the CDU/CSU towards Germany and Eastern Europe.)
Christian Hacke. Cologne, FRG: Verlag Wissenschaft und Politik, 1975. 152p. bibliog.

Given the Kohl government's success in developing relations with East Germany, it is interesting to recall the attitudes of the Christian Democratic Union (CDU)/Christian Socialist Union (CSU) as opposition parties to Willy Brandt's *Ostpolitik*. Reaction was almost exclusively negative as far as Bundestag votes were concerned. However, it was widely known that a number of different opinions were actually represented within the Party and here the most positive attitude was taken by Walther Leisler-Kiep with whom the author worked at the time. It is not surprising, therefore, that the Party is quite sharply criticized for taking a 'wrong turning' in not recognizing that the time had come for détente. Interestingly, Helmut Kohl is seen here as something of a closet Kiep supporter and Hacke calls upon him and like-minded senior CDU politicians to display active leadership especially in the face of resistance within the Party. Ten years later, the author must have been pleased at the turn events have taken.

345 **Deutschlands doppelte Zukunft.** (Germany's double future.)
Peter Christian Ludz. Munich: Hanser, 1974. 181p. Paris: Atlantic Institute for International Affairs, 1974. Published in England as *Two Germanies in one world*.

Taking the new situation created by the *Ostpolitik* as his starting point, Ludz highlights a number of key areas for attention. How does *Ostpolitik* affect West German relations with the Atlantic Alliance and the GDR's relations with her Eastern Bloc partners? What effect will *Ostpolitik* have on relations between the two German states themselves and where are the limits to conflict and cooperation? How will *Ostpolitik* influence the two German states in Europe and the rest of the world? The answers Ludz gave to these questions were necessarily speculative and subjective at the time of writing – hence the essay form adopted. Moreover, some issues which have since proved relevant in the context of East-West German relations (for example, *Ostpolitik* managed by a Christian Democrat-led government, environmental protection, the peace movement and the attitudes of young people) were not raised at all. Overall though, Ludz's conclusions have generally been confirmed by subsequent events.

346   **Foreign policy in Germany: ideological and political aspects of intra-German relations.**
Peter Christian Ludz.   In: *Germany in world politics.* Edited by Viola H. Drath. New York; London: Cyrco Press, 1979, p. 54–77.

In this thorough and scholarly analysis, Ludz reviews developments and highlights some ideological tensions in relations between the two German states. These arise from the fact that the 'political élites in the FRG and the GDR view one another as "negative reference groups" in all conceivable sets of arguments', and also that the Basic Treaty governing intra-German relations 'skirted fundamental ideological reservations'. The result is, according to Ludz, that ideological issues now arise more often in specific form, such as citizenship, or the GDR's tendency to regard itself as heir to the 'progressive' traditions of German history. Ludz makes a strong criticism of the Federal Republic for failing to take effective measures to 'promote a politically responsible awareness of German history and culture and, in particular, a democratic re-evaluation and interpretation of recent German history'.

347   **East Germany and détente: building authority after the Wall.**
A. James McAdams.   Cambridge, England: Cambridge University Press, 1985. 233p. bibliog.

McAdams undertakes the task of explaining why, after setting its face so determinedly against détente in the late 1960s and early 1970s, the GDR not merely accommodated itself to that policy but actually became one of its most enthusiastic supporters. In essence, his thesis is that the régime demonstrated a surprising degree of adaptability to the opportunities unexpectedly offered by what seemed initially to be unfavourable new circumstances. In developing this thesis, he shows a keen eye for the ironies of GDR policy development since the early 1970s. In particular, he stresses how the process of détente, once so fiercely resisted because it appeared certain to undermine the domestic authority which the régime was struggling with limited success to establish, was one which brought: first the diplomatic recognition which the country had sought for over two decades; then important economic advances through improved access to foreign markets (not least in West Germany); and finally the all-important psychological benefit of being able to demonstrate to its own population the GDR's accepted role as an equal partner with the Federal Republic on the international stage. That all this proved to be the case will have surprised no-one more than the régime itself, but McAdams justifiably awards it high marks for eventually showing the ability to respond quickly and skilfully to a momentous change in its circumstances.

348   **German foreign policies, West and East.**
Peter H. Merkl.   Santa Barbara, California: ABC-Clio; Oxford: Clio Press, 1974. 232p. map. bibliog.

On the surface there would seem to be few subjects which lend themselves as readily to a political culture analysis as the attitudes of the two German states to themselves and one another. However, observers of German affairs will know how many factors have to be taken into account to do the subject justice – German history, Germany's guilt, the division of Germany and the role of the German states' new allies. Moreover, there is the question of German reunification. Peter Merkl has marshalled all this information, and more, into a brilliant comparative study of German foreign policies, focussing on Willy Brandt's *Ostpolitik* and the debt it owes to Konrad Adenauer's *Westpolitik*. Far from seeing *Ostpolitik* as a threat to the stability of the GDR, Merkl concludes that the Socialist Unity Party (SED) will eventually accept that the 'new era of cooperation and understanding . . . presents no threat to either one of the two Germanies'.

349 **Freikauf. Menschenhandel in Deutschland.** (Buying freedom: trade in human beings in Germany.)
Michel Meyer, translated from the French by Marianne Lipcowitz.
Vienna; Hamburg, FRG: Paul Zsolnay Verlag, 1978. 224p.

This book, originally produced in France under the title *Des hommes contre des marks*, deals with the procedure practised by the government of the FRG of purchasing the freedom of prisoners in GDR jails. The style is highly journalistic with much of the information personalized. Indeed, a fictional person 'Dagmar Winkler' is invented to dramatize the course of the bus journey out of the GDR. In this way, the origin of the work as a television documentary is clearly visible. This is not to say that it is not informative; there are, for example, reproduced interviews with Rainer Barzel and with the two lawyers, Jürgen Stange (FRG) and Wolfgang Vogel (GDR), who arrange the deals. Meyer's general standpoint is one of moral revulsion against the practice, which he nevertheless views as destined to continue.

350 **The GDR and the German question in the 1980s.**
Günter Minnerup. In: *The GDR in the 1980s*. Edited by Ian Wallace. Dundee, Scotland: GDR Monitor, 1984, p. 3–13.

The central thesis of this contribution is that in the 1980s various factors will combine to challenge the *status quo* as it obtains after the normalization of relations between the two German states. In Minnerup's view, we are witnessing today the end of the prosperous, stable post-war era in Europe and may, in fact, be entering an era reminiscent of the pre-war period. If accepted, this thesis is deeply depressing, but the author argues that at least Germans may derive some hope from the perception that the seemingly immutable division of their country and of Europe may now be open to challenge.

351 **Eastern Europe in the 1970s.**
Sylva Sinanian, Istvan Deak, Peter C. Ludz. New York; London: Praeger, 1972. 260p.

Contains two sets of contributions for a 'Roundtable Discussion' at an international conference on Eastern Europe held at Columbia University in 1971. One discussion deals with the normalization of relations between the FRG and Eastern Europe while the second refers to the role of the GDR within Eastern Europe. Dominated by the prospects of détente, by the advent of Honecker and a

Foreign Relations. Détente, *Ostpolitik* and relations with the FRG

future agreement between East and West Germany, various viewpoints are put on then current aspects of *Ostpolitik* and inter-German relations. A recurring view is that an East-West German agreement, while promoted by the USSR, has been resisted by the GDR and presents problems for the GDR leadership on the issue of German nationhood. Contributors include scholars, journalists and representatives of the Polish government and the FRG.

352 **Der kalte Krieg gegen die DDR. Von seinen Anfängen bis 1961.**
(The Cold War against the GDR: from its beginnings until 1961.)
Hans Teller. Berlin (East): Akademie, 1979. 265p. bibliog.

A highly polemical attack on the alleged 'Cold War' consistently waged by West Germany against the GDR with the aim of undermining and destroying it. The author argues that even the outwardly more conciliatory policy adopted by Bonn in recent years cannot conceal that this fundamental aim has not been abandoned. The volume also includes a chronological table of major events pertinent to its theme and a section of black-and-white photographs.

353 **The quest for a united Germany.**
Ferenc A. Vali. Baltimore, Maryland: Johns Hopkins Press, 1967. 318p. bibliog. map.

Written in the mid-1960s, when progress in the German question was proving very slow in coming, despite the new climate of super-power détente, this book sets out to examine German reunification from many angles and points of view. Adopting a largely historical approach, the author places the division of Germany in historical perspective and examines the attitudes of the main West German political parties to the question of a united Germany. A similar approach is taken to describe the position both of the Socialist Unity Party (SED) and of the people of the GDR. Given the current preoccupation in the GDR with 'progressive' German traditions and history, Vali's section on the presentation of history makes extremely interesting reading. National heroes presented to young people in the GDR include Bismarck and Luther and, in the author's view, this attempt 'to divert German animosity from its natural (eastern) direction into a rather artificial western course was no small feat of historical acrobatics for the leaders of the D.D.R.'. In the conclusion, a number of conditions for German reunification are identified, the most important of which is probably 'patience and time'.

354 **Aspects of the German question.**
Edited by Peter R. Weilemann. Sankt Augustin, FRG: Konrad-Adenauer-Stiftung, 1986. 77p.

In June 1985 a small group of British and West German political scientists came together at Wiston House, Wilton Park, England, to discuss aspects of the German question. This volume contains some of the papers delivered by the German participants, revised and subsequently updated. As the conference was hosted by the Konrad Adenauer Foundation, it is the Christian Democrat view which prevails. The fundamental question underlying the whole collection is that of German identity, and the pain of the division of Germany is coupled with a desire for the Federal Republic's Western partners to understand more clearly than sometimes appears what it is the Germans want. The collection concludes with an essay outlining some of the difficulties involved in comparative research into the two Germanies. An interesting set of reflections by some very distinguished West German academics but it is a shame that the editor has been content with such a laboured translation.

355 Germany's *Ostpolitik*.
Lawrence L. Whetten. London; Oxford, England: Oxford University Press, 1971. 244p. bibliog.

This was one of the first books in English to offer an historical analysis of the change in the relationship between the Federal Republic and the Warsaw Pact countries and, as such, is still a useful reference source. The method employed examines the changes in the positions of the principal states on these key issues: 'the German threat, regional stability, collective security and political accommodation'. The result is a comprehensive coverage of major influences contributing to détente and of some of the tensions and conflicts arising from it. Unfortunately, the book was completed before Walter Ulbricht's overthrow and that event sheds some doubt on the author's assertion that 'it is now possible for East Germany to act virtually as independently as has Romania for the last ten years'.

356 Germany East and West.
Lawrence L. Whetten. New York; London: New York University Press, 1980. 215p.

There are still relatively few sources in English tracing the development of relations between the two German states. This book seeks to plug that gap and to put these relations into an historical perspective. It is the author's basic contention that the two states 'share a common cultural and social background which continues to influence national policy and public behavior', but that 'there are also tendencies . . . that encourage separateness and distinctive national development'. In his earlier book on *Germany's Ostpolitik* (q.v.) the author was unable to comment on the long-term implications of *Ostpolitik* for the GDR. Here he deals with the subject in terms of various problems of social organization, leadership, dissent, authority and legitimacy. He concludes that the Socialist Unity Party's (SED) 'persisting insecurity places limits on both the degree and nature of co-operation it will be able to engage in with Bonn'. A useful appendix lists formal agreements between the two states from 1949–79.

357 Germany and the management of détente.
Philip Windsor. London: Chatto & Windus for the Institute of Strategic Studies, 1971. 207p. (Studies in International Security, no. 15).

Germany's geographical position at the heart of Europe and Germany's division between East and West have obviously increased the country's vulnerability to winds of change in East-West relations. The wind of détente, though gentle, posed new problems for the two German states to solve, specifically in terms of the scope for developments in their relations. These interactions are put under scrutiny in this book, which examines the nature of détente and its implications for the two Germanies during the 1960s. The author contends that, until the mid-

121

60s, détente was managed within the framework of the alliances. Whereas the West moved away from this 'to a pattern of individual initiatives', this coincided with 'a new insistence on the importance of the Warsaw Pact'. How this pattern is reflected in the responses to the Federal German government's new policy initiatives is discussed in detail in the penultimate chapter on the two Germanies.

with Developing Nations

358 **A new Afrika Korps?**
Melvin Croan. *Washington Quarterly*, vol. 21 (winter 1980), p. 21–37.

Croan highlights an important shift which occurred in the early 1970s in the GDR's involvement with Africa. Whereas diplomatic recognition had once been the GDR's aim, this now gave way to the wish to promote the advance of socialism. Besides the considerable material aid and technical advice given to various national liberation movements such as the Popular Movement for the Liberation of Angola (MPLA), Front for the Liberation of Mozambique (Frelimo), South West African People's Organization (SWAPO) and the African National Congress (ANC), the GDR became active in consolidating 'proto-Leninism' in the established African states of a socialist orientation. In Croan's view, it did this primarily to accord with the needs of Soviet policy and to secure greater legitimation for the Socialist Unity Party (SED) at home. At its disposal it had long-standing contacts with liberation movements as well as a strong body of selected cadres and academic specialists trained in African affairs. Although, compared to its military assistance, East German development aid has remained 'rather unsubstantial', the GDR's overall involvement in Africa represents a considerable drain on resources, but one certain reward is that it now 'enjoys considerable prestige throughout the continent'.

359 **Erkennt Ihr, warum wir Euch lieben? (Do you realise why we love you?): the GDR and the states of Southern Africa in the 1980s.**
Geoffrey Davis. In: *The GDR in the 1980s.* Edited by Ian Wallace. Dundee, Scotland: GDR Monitor, 1984, p. 43–70. (GDR Monitor Special Series, no. 4).

The title of this article comes from a speech Kenneth Kaunda made in the GDR in August 1980 and it is an apt choice to illustrate the main thrust of the GDR's policy stand on Southern Africa: support for black liberation and for the key front-line states in their struggle to establish socialist societies. It is widely known that the GDR is involved in military activities in Southern Africa and this article provides useful information about this subject together with a short section devoted to GDR involvement in Angola. Davis dates the GDR's activity from the beginning of the decolonization process and concludes that the differences between West and East German policy in this part of the world are all grist to the mill of *Abgrenzung* (the GDR's policy of demarcation from the West).

360   **East Germany in black Africa: a new special role?**
       George A. Glass.   *World Today*, vol. 36 (Aug. 1980), p. 305–12.

The increased presence of the GDR in black Africa in the last years of the 1970s,
and the extent of East German cooperation with black Africa in a number of
areas, form the starting point of this article. As the author sees it, the GDR's
involvement in this region is linked with GDR membership of the United Nations
and Portuguese withdrawal from Angola and Mozambique in 1975–76. Of course,
this presence is closely linked with the GDR's need to increase its own status and
black Africa is a convenient springboard for establishing the GDR's position on
the world stage. The author catalogues the extent of the presence: the GDR has
relations with over forty African countries but concentrates on a select number
and on specific groups, such as the Popular Movement for the Liberation of
Angola (MPLA), the South West African People's Organization (SWAPO), the
African National Congress (ANC), the Zimbabwe African People's Union
(ZAPU) and the Zimbabwe African National Union (ZANU). Apart from
Romania, no other country of Eastern Europe has as much contact in the form of
visits, agreements and exchanges. The author asserts that, although the policy is
active and expanding, the GDR 'has not yet sought to do more than generally
increase its presence and support in black Africa'.

361   **The GDR and the Third World: supplicant and surrogate.**
       Michael Sodaro.   In: *Eastern Europe and the Third World. East
       vs. South*. Edited by Michael Radu. New York: Praeger, 1981,
       p. 106–41.

Sodaro shows how the GDR first presented itself in the Third World as a
supplicant anxious to gain diplomatic recognition as a sovereign, independent
German state. After this status had been attained (by 1973), the GDR became
more active in the Third World as a surrogate of Soviet foreign policy. By the late
1970s, however, it had to combine its role as surrogate with a supplicant's desire
to secure oil supplies at prices more affordable than those charged by the Soviet
Union from 1975. Sodaro concludes with the justifiable speculation that, given the
unpredictable nature of political realities in the Third World as well as the severe
strain imposed on the GDR economy by its surrogate rôle, the country's Third
World ventures may ultimately bring more burdens than benefits.

362   **East German security policies in Africa.**
       Jiri Valenta, Shannon Butler.   In: *Eastern Europe and the Third
       World. East vs. South*. Edited by Michael Radu. New York:
       Praeger, 1981, p. 142–68.

This essay focuses on East Germany's assertive foreign policy in the Africa of the
1970s, when the GDR placed increased emphasis on military and security
considerations and concentrated its activity both on Angola, Mozambique and
Ethiopia because of their Marxist-Leninist orientation and also on the national
liberation movements – Zimbabwe African People's Union (ZAPU), the African
National Congress (ANC) and the South West African People's Organization
(SWAPO). The authors rightly emphasize, however, that a number of factors,
notably the unstable political situation in new, or emerging, African states as well
as the constraints imposed by the GDR's own economic problems, mean that the
ultimate success of this policy in Africa is by no means certain.

with Western Nations

363 **Alternative to partition.**
Zbigniew K. Brzeziński.   New York: McGraw Hill, 1965. 208p.
(Atlantic Policy Studies Program, Council on Foreign Relations).

Brzeziński challenges the belief that division is a satisfactory way to resolve affairs in Europe and perceives a 'reemergence of the German issue as the key problem for U.S. foreign policy'. Given post-Cold War conditions in Europe, it is the author's belief that the West, particularly the United States, must take the 'creative initiative' to overcome the legacy of World War II. Five policy goals are defined, of which the first seeks to convince Czechs and Poles, in particular, that 'the existence of East Germany limits their freedom without enhancing their security'. The author urges a policy of isolation towards East Germany which would reduce the GDR to an embarrassing anachronism and, by contrast, a policy of peaceful engagement for Eastern Europe where economic factors would play an important role.

364 **The German Democratic Republic and the United States.**
David Childs.   In: *Honecker's Germany*. Edited by David Childs.
London: Allen & Unwin, 1985, p. 166–87.

Diplomatic relations between the United States and the GDR were established in September 1974 and, according to Childs, they have been 'formally correct, at times cordial, without being of central importance to either side'. As such, they have received scant attention elsewhere and this review fills a gap by providing some useful information in a number of areas, including trade and political and cultural relations. Interestingly, despite considerable official encouragement and McCarthyism as a factor influencing communist émigrés to the United States to return to the GDR, anti-Americanism appears not to be widespread in the GDR. In fact, the opportunities for East Germans to read American authors and to see American plays and films (in addition to US films and series screened by West German television) are far greater than might be assumed.

365 **Desirability, objectives and possibilities of a common *Ostpolitik*.**
Pierre Hassner.   In: *EEC policy towards Eastern Europe*. Edited by Ieuan John. Farnborough, England: Saxon House, D. C. Heath; Lexington, Massachusetts: Lexington Books, D. C. Heath, 1975, p. 125–43.

The enlargement of the European Economic Community (EEC) in the early 1970s led to several new problems for the Community, including the question of a jointly formulated policy towards Eastern Europe. Pierre Hassner focuses on the opportunities afforded by such a policy for political influence in Eastern Europe, aware though that 'different traditions and interests are more likely to lead to conflicts than to a common policy'. West Germany has 'massive direct interests' because of the country's geographical position and relationship with the GDR. In an EEC context, the question of intra-German trade can be answered very differently depending on the country concerned and, as the author notes, though this may not be a burning issue today, things could change and bring the German problem back to 'the centre both of European integration and of *Ostpolitik*. And it will be as desirable as ever not to let the two dimensions conflict but to make of the former the preferred framework of the latter'.

366   **East Germany at Westminster – the campaign for recognition.**
      Marianne Howarth.   *GDR Monitor,* no. 5 (summer 1981),
      p. 1–12.

International diplomatic recognition by as many states as possible was the GDR's major foreign policy goal until the winter of 1972. Then, the signing of the Basic Treaty removed all remaining obstacles to recognition and Britain was one of the first states to normalize its relations with the GDR. Recognition by Britain was a prize the GDR had long coveted and since the early 1950s many efforts had been made to weaken the British government's loyal support for Bonn's stand on this question. In this closely researched and informative article, the author surveys these efforts as they involved British MPs. A variety of arguments was advanced, of which the damage to trade relations was potentially the most persuasive, and a large number of groups within and outside Parliament were established. The author concludes, though, that there was never any real chance that Britain would recognize the GDR in a unilateral move and that the recognition campaign's successes are of a more modest nature.

367   **The GDR's relations with the advanced industrial countries of the West.**
      J. M. Starrels.   In: *Germany in world politics.* Edited by Viola
      Harms Drath. New York: Cyrco Press, 1979, p. 78–96.

The author's basic thesis proposes that the GDR, uniquely among the states of Eastern Europe, 'continues to possess a Western identity' which derives from its geographical position and history. Thus the GDR cannot separate itself from 'Western economic, political and sociological dynamics' and its relations with the West (defined here as Western Europe, North America and Japan) are of great importance. In the long-term, although the GDR's *Westpolitik* is dependent on the policy objectives of both Moscow and Bonn, this will not prevent the GDR from being an important actor in international affairs. Indeed, the author predicts 'an increasingly pronounced East German approach towards dealings with the West'.

with the USSR/Warsaw Pact

368   **East Germany: the Soviet connection.**
      Melvin Croan.   Beverly Hills, California; London: Sage, 1976.
      71p. 2 maps. bibliog. (The Washington Papers, vol. 4, no. 36).

Arguing from the vantage point of the mid-1970s that the East German-Soviet relationship must be central to any analysis of the problem of the divided Germany, Croan admits that initial information about this relationship is inaccessible but sees the available data as nevertheless ample to furnish 'an analysis of the general characteristics of the relationship' and to suggest 'plausible inferences for the future'. He regards the period since 1972 as qualitatively different from anything that preceded it in the GDR's history (the result of détente) and asks how this will affect the East German-Soviet connection. The 'single most tantalizing aspect' is a possible change in the GDR's definition of its own vital interests, particularly as regards relations with West Germany, and of crucial importance in this respect will be the extent to which the GDR's overall relationship with the FRG is influenced by the domestic impact of increased contacts with West Germany [this perceptive observation has been fruitfully followed up by more recent commentators, notably A. James McAdams in his book *East Germany and détente* (q.v.)]. In Croan's judgement, the FRG is unlikely to derive a substantial advantage from these developments, firstly because the East German system's ability to withstand the initial shock of a massive influx of visitors from the West 'is now beyond any serious doubt', and secondly because 'the key to East Germany . . . remains in the safekeeping of the Kremlin'.

369   **Germany and Eastern Europe since 1945.**
Keesing's Research Report.   New York: Charles Scribner's, 1973. 322p. map.

An essential reference book of documents in English compiled to provide a comprehensive survey 'from the Potsdam Agreement of 1945 to the efforts of Chancellor Brandt . . . to find a *modus vivendi* for his country with those of Communist Europe'. It is divided into four main sections, covering: the occupation period (and including the text of the Potsdam Agreement); the integration of the two German states into their respective blocs; developments between 1955 and 1965 (in particular the Hallstein doctrine and the Berlin Passes Agreement of 1963–66); and developments from 1966 to 1972 which covers all the Eastern Treaties except, unfortunately, the Basic Treaty itself. The documents are linked by short explanatory texts which are a model of clarity and conciseness.

370   **Soviet-GDR relations in the Honecker era.**
Henry Krisch.   *East Central Europe*, vol. 6, part 2 (1979), p. 152–72.

Henry Krisch, one of the foremost American commentators on relations between the GDR and the Soviet Union, addresses himself to two main themes in this informative article: a survey of the current state of GDR-Soviet relations and an analysis of some critical issues in this relationship. He takes as his starting-point the premise that 'assimilation with the "socialist community" in general, and the Soviet Union in particular' is not an area over which the GDR can exercise any choice. This assimilation can take many forms, ranging from personal associations – by 1977 no fewer than 94 marriages had come about from the involvement of the Free German Youth in the 'Friendship' natural gas pipeline project – through to inter-governmental and inter-Party contact. However, the loyalty the Soviet Union can command from the GDR in certain areas has to be seen in wider perspective: while GDR engagement in the Third World is a good example of a relative identity of interest between GDR and Soviet foreign policy, the same cannot be said of attitudes to the West. Indeed Krisch detects 'a growing divergence of perspective' in this area, though this may be less pronounced in the Gorbachev era. Fundamentally though, the twin forces of 'Soviet power and German partition' will continue to beset GDR foreign and domestic policy.

371 **Gorbachev and Eastern Europe.**
Vladimir V. Kusin. *Problems of Communism* (Jan.-Feb. 1986),
p. 39–53.

When Mikhail Gorbachev took over, the question in many Western observers'
minds was the direction the new leadership in the USSR would encourage the
Eastern European states to take. Would there be greater uniformity, or greater
latitude? The author attempts to answer the question for a number of Eastern
European states including the GDR, noting here that Erich Honecker was urged
to broaden his *Westpolitik* horizons in an attempt to drive a wedge between the
supporters and opponents of President Ronald Reagan's plans for Strategic
Defence Initiative (SDI) ('Star Wars'). Specifically, this implies that relations with
the Bonn government should be soft-pedalled while contacts with the Social
Democratic Party (SPD) were to be cultivated. The author recognizes, though,
that such issues cannot necessarily be regarded in isolation and concludes that
'Soviet chastisement for GDR foreign policy transgressions is likely to be carefully
balanced with good marks for East Berlin's useful domestic policies'.

372 **The German Democratic Republic and the Soviet Union.**
Martin McCauley. In: *Honecker's Germany*. Edited by David
Childs. London: Allen & Unwin, 1985, p. 147–65.

An awareness of Soviet thinking on Germany and the GDR is essential for a
proper understanding of GDR politics and foreign policy. The fundamental
problem for the USSR remains the need to protect Soviet security interests and it
has never satisfactorily resolved the question whether these interests are 'better
served by one Germany or two'. Between 1945 and 1955 Soviet policy reluctantly
moved from its original aim of the eventual creation of a united socialist Germany
to an acknowledgement of the division. Likewise, the GDR has always faced a
delicately balanced situation where loyalty to Moscow has had to be set against
the defence of vital GDR interests. It was this conflict which came to a head at
the time of the *Ostpolitik* and which resulted in Ulbricht's resignation. Though
Soviet-GDR relations have improved since then, so too has the GDR's self-
confidence in its relationship with West Germany. Could this 'lead to a Soviet
decision to play its all-German card'? McCauley does not exclude the possibility.

373 **East Germany and the Warsaw Alliance: the politics of détente.**
N. Edwina Moreton. Boulder, Colorado: Westview Press, 1978.
267p. bibliog.

Noting that previous Western accounts of the German problem tended to ignore
the East German point of view, Moreton successfully sets out to redress the
balance and in doing so throws much light on the impact of the German problem
on the Warsaw Alliance, with particular emphasis on the period between the late
1960s and the mid-1970s. She identifies within the Warsaw Pact a process of
change from a Soviet-dominated system towards 'a more mature political
alliance', highlighting also 'a process of East German integration within the
Warsaw alliance on a more rational and equal basis than hitherto'. At the same
time, she discusses the claim often found in East German sources that the
German problem was 'solved' by the Four Power Berlin Agreement and the Basic
Treaty. A scholarly and judiciously argued book.

Foreign Relations. with the USSR/Warsaw Pact

374 **Soviet allies: the Warsaw Pact and the issue of reliability.**
Edited by Daniel N. Nelson. Boulder, Colorado; London:
Westview Press, 1984. 240p.

In this collection of essays a team of scholars consider the degree to which
Warsaw Pact leaders can be assured of non-Soviet military support in hostile
circumstances. In a case study devoted to the GDR, Henry Krisch argues
(p. 143–83) that the GDR's armed forces would prove to be of varying reliability
as an instrument of Soviet policy in a major conflict depending on where that
conflict took place – in Europe, within the GDR, in Eastern Europe, or in the
Third World. However, trade patterns, high levels of cooperation in various
spheres, and the current leadership's close identification with Soviet policies, all
serve to increase the GDR's reliability as an ally.

375 **Eastern Europe: a divergence of conflicting interests.**
Otto Pick. *World Today*, vol. 41, nos. 8–9, (Aug.-Sept. 1985),
p. 141–44.

When Mikhail Gorbachev became the new Soviet political leader, opinion was
divided over the line he would take towards the trend, then recently apparent in
the GDR and some other Eastern European countries, of pursuing a more
independent line in foreign policy. In this article, Professor Pick analyses the
implications for a number of Eastern European countries. For the GDR, he
observes that Erich Honecker's purpose in pursuing 'his mini-détente with West
Germany' is closely linked with the need to raise the 'level of the régime's
legitimacy'. However, as the author reminds us, when the *Westpolitik* stance
threatened to undermine the Soviet propaganda campaign against INF (intermediate-range nuclear forces), the limits set on this freedom became clear. The
cancellation of Honecker's planned visit to Bonn in 1984 has to be seen in this
light.

376 **The Warsaw Pact: case studies in communist conflict resolution.**
Robin Alison Remington. Cambridge, Massachusetts; London:
MIT Press, 1971. 268p. bibliog. (Studies in Communism,
Revisionism and Revolution, no. 17).

The case study on East Germany in this treatment focuses on GDR-Warsaw Pact
relations at the onset of *Ostpolitik* negotiations, placing these also in the context
of 'escalating Sino-Soviet polemics' and the 'Sino-Soviet-Rumanian triangle' – an
interesting dimension. The difficulties inherent in making a serious analysis of a
current situation do sometimes surface in the chapter entitled 'East Germany: the
politics of persuasion' (p. 134–64), which is occasionally more journalistic than
academic, and the author is tentative in reaching conclusions, preferring to stick
to a descriptive approach. This remains, however, a useful account of Warsaw
Pact reactions to Bonn's new policy initiatives.

77 **Braucht der Osten die DDR?** (Does Eastern Europe need the GDR?)
Eberhard Schulz, Hans Dieter Schulz.   Opladen, FRG: Leske, 1968. 119p.

oth German states owe their origins to the foreign policies of their respective ccupying powers and some would argue that the GDR, at least, owes its ontinuing existence to a Soviet desire to maintain the *status quo*. Can the same e said of Eastern Europe? Are the interests of these countries better served by vo Germanies rather than by one? It is these questions which this book seeks to nswer by analysing the political, ideological, economic and military significance f the GDR for her Eastern neighbours. As the author demonstrates, the mportance of the GDR varies in degree and in kind, depending on the state oncerned. However, behind this lies a more tantalizing question: could the oviet Union and the other Eastern European states be induced by barter, or by ther means, to surrender the GDR and thus facilitate the reunification of jermany in 'peace and freedom'? A realistic answer, the author concludes, must lso be a negative one.

78 **Soviet policy toward the German Democratic Republic.**
Angela E. Stent.   In: *Soviet policy in Eastern Europe.* Edited by Sarah Meiklejohn Terry. New Haven, Connecticut; London: Yale University Press, 1984, p. 33–60. (A Council on Foreign Relations Book.)

oviet-East German relations rest on a traditional 'love-hate' relationship etween Russia and Germany: Russian fear of Germany as a security threat has o-existed alongside Russian admiration for many of Germany's technological and ultural achievements. What this implies today is 'a complex mixture of enmity nd entente' as a characteristic of Soviet attitudes to the GDR. Although the jDR owes its existence to the will of the Soviet Union, the current importance of he GDR to Soviet *Westpolitik* is potentially destabilizing. It is this combination of ictors which the author analyses in this chapter, focusing particularly on the political and economic aspects of trilateral Soviet ties with both Germanys'. Attention is paid to a number of issues, including military contacts and Moscow's nterest in encouraging East-West German relations, though this interest naturally tops short of encouraging these relations to 'develop an independent momentum'. n the 1980s, the author predicts that the Soviet Union will pursue both the defensive and assertive sides of the German triangle' and analyses this in the light f events in Poland, INF (intermediate-range nuclear forces) negotiations, and frich Honecker's proposed visit to Bonn. Unfortunately, the author's rather vordy style tends to obscure the quality of the research involved in arriving at ome quite sound conclusions.

79 **The German Democratic Republic: Moscow's faithful 'ally'.**
Eric Waldman.   In: *East Central Europe.* Edited by Milorad M. Drachkovitch. Stanford, California: Hoover Institution Press, 1982, p. 267–85.

Waldman traces the distinctive phases in the development of East Germany, from he occupation to the 1981 economic plan. The leitmotif is the GDR's adherence to the Kremlin throughout – with a brief interlude when Ulbricht apparent sought ideological parity with its senior partner. The strengths of the article lie its review of East German foreign policy and of the division between the GD and the USSR concerning overseas activities in the promotion of communi influence, especially in the Third World. The reaction of the ordinary Ea German to the Polish crisis from 1980 is described in some detail as a considerab shock to the Socialist Unity Party (SED). In summary, Waldman concludes th price support for consumer goods in the 1980s will threaten political tranquilli although there are no signs that the innate momentum of industrial progress likely to make the system less rigid.

380   **Community and conflict in the socialist camp.**
Gerhard Wettig, translated from the German by Edwina Moreton Hannes Adomeit.   London: C. Hurst, 1975. 161p.

This book analyses the attitudes of both the Soviet Union and the GDR to t German problem during the period 1965–72. These years were characterized by reappraisal of previous policy positions in the West and by the effects of a déten process in the East. Relations between the Soviet Union and her allies we naturally deeply affected by these developments and, whereas most Easte European states could be allowed, subject to Soviet control, to enjoy som measure of rapprochement with Bonn, this did not apply to the GDR. 'On tl contrary, the East German leaders were extremely apprehensive of such normalisation, whether it were their own or that of their allies.' To examine the relationships more closely, the author has selected eight case studies from t period, five of which are closely interrelated as they refer to the period Ostpolitik negotiations, in order 'to illuminate relative interests, processes coordination, instruments of exerting influence and outcomes'.

Law and the Legal System

381 **Die Rechtsauffassung im kommunistischen Staat.** (The view of law
  in the communist state.)
  Ernst-Wolfgang Böckenförde.   Munich: Kösel-Verlag, 1967.
  110p.

This book is in three parts. The first deals with the nature of communist justice,
the second with the legal system of the GDR and the third provides a comparison
of Western and Eastern concepts of law. The final part of the last section criticizes
the West German practice of regarding its law as applicable throughout Germany,
not just as a politicization of law but also as a contravention of the principle that
the law should provide protection, something which West German law cannot do
for the normal citizen of the GDR. As for the legal system of the GDR itself,
Böckenförde notes, not only the subordination of law to politics, but also the
moral dimension of communist law, the attempt to use law, particularly in 'social
courts', to educate people into the correct consciousness. All in all, this book
provides an objective, comprehensible survey.

382 **Einführung in das Recht der DDR.** (An introduction to the legal
  system of the GDR.)
  Georg Brunner.   Munich: C. H. Beck'sche Verlagsbuchhandlung,
  1975. 210p. (Schriftenreihe der Juristischen Schulung 29).

Provides a broad introduction to the subject. The first part, which deals with the
foundation of GDR law, includes an explanation of the East German concept of
law – namely that it is subordinate to politics – an historical survey, a catalogue of
the various legislative channels and a brief introduction to various types of law.
The second part concentrates on the political system and contains a section on
basic rights. The third and final part turns in more detail to individual aspects of
the law, namely economic, labour, family and criminal law. The general approach
of the book is factual, although its critical tone is unmistakable.

131

Law and the Legal System

383 Manual of German law.
E. J. Cohn. London: British Institute of International and Comparative Law, 1968, 2 vols.

The final chapter of the second volume is devoted to two aspects of GDR family law – the law of divorce and private international law in the field of family law.

384 Die Lage des Rechts in Mitteldeutschland. (The legal situation in Middle Germany.)
Karlsruhe, FRG: C. F. Müller, 1965. 177p.

Reprints a series of Freiburg University lectures (delivered by several academics) on GDR law. There are eight lectures in all which range over the Marxist view of law and various aspects of criminal and civil law in the GDR. Specific topics dealt with include the question of ownership, family law, labour law and administrative law.

385 Politischer Strafvollzug in der DDR. (The penal system for political prisoners in the GDR.)
Gerhard Finn with the cooperation of Karl Wilhelm Fricke.
Cologne, FRG: Verlag Wissenschaft und Politik, 1981. 168p.

Concentrates on such questions as the organization of the penal system, the various types of prison and the treatment of political prisoners. The work also contains a section which includes details of various amnesties and of the Federal Republic's practice of purchasing the freedom of certain prisoners. A final documentary section reproduces the GDR laws relating to the penal system and the rehabilitation of prisoners. In the case of political prisoners, rehabilitation would often appear to be a difficult problem, unless the prisoner renounces the views which placed him in prison in the first place. Nevertheless, Finn does detect a general improvement in the penal system of the GDR.

386 Politik und Justiz in der DDR. Zur Geschichte der politischen Verfolgung 1945–1968. Bericht und Dokumentation. (Politics and justice in the GDR: the history of political persecution 1948–68; a report and documentation.)
Karl Wilhelm Fricke. Cologne, FRG: Verlag Wissenschaft und Politik, 1979. 676p. bibliog.

This extensive work provides in many respects a history of political justice in the GDR until 1968. The documents which are incorporated into the text range from autobiographical statements by former prisoners, to an official letter informing a relative that a death sentence has been carried out. Fricke stresses that there can be no question of an independent legal system in the GDR where the law is subject to the political aims of the régime. Although he concludes that the GDR has established an ordered legal process, he is unwilling to conclude that there could not be a return to the arbitrary judicial terror of the Stalin era. He estimates that there were up to 300,000 political prisoners in the years up to 1968, more than a quarter of whom died, principally people interned by the Soviet authorities after the war.

387 **Der Rechtsstatus Deutschlands aus der Sicht der DDR.** (The legal
   status of Germany from the viewpoint of the GDR.)
   Jens Hacker. Cologne, FRG: Verlag Wissenschaft und Politik,
   1974. 509p. bibliog. (Abhandlungen zum Ostrecht – Eastern
   European Law Series, vol. 13).

What is the legal status of Germany today? Did the German Reich disappear
once and for all with the unconditional surrender in 1945? Or did it simply cease
to operate? What is the legal nature of the two German states? These are the
questions which the author seeks to answer. Clearly this is an extremely complex
area and one which goes well beyond being just a legal question. Historical,
ideological and political factors all have an important part to play. Whereas the
Federal Republic has largely taken the view that the German Reich did not
disappear and that, in legal terms, the FRG is identical with it, the perception of
the GDR has changed over the years. The current policy of ideological
demarcation disavows a shared heritage with the Federal Republic but the
contradictions and inconsistencies of this position cannot be satisfactorily
resolved. Hacker acknowledges the complexity of the issue and analyses the
implications arising from it in what one commentator has described as 'a complete
and exceptionally good survey'.

388 **Subjektives Recht und Wirtschaftsordnung. Untersuchungen zum
   Zivilrecht in der Bundesrepublik Deutschland und der SBZ.**
   (Private law and economic order: studies in the civil law of the
   Federal Republic of Germany and the Soviet Zone of Occupation.)
   Paul Hofman. Stuttgart, FRG: Gustav Fischer Verlag, 1968.
   346p. bibliog.

This volume is primarily concerned with the law relating to such economic
questions as ownership, patents and dismissal. Generally, Hofman describes the
legal position in the two German states and then contrasts the two systems in
summary form at the end of each chapter. In conclusion, he sees a strong affinity
between the economic and the legal system in each state. Hence in the GDR,
laws relating to the individual are bound to duties and are intended to enable the
individual to work in the community.

389 **The administration of justice and the concept of legality in East
   Germany.**
   Otto Kirchheimer. *Yale Law Journal*, vol. 68, no. 4 (March
   1959), p. 705–49.

Provides a broad survey of the legal system of the GDR in the late 1950s. The
first part is devoted to legal institutions and the roles of various members of the
legal profession such as judges, prosecutors and lawyers. The second part is
devoted to the concept of socialist legality and summarizes the legal history of
both the Soviet Union and the GDR. Kirchheimer notes periods of relaxation in
1953 and 1956 but sees a general tendency for the Party to keep a tight control
over judicial processes. In conclusion, he claims that the legal profession must
follow not just written statute but other orders and signals from above. There is
no question of judges helping to create a balance between the claims of the
individual and those of the state.

390 **Probleme des DDR-Rechts.** (Problems of GDR justice.)
Edited by Richard Lange, Boris Meissner, Klemens Pleyer.
Cologne, FRG: Verlag Wissenschaft und Politik, 1973. 183p.

This volume results from a conference on GDR law held in 1971. It consists of modified versions of papers given there by a number of experts. The topics covered are: the legal position of the Socialist Unity Party (SED) and other parties; the role of local authorities in the GDR political system; the protection (or otherwise) of the individual in the legal system; the problem of freedom of contract in civil law; the question of the conflict of interest in civil and labour law; the purpose of punishment; the criminal law relating to young people; and the position of international law as an academic discipline. The general tone is critical.

391 **Law and justice in a socialist society: the legal system of the German Democratic Republic.**
Berlin (East): Panorama DDR, 1976. 64p.

This booklet is not just an explanation of the judicial system, but also contains a limited amount of documentation in the form of extracts from the constitution and various statutes. The main body of the text explains the proposition that 'a new society requires new law' – others might say this means the removal of vital legal safeguards – and provides a historical survey as well as considering labour, the family and civil law and crime prevention. Although Western justice is criticized and the GDR is seen as a state where social conditions have reduced the volume of crime, the tone is not only one of self-congratulation. Moreover, a degree of genuine information is provided and the existence of the death penalty is admitted, even if elsewhere the proposition is advanced that 'punishment is not revenge' and much stress is laid on the alternatives to custodial sentences.

392 **DDR-Gesetze Textausgabe.** (GDR laws, textual edition.)
Edited by Erika Leiser-Triebrigg, Dietrich Müller-Römer.
Cologne, FRG: Verlag Wissenschaft und Politik, 1971. 2,650p.

As its size indicates, this collection will cater for the needs of those requiring exact details of GDR statutes.

393 **Kriminologie. Theoretische Grundlagen und Analysen.**
(Criminology: theoretical bases and analyses.)
John Lekschas (et al.). Berlin (East): Staatsverlag der Deutschen Demokratischen Republik, 1983. 496p.

This book describes itself as a system of theoretical statements on criminology. It provides an introduction to the discipline of criminology, an investigation of the roots of criminal behaviour, and a history of the development of crime in capitalist and socialist countries. Its principal concern, however, is with crime in the GDR, the causes of which are investigated. Happily, Western media and influence are not seen as a sole, or even major, cause. In conclusion, the book postulates steps towards the further reduction of crime; the ideal should be to achieve the social integration of the individual, which in turn will result in the 'total identification of individuals with society's goals and the development of their creative powers in a fertile cross-relationship with society'. Following the text, there is a brief summary of the book's contents in a number of languages, including (somewhat opaque) English.

394 **Sozialistisches und bürgerliches Zivilrechtsdenken in der DDR.**
(Socialist and bourgeois concepts of civil law in the GDR.)
Inga Markowits. Cologne, FRG: Verlag Wissenschaft und
Politik, 1969. 200p. bibliog.

This volume is an historical survey of the development of GDR civil law from 1945 until the 1960s. Markowits claims that the attempts to create a new kind of socialist civil law following the 1958 Babelsberg Conference, at which Walter Ulbricht spoke, largely failed. Her conclusion is that the GDR has had to accept traditional bourgeois legal structures and that civil law probably cannot stand in the vanguard of revolutionary social change.

395 **Strafrecht. Allgemeiner Teil.** (Criminal law: general part.)
Berlin (East): Staatsverlag der Deutschen Demokratischen
Republik, 1978. 560p.

This book, produced by the law department of the Humboldt University in Berlin (East) and the Academy for Law in Potsdam-Babelsberg, is a general explanation of the principles underlying GDR criminal law. It is conceived as a teaching manual (Lehrbuch) and contains eight chapters on the following subjects: socialist criminal law and the academic study of socialist criminal law; the development of GDR criminal law; the doctrine of GDR criminal law; the theory of crime and the criminal; the concept of criminal responsibility; the measures (punishments) available in relation to criminal responsibility; the possibilities for not taking such measures (amnesties, for example); and the criminal law realting to young people.

396 **Strafrecht. Besonderer Teil.** (Criminal law: specific part.)
Berlin (East): Staatsverlag der Deutschen Demokratischen
Republik, 1981. 271p.

This companion volume to *Strafrecht. Allgemeiner Teil.* [Criminal law: general part] (q.v.) is the attempt to put flesh on the earlier volume's statements of principle. It attempts to show which concrete actions are punished by GDR law. Thus the index primarily contains references to various types of crime and criminal. Many of these would be common to any work on this subject, for example murder and bribery, but others such as 'agitation against the state' or 'the misleading of children into an anti-social way of life' reflect the nature of GDR society.

397 **Strafrecht der Deutschen Demokratischen Republik. Kommentar zum Strafgesetzbuch.** (Criminal law of the German Democratic Republic: commentary on the criminal code.)
Berlin (East): Staatsverlag der Deutschen Demokratischen
Republik, 1984. 636p.

This volume produced by the GDR Ministry of Justice deals systematically with the individual provisions of the Criminal Code, each of which is reproduced and

135

commented on. An index refers to the various areas of the law so that it is easily possible to use this book for reference purposes.

398 **Das neue Zivilrecht der DDR nach dem Zivilgesetzbuch von 1975.**
(The new civil law of the GDR according to the Civil Code of 1975.)
Edited by Klaus Westen.   Berlin (West): In Kommission bei Nomos Verlagsgesellschaft, Baden-Baden, 1977. 320p.

This volume gathers together essays on various aspects of GDR civil law and deals with such topics as the law relating to tenancy, insurance, purchase, inheritance and damages. It does not, however, deal systematically with every aspect of civil law. In the opening chapter, Westen notes a confusing attitude to civil law in the GDR which is reflected in a tendency to follow the example of capitalist countries. Even after the reforms of 1975, he cannot discern a clear corpus of civil law and such areas as family and labour law, for example, are not regarded as civil law.

The Military and Defence

399 Die Nationale Volksarmee der DDR im Rahmen des Warschauer Paktes. (The National People's Army of the GDR in the context of the Warsaw Pact.)
Arbeitskreis für Wehrforschung. (Work group on military research.) Munich: Bernard & Graefe, 1980. 238p.

A group of authors, one of them a British officer, examine different aspects of the National People's Army (NVA) such as: internal structure; military tradition; comparisons between the NVA and the other Warsaw Pact forces; 'socialist defence education'; the relations between the military, the Socialist Unity Party (SED) and society; the GDR navy; and military doctrine.

400 Taschenbuch für Wehrpflichtige. (Handbook for conscripts.)
Autorenkollektiv. (Authors' collective). Berlin (East): Militärverlag, 1965 and regular revised reprints since then, 380p.

As the title suggests, this volume contains everything the Socialist Unity Party (SED) thinks the conscript needs to know about military service from medals, ranks and brief histories of the individual Warsaw Pact armed forces, to rights and duties, call-up and discharge, uniforms, food, accommodation and leave.

401 Civil war in the making: 'the combat groups of the working class' in East Germany.
W. Bader, translated from the German by Major Eugen Hinterhoff, Philip Windsor, introduction by the Right Honourable Lord Morrison of Lambeth, C. H. London: Independent Information Centre, [n.d.] (ca. 1963). 128p. maps.

Today's combat groups can be traced back to the old Marxist idea of an 'armed working class' and their traditions stem specifically from the communist risings of

137

the early years of the Weimar Republic and from the *Rotfrontkämpferbund* (League of Red Front Fighters, 1924–33). Combat groups are based in the factory or workshop and are formed by men in employment there. This booklet discusses the history of their growth since the early 1950s, the way they are organized, their equipment and training, their political education and tradition, their readiness for action (for example at the time of the building of the Berlin Wall), and their value. Liberally illustrated with photographs, it takes a totally hostile view towards the 'totalitarian' GDR, making comparisons with Nazism, but argues that it has in its combat groups a valuable instrument 'which can fight both according to military rules and by unconventional methods'.

402 **Ökonomie und Landesverteidigung.** (Economy and national
defence.)
Autorenkollektiv. (Authors' collective.) led by Colonel Dr. Horst
Fiedler.   Berlin (East): Militärverlag, 1973. 160p.

A brief, general look at how the economy is needed to back up the armed forces. An admission that defence is expensive but very necessary in view of the threat from Western imperialism.

403 **The East German Army: the second power in the Warsaw Pact.**
Thomas M. Forster, translated from the German by Deryck Viney,
introduction by General Sir Harry Tuzo, GCB, OBE, MC,
MA.   London: George Allen & Unwin, 1980. 5th ed. 310p.
bibliog.

Described by General Sir Harry Tuzo in his introduction as a standard work (it appears in English, French and Italian translations as well as in the original German), this volume offers a comprehensive and detailed overview of the important role played by the military in GDR society. The author quotes freely from GDR sources to underline the deliberate all-pervasiveness of that rôle, the aim of socialist military education in his view being to produce 'not just a militarized society but at the same time . . . militarized individuals'. Chapters are devoted to such topics as frontier troops, political organization within the army, weapons and other equipment, military training, and political-ideological education and training. The book is liberally illustrated with photographs, tables and figures, including colour reproductions of the badges associated with all military ranks.

404 **Fassonschnitt.** (Military cut.)
Jürgen Fuchs.   Reinbek, FRG: Rowohlt, 1984. 384p.

Jürgen Fuchs, who now lives in West Berlin, here gives a detailed and sensitive account of the first phase of his compulsory military service (1969–71) in the GDR's National People's Army (NVA). The writing is lively and has the ring of authenticity. This worm's eye view of life in the NVA adds an important new dimension to our study of the military when read in conjunction with Dale Roy Herspring's *East German civil–military relations: the impact of technology, 1949–72* (q.v.), Thomas M. Forster's *The East German Army: the second power in the Warsaw Pact* (q.v.) and Gero Neugebauer's *The military and society in the GDR* (q.v.).

405 **East German civil–military relations: the impact of technology 1949–72.**
Dale Roy Herspring, foreword by Peter Christian Ludz. New York; Washington, D.C.; London: Praeger, 1973. 216p. bibliog.

Herspring's study represents an important milestone in the study of the GDR military. He defines his major goal as 'to determine whether political control increases, decreases, or remains the same as the level of technology rises' within this skill group. Using seventeen empirical indicators for technology on the one hand and fifteen for political control on the other, he establishes that in the officer corps of the military a kind of dual (politico-technical) military executive has emerged, or, in less technical terms, one which is both 'red' and 'expert'. He divides the period 1949–72 into five distinct sub-periods and convincingly demonstrates how the levels of both technology and political control rise over time. This finding differs interestingly from the conclusion reached by Peter Christian Ludz in his excellent study *The changing Party élite in East Germany* (q.v.), namely that, in the economic (as opposed to the military) sphere, the Party requires of its technocrats no more than Party membership, i.e., a relatively low degree of politicization. The text includes ten tables and five figures.

406 **Militärwesen in der DDR.** (The military in the GDR.)
Günter Holzweissig. Berlin (West): Verlag Gebr. Holzapfel, 1985. 160p. bibliog.

The author manages to cram a great deal into this slim volume with chapters on the frontier police, civil defence, the armed units of the Ministry of Interior, the Ministry of State Security, the armed factory units and, of course, the National People's Army (NVA). It is well illustrated with official GDR photographs.

407 **100 Fragen 100 Antworten zur Wehrpflicht.** (100 questions 100 answers on conscription.)
Major Erna Jäpel. Berlin (East): Deutscher Militärverlag, 3rd ed., 1967. 159p.

A brief official guide for conscripts to military service.

408 **Der Einsatz der Truppen bei der Anwendung von atomaren, chemischen und bakteriologischen Waffen.** (The use of troops in the application of atomic, chemical, and bacteriological weapons.)
Ministerium für Nationale Verteidigung. (Ministry for National Defence.) Berlin (East): Verlag des Ministeriums für Nationale Verteidigung, 1956. 144p.

A well-illustrated document which reveals that the National People's Army (NVA) took atomic, chemical, and bacteriological weapons seriously even in the mid-1950s.

The Military and Defence

409 **Die Verteidigung des sozialistischen Vaterlandes.** (The defence of
the socialist fatherland.)
Autorenkollektiv (Authors' collective) led by Colonel Dr Hermann
Müller. Berlin (East): Deutscher Militärverlag, 1971. 110p.

Strongly supports the defence policy of the Communist Party of the Soviet Union
(CPSU) and the Socialist Unity Party (SED) and its application in the GDR. The
volume examines such issues as: the unity of the people and the armed forces;
military discipline; the leading rôle of the Party; the economy and defence;
defence education; and military integration in the Warsaw Pact.

410 **The military and society in the GDR.**
Gero Neugebauer. In: *Studies in GDR culture and society 5:
selected papers from the tenth New Hampshire Symposium on the
German Democratic Republic.* Edited by Margy Gerber (et al.).
Lanham, Maryland; New York; London: University Press of
America, 1985, p. 81–93.

Neugebauer completely rejects the view that the GDR is a *militaristic* society and,
in a cogently reasoned case, argues that it cannot even be called a *militarized*
society despite the important rôle accorded to the military as an instrument of
political socialization. His conclusion is that, so long as the GDR continues to
develop its economic and social system 'without using the military as a means of
securing domestic power, the decisive step to a militarized system will not have
been taken'.

411 **Die bewaffneten Verbände der DDR.** (The armed organizations of
the GDR.)
Hans Ullrich Rühmland. PhD thesis, Philosophy Faculty of the
Westfälische Wilhelms-Universität Münster, 1981. 329p. bibliog.

The author deals with the history of the various armed organizations in the Soviet
Zone/GDR, their present structure and functions, their integration in the GDR's
political system and into the Warsaw Pact.

Economy

412 **Neues ökonomisches System und Investitionspolitik.** (The New
Economic System and investment policy.)
Erich Apel, Günter Mittag. Berlin (East): Dietz Verlag, 1965.
208p.

The official version of how the New Economic System was supposed to deal with
investment policy. It also contains the official regulation of 25 September 1964
related to investments.

413 **Die Volkswirtschaft der DDR.** (The economy of the GDR.)
Autorenkollektiv. (Authors' collective.) Berlin (East): Verlag
Die Wirtschaft, 1979. 296p.

This is the official view of the GDR's economy and its development produced by
the Central Committee of the Socialist Unity Party's (SED) Akademie für
Gesellschaftswissenschaften (Academy of Social Sciences). It is full of quotations
from Lenin, Marx, Engels and, above all, Erich Honecker. Joseph Stalin, Walter
Ulbricht and Otto Grotewohl are all 'unpersons'. The difficulties of the GDR are
regarded as being solely to the relatively undeveloped nature of the economy
it inherited and the activities of the imperialists. There is no attempt to
discuss – or even mention – the damage done by SED policies introduced with
great enthusiasm and then abandoned as erroneous. The volume abounds with
statistics showing the SED's victorious struggles, with international comparisons
only when it is thought these will be to the advantage of the GDR. It is admitted,
for instance, that the GDR has a housing problem (something everyone in the
GDR well knows) but a table of international housing statistics is provided to
reveal how by 1975–76 the GDR was building more homes proportionate to the
population than virtually any other state (only Czechoslovakia is seen as being
ahead in 1976). There is no attempt to discuss quality, size or choice, or to point
out that, if certain states, West Germany for instance, have consistently had a
high level of home-building activity with a stagnant population, a time will be

141

Economy

reached when demand for new housing slackens. The volume is another example
of how, in some respects, East German writing on developments since 1945 has
actually declined in quality since 1971.

414   **Zu aktuellen Fragen der Ökonomie. Beiträge aus der Forschung.**
(The current economic questions: research papers.)
Autorenkollektiv. (Authors' collective.)   Berlin (East): Verlag
Die Wirtschaft, 1966. 239p.

A high-powered team of Socialist Unity Party (SED) professors deal with a
variety of problems in connection with the New Economic System.

415   **Zu den wissenschaftlichen Grundlagen des neuen ökonomischen
Systems.** (The scientific foundations of the New Economic
System.)
Wolfgang Berger, Otto Reinhold.   Berlin (East): Dietz Verlag,
1966. 158p.

An attempt by two Socialist Unity Party (SED) war horses to explain that the
New Economic System represented a totally consistent development of what had
gone before, with many quotes from Walter Ulbricht to prove it. In the final part
of the volume the writers defend the GDR against claims by Western
commentators that the New Economic System represented a partial return to
capitalism.

416   **The GDR economy between East and West: problems and
opportunities.**
Pieter A. Boot.   In: *Studies in GDR culture and society 6: selected
papers from the eleventh New Hampshire symposium on the
German Democratic Republic.* Edited by Margy Gerber (et al.).
Lanham, Maryland; New York; London: University of America
Press, 1986, p. 17–30.

Reviews the history and current economic health of the Council for Mutual
Economic Assistance (Comecon) and the GDR's economic relationship with the
Soviet Union. The failure of Comecon to fulfill its ambitious programme of long-
term planned integration by the end of the 1960s, however, has increased the
importance of trade with the West, especially for the GDR which is striving to
reduce shortages and re-export finished goods. The structure of trade with the
West is not favourable for the GDR as a whole, however, as few enterprises are
orientated towards Western markets and the imported technology does not
benefit other industries, which are more involved with Comecon. Through
organizational reform, balanced investment and technology imports for priority
areas, however, the GDR may be able to halt its ongoing losses of market shares
in manufactured products in the West now that it has realized a foreign trade
surplus and reduced its net debt.

417 **Die Wirtschaft der DDR.** (The economy of the GDR.)
Werner Bröll. Munich: Olzog Verlag, 1974. 200p. bibliog.
This is the sixth volume in the series Gegenwartsfragen der Ost-Wirtschaft
(Contemporary problems of the Eastern economy) bearing the imprint of the
Osteuropa-Institut (East European Institute) in Munich. A brisk, brief but
comprehensive survey on the GDR's relations with the other Council for Mutual
Economic Assistance (Comecon) states with sections devoted to trade relations
with each of the GDR's East European allies. Bröll concludes that the trade of
the two German states with Eastern Europe and the Soviet Union, taken
together, has roughly the same significance as the trade of the German Reich had
with these areas before World War II. The book does not have the questioning
quality of Werner Obst's *DDR-Wirtschaft. Modell und Wirklichkeit* (q.v.).

418 **The consumer under socialist planning: the East German case.**
Phillip J. Bryson. New York: Praeger, 1984. 207p. bibliog.
Since the 8th Party Congress of the Socialist Unity Party (SED) in 1971, the
principal task (*Hauptaufgabe*) of economic planning in the GDR has been
proclaimed as the enhancement of the material and cultural living standards of the
people, and this was enshrined in the country's new constitution in 1974. Taken in
conjunction both with the country's relatively impressive economic development
and also with the natural comparison that may be drawn with West Germany, this
fact makes the GDR (rather than the Soviet Union) 'an ideal case study of
consumption in affluent socialism'. As Bryson shows by drawing on relevant East
and West German studies, progress in the 1970s was significant and, in spite of
current problems, East German consumers remain the richest in East Europe.
They are many years ahead of their Soviet counterparts, but Bryson's prediction
is that 'no substantial improvements' are likely in the immediate future and that
the GDR's wish to catch up with West Germany will therefore not be fulfilled.

419 **Workshop on the GDR economy: proceedings.**
Edited by Irwin L. Collier, Jr. Washington, DC: American
Institute for Contemporary German Studies, 1986. 92p. bibliog.
A collection of four papers: Jan Vanous's 'The GDR within CMEA'; John E.
Parsons's 'Forms of GDR economic cooperation with the nonsocialist world';
Phillip J. Bryson's 'GDR economic planning and social policy in the 1980s'; and
Irwin L. Collier, Jr's 'The GDR Five Year Plan 1986–1990'; to which is appended
an interesting section of comments by Wolfgang Heinrichs of the Central Institute
for Economics at the Academy of Sciences of the GDR. A summary of the
discussion which followed the papers is included in a final section. This is a useful
source for specialists on the GDR economy.

420 **Handbuch DDR-Wirtschaft.** (Handbook of the GDR economy.)
Deutsches Institut für Wirtschaftsforschung Berlin. Reinbek,
FRG: Rowohlt, 1985. 439p. bibliog.
This is the paperback version of the fourth edition of this authoritative survey of
the GDR economy. The first edition was published in 1971. It is written by a team
of specialists led by that veteran researcher on the GDR economy, Doris
Cornelsen. All the areas that the economist would expect are covered: the major

143

factors underlying the GDR's economic development; economic organization and planning; national economic accounting; production in the individual sectors of the economy; use and division of produce and income; foreign economic relations; the GDR in the Council for Mutual Economic Assistance (Comecon); and there is also a statistical appendix. There is a brief section which attempts to clarify the differences between Western and GDR/Soviet terminology and methods of accounting. Many non-economists would expect to find such a volume rather narrowly drawn and forbidding but there are at least several sections which will be of great interest to those concerned with the GDR's way of life. Thus there is an attempt to analyse the social security system of the GDR, health care, environmental protection, hotels and restaurants, tourism and foreign travel. On the GDR's social security, the authors conclude that, although it is comprehensive, the benefits, up to now, are low, at least for those who are not yet, or are no longer, contributing to the building or maintenance of the state and society. For those who are contributing, the benefits are good or even exemplary. They conclude on the health service that there is a shortage of doctors and other medical personnel, overcrowding in hospitals, long waiting lists for treatment, shortages of medicine and drugs, out-of-date techniques and equipment. In the section on environmental protection, we learn that the inhabitants of the GDR are rather badly off for drinking-water. It will come as no surprise to readers who have visited the GDR that the survey concludes that there are not enough hotels and restaurants. In their examination of the development of agriculture, the writers conclude that, although the Socialist Unity Party (SED) claims that the GDR agricultural system is superior to that in the West, this cannot be proved, although on the other hand, it cannot be concluded that GDR agriculture is a failure. This judicial summing-up is typical of the team's attempt to strive for objectivity. Perhaps it could be argued that they are too diplomatic, wishing to get at the truth but at the same time not wanting to do anything to burden the FRG's relationship with the GDR. This volume is a 'must' not only for specialists concerned with the GDR economy but for anyone interested in GDR society and way of life. An English version has also been published, ed. by Reinhard Pohl, translated from the German by Lux Furtmüller, and entitled *Handbook of the economy of the German Democratic Republic* (Westmead, England: Saxon House, 1979. 366p.).

421   **East Germany.**
Economist Intelligence Unit.   In: *EIU Regional Review. Eastern Europe and the USSR 1986. Economist Intelligence Unit.* London: Economist Publications, 1986, p. 55–64. map.

A highly concentrated summary of GDR affairs in 1985, preceded by an overview of GDR history and followed by a brief consideration of 'implications for the future'. In essence, a picture emerges of a country which has its fair share of problems but which is basically stable and can look forward to modest progress in the year ahead. Of particular interest is the prediction that exports to and imports from West Germany should both grow, given that economic ties between the two countries continue to become ever closer despite their uncertain political relations.

422   **The economy of the GDR.**
Stephen F. Frowen.   In: *Honecker's Germany*. Edited by David
Childs. London: Allen & Unwin, 1985, p. 32–49. bibliog.
This expert from the University of Surrey, England, paints an optimistic picture
of the GDR economy. He is impressed not only by the GDR's success in
overcoming its early difficulties – devastation, reparations, emigration of labour
to the West, lack of raw materials and fuels – but also its recent efforts to reduce
its Western debt and raise productivity. He is not concerned with the politics and
dogmatic ideological view of economics which led to many of the difficulties in the
first place. Frowen concludes that the ambitious growth rates aimed at 'will also
require more imports of high-technology investment goods from the West and this
will require stepping up exports. It is likely to take some time before the GDR
can hope to raise the standard of living of its population to anything like the level
achieved by West European industrial countries, although the progress made in
that direction so far is certainly remarkable.'

423   **The GDR's economy in the '80s: requirements, problems,
possibilities.**
Berlin (East): Panorama DDR, 1981. 80p.
One of a series of official pamphlets on various aspects of GDR life. This one is
illustrated with attentive children, joking foremen, laughing miners, studious
women, healthy cattle and wise Party leaders.

424   **Enterprise guidance in Eastern Europe: a comparison of four
socialist economies.**
David Granick.   Princeton, New Jersey: Princeton University
Press, 1975. 505p.
The four economies under scrutiny in this volume are those of Romania, the
GDR, Hungary, and Yugoslavia. Based on field research and, in particular,
numerous interviews carried out in the various countries in 1970–71, the study
focuses on the variations in management which are the consequence of the
different economic reforms introduced in each country in the second half of the
1960s. In the case of the GDR this was the New Economic System, and this is
carefully discussed by the author as are both the educational backgrounds of
industrial managers and professionals and also the role of trade unions. Granick's
work therefore represents a carefully researched analysis of a particularly
important phase in the development of the GDR economy and of economic
policy.

425   **Zentralverwaltungswirtschaft am Beispiel der SBZ.** (Central
      administration of the economy: the example of the Soviet Zone of
      Occupation.)
      Joachim Hoffmann, with an introduction by Karl C.
      Thalheim.   Frankfurt am Main, FRG: Verlag Moritz Diesterweg,
      1966. 155p.

A lively little book in which the author usefully quotes from many GDR sources
in his attempt to describe how the GDR economy was nationalized and then
administered (1950s–66).

426   **The convergence theory: the debate in the Federal Republic of
      Germany.**
      Jutta Kneissel, translated from the German by Andreas Huyssen,
      Johanna Moore.   *New German Critique*, no. 2 (spring 1974),
      p. 16–27.

According to the convergence theory, which was first articulated in the early
1960s, the economic systems of East and West are gradually becoming
increasingly similar and developing towards a uniform industrial society. This
article concentrates on the debate about this theory in the Federal Republic of
Germany, but in a useful final section it explains that the theory is completely
rejected in the GDR largely on two grounds: firstly because of the fundamental
difference in the socioeconomic base of the two countries; and secondly because
of the planned control of the economy in the GDR as opposed to the unplanned,
crisis-ridden production of Western countries. In addition, the theory is seen as a
form of 'ideological diversion', i.e., a calculated attempt to disrupt the growth of
socialism in the GDR.

427   **Economic integration in the Soviet bloc with an East German case
      study.**
      Heinz Köhler.   New York: Praeger, 1965. 402p. bibliog.

This volume is very much a work for specialists by an expert economic detective.

428   **The German Democratic Republic.**
      Gert Leptin.   In: *The new economic systems of Eastern Europe*.
      Edited by Hans-Hermann Höhmann, Michael Kaser, Karl C.
      Thalheim. London: Hurst, 1975. p. 43–77.

An appraisal of the New Economic System, initiated in the GDR in 1963, and of
the reasons why it was abandoned in the late 1960s.

429   **The GDR – economic policy caught between pressure for efficiency and lack of ideas.**
Manfred Melzer.   In: *The East European economies in the 1970s.*
Edited by Alec Nove, Hans-Hermann Höhmann, Gertraud
Seidenstecher. London: Butterworth, 1982, p. 45–90. bibliog.

In autumn 1970 the GDR abandoned the 'New Economic System of Planning and Management' (NES) which it had adopted in 1963. Essentially, this meant that the decentralizing impetus of the NES, which gave increased decisionmaking powers to the lower levels of management, had exhausted itself. With the move back to centralization the old planning problems of 1963 had resurfaced. Indeed, they are more acute than ever because of the rise in the volume of output, increased product differentiation, and more complex production processes. This is particularly true of the difficulties involved in setting prices. Melzer identifies the two major weaknesses of the GDR's economic system as inflexibility in response to external or internal pressures, and inefficiency (low productivity). Changes in the second half of the 1970s have sought to offset these weaknesses but in fact have only underlined the difficulties. This gives rise to Melzer's main thesis: 'increases in performance were supposed to be achieved by more exact, precise formal planning processes rather than by real attempts to solve problems of substance – evidently the relevant ideas for this are lacking.'

430   **Wirtschaftswunder DDR.** (Economic miracle GDR.)
Hans Müller, Karl Reissig.   Berlin (East): Dietz Verlag, 1968.
531p. bibliog.

As the title suggests this volume is designed to show that the Socialist Unity Party (SED) produced an economic miracle in the part of Germany under its control. Well illustrated, this is a far better presented book than most in this genre. From the SED's point of view the authors did a reasonable job, giving a more convincing account than most Party writers.

431   **Das geplante Wunder.** (The planned miracle.)
Joachim Nawrocki.   Hamburg, FRG: Christian Wegner Verlag,
1967. 290p. bibliog.

A lively, well-written and researched book by a journalist who publishes in the West German weekly, *Die Zeit.* This was one of the first West German books to get away from Cold War polemics and attempt to analyse the GDR's economic successes as well as its failures. It is something of a classic which can still be read with interest. The photographs are also interesting, having a documentary quality of their own.

432   **DDR-Wirtschaft. Modell und Wirklichkeit.** (The GDR economy: model and reality.)
Werner Obst.   Hamburg, FRG: Hoffmann und Campe, 1973.
279p. bibliog.

A useful book by a former GDR insider – an economic expert at the *Ministerrat* (Council of Ministers) – whose thesis is that, although the GDR economic system works, the difference between effort and achievement, input and output, use of capital and private consumption, is most unsatisfactory, especially compared with the Federal Republic. He believes the GDR achieved a technological revolution in the 1960s but that it did not bring the economic benefits expected. He claims that capital investments bring a return of only half what they would bring in West Germany. His underlying theme seems to be that GDR Germans are the same people as the Germans of the Federal Republic, with the same abilities and values, and it is the system which frustrates all their efforts. Take foreign trade, for example: it is not that GDR experts cannot negotiate as effectively as West Germans; it is simply that political considerations are more important than economic ones. He reveals how the GDR economy was sacrificed to Soviet interests and cites, for example, the case of the ship-building industry which was built up to please the Soviet Union and which had capital poured into it without any chance of even costs being covered. He also quotes the example of Soviet energy supplies. In 1967 Ulbricht accepted, without discussion, a Soviet price of ten pfennigs per cubic metre of natural gas, while the Federal Republic paid the Russians only half that price. The same happened in the case of coal which could have been bought much more cheaply from West Germany. Obst cautions Western users of GDR statistics and the use of the word 'miracle' in connection with GDR economic progress. He prefers to describe it as economic development of the kind there has been all over the world. Finally, he also dismisses the constantly repeated remark used in the West that the GDR's achievement is that it has reached the highest standard of living in the Soviet bloc. This, he points out, was traditionally the case, but what matters is the GDR standard of living relative to that of the Federal Republic.

433 **The economy.**
Arthur A. Stahnke.   In: *East Germany: a country study*. Edited by Eugene K. Keefe. Washington, DC: Department of the Army, 1982, p. 105–49. bibliog.

A good overview of the GDR economy based on a wide variety of sources and attempting to be fair.

434 **Progress and the GDR economy: GDR economic performance and its measurement.**
Arthur A. Stahnke.   *Studies in GDR culture and society 6: selected papers from the eleventh New Hampshire symposium on the German Democratic Republic.* Edited by Margy Gerber (et al.). Lanham, Maryland; New York; London: University of America Press, 1986, p. 1–16.

Despite difficulties of access to objective data and differences between East and West as to the criteria of evaluation, Stahnke attempts a cautious review and interpretation of the available evidence on the performance of the GDR's economy. He analyses a number of different indicators ranging from macro-growth rates such as Gross National Product to living standards, social welfare, foreign trade and efficiency in the utilization of labour and materials ('intensification'). He concludes that, while produced national income has grown and the trade balance has improved, consumer welfare and productivity results continue to disappoint and much needs to be done in improving product quality. In view of the difficult internal and international conditions, however, the GDR has performed much better than expected in the 1980s.

435 **Economic system and economic policy: the challenge of the 1970s.**
Jürgen Strassburger. In: *Policymaking in the German Democratic Republic*. Edited by Klaus von Beyme, Hartmut Zimmermann, translated from the German by Eileen Martin. Aldershot, England: Gower for the German Political Science Association, 1984, p. 109–43. (German Political Studies, vol. 5).

A political and sociological analysis of the changes which took place in the economic policy of the GDR in the 1970s. The author argues that the changes came about, not because Honecker replaced Ulbricht as leader, but mainly because serious economic (and social) problems had emerged which demanded new initiatives.

436 **Germany between East and West.**
Wolfgang F. Stolper, foreword by Henry G. Aubrey. Washington, DC: National Planning Association, 1960. 80p.

This volume is part of a series entitled 'The economics of competitive cooexistence'. After outlining the course of economic development in the two Germanies since the war, Stolper describes the political alternatives open to West Germany as it faces the future. He then discusses the economic prospects of West and East Germany 'for the next 15 years or so' before considering the economic implications of the major political options (reunification, neutralism) facing West Germany. He concludes that West Germany has 'outproduced, outconsumed, and outtraded' East Germany so far but that an improved performance by the GDR economy is 'possible and indeed likely'.

437 **The structure of the East German economy.**
Wolfgang F. Stolper, with the assistance of Karl W. Roskamp. Cambridge, Massachusetts: Harvard University Press, 1960. 478p. bibliog.

A comprehensive analysis of the East German economy prior to 1958. The book also offers a systematic comparison of all aspects of the GDR's economic performance with that of West Germany, although the difficulty of working with East German statistics is acknowledged to involve a high degree of arbitrariness for the researcher. The study is divided into six sections: population movements and the labour force in East Germany; East German methodology in producing statistical data; industrial production; agriculture and forestry; construction, transportation and communication, and trade; Gross National Product. The author's general conclusion is that 'the East German economy has performed more poorly than the West German economy by whatever test one wishes to apply'.

438 **Betriebswirtschaftliche Probleme in der DDR und in andern RGW-Ländern.** (Management problems in the GDR and in other Comecon countries.)
Edited by Karl C. Thalheim. Berlin (West): Forschungsstelle für Gesamtdeutsche Wirtschaftliche und Soziale Fragen, Sonderheft 1977. 203p. bibliog.

A series of short, but useful, essays on different aspects of socialist economic enterprise in the GDR and Poland.

439 **Die Wirtschaftspolitik der DDR im Schatten Moskaus.** (The economic policy of the GDR in the shadow of Moscow.)
Karl C. Thalheim. Hanover, FRG: Niedersächsische Landeszentrale für politische Bildung, 1979. 107p.

In this short book Thalheim argues that the difference in the economic performance of the two Germanies can be explained above all by: the imposition of the Soviet economic system on the GDR; the considerable integration of the GDR's economy in the Soviet bloc and in particular the one-sided emphasis on the USSR and the Council for Mutual Economic Assistance (Comecon) countries in its foreign trade; and the investment of huge resources in those branches of the economy where competition with West Germany was at its most intense but where the GDR also started from a position of real disadvantage. All this was possible only because the GDR's economic policy was decided 'in the shadow of Moscow'.

440 **Die wirtschaftliche Entwicklung der beiden Staaten in Deutschland.** (The economic development of both states in Germany.)
Karl C. Thalheim. Opladen, FRG: Westdeutscher Verlag, 1981. 254p. bibliog.

A significant comparative study of the two German economies by an acknowledged expert.

441 **Das Neue Ökonomische System der Planung und Leitung der Volkswirtschaft in der Praxis.** (The New Economic System for the planning and management of the economy in practice.)
Walter Ulbricht, with Erich Apel. Berlin (East): Dietz Verlag, 1963. 298p.

These are the published minutes of the economic conference of the Socialist Unity Party's (SED) Central Committee and Council of Ministers which was organized to discuss the New Economic System.

442 **The two German economies: a comparison between the National Product of the German Democratic Republic and the Federal Republic of Germany.**
Herbert Wilkens, translated from the German by Lux Furtmüller. Farnborough, England: Gower, 1981. 180p. bibliog.
Recognizing that objective comparison of the GDR economy with any other is made difficult by other very different procedures of National Product accounting, Wilkens rearranges the available data on the GDR economy in a form comparable with Western procedures. This produces a number of suggestive insights, although it should be noted that the data used relates only to the period up to 1977.

443 **Die Wirtschaft im geteilten Deutschland 1945–1970.** (The economy in divided Germany 1945–70.)
Harald Winkel. Wiesbaden, FRG: Franz Steiner Verlag, 1974. 217p. bibliog.
After an outline of the developments in the four zones of occupation to 1949 the author moves on to a competent, straightforward description of the progress of first the West German economy and then the GDR economy.

444 **Soviet economic policy in postwar Germany: a collection of papers by former Soviet officials.**
Vasili Yershov, Vladimir Alexandrov, Vladimir Rudolph, Vlas Leskov, Mikhail Mab, Viacheslav Nevsky, Nikolai Grishin, edited and with an introduction by Robert Slusser. New York: Research Program on the USSR, 1953. 184p. maps. bibliog. (Studies on the USSR, no. 3).
The subjects covered in this extremely useful collection of papers by former Soviet officials in the Soviet Zone of Occupation are: confiscation, plunder, and dismantling during the first phase of occupation; the administrative organization of Soviet control; Soviet agricultural policy; and the 'Vismut' uranium mining operation in Saxony. The authors are able to provide telling insights into the thinking of top Soviet officials as to how the USSR might best use its control over its zone.

Trade, Industry and Transport

445 The red robots are here!
Michael Dennis. *GDR Monitor*, no. 12 (winter 1984–85),
p. 1–17.

An assessment of the importance of industrial robots in the GDR's economic strategy since the beginning of the 1980s. The robots were introduced to increase productivity and to maintain a stable rate of economic growth.

446 Postwar trade in divided Germany: the internal and international issues.
Kevel Holbik, Henry Myers. Baltimore, Maryland: Johns
Hopkins Press, 1964. 138p. bibliog.

This book is of interest as the first Western study of postwar intra-German trade. Its main conclusion is that neither the Federal Republic nor East Germany, for different reasons, appears interested in expanding East-West trade substantially and that this is unlikely to change until a relaxation of tensions can be achieved (as in fact happened with the coming of détente and the Federal Republic's *Ostpolitik* at the end of the 1960s).

447 The policy process in communist states: politics and industrial administration.
Leslie Holmes, foreword by Roger E. Kanet. Beverley Hills,
California; London: Sage, 1981. 280p. bibliog.

A comparative study of the growth and development of production associations in the Soviet Union and the GDR (for the GDR, primarily Vereinigungen Volkseigener Betriebe [Associations of State Enterprises] (VVBs) and *Kombinate*) as monopolistic, or oligopolistic, organizations for whole sub-branches of industry. The author focusses on one set of legislation (1973–74 in the USSR and 1973 in the GDR) and looks backward to establish the 'demand' inputs that gave rise to it. He also considers the implementation of the policy and its likely future results. Holmes describes the industrial structures of both economies before assessing the agencies through which demand is articulated as well as the nature of the demand itself, the Party policy and legislative response followed by policy implementation, with a final, extended section on opposition to the policy. The conclusions confirm the role of Party leaders as initiators and managers of policy innovation. An essential source for the serious student of the GDR.

448 **Economic reform in East German industry.**
Gert Leptin, Manfred Melzer, translated from the German by Roger A. Clarke.   Oxford, England: Oxford University Press, 1978. 200p. (Economic Reforms in East European Industry Series of the Institute of Soviet and East European Studies, Glasgow.)
Very much a scholarly book written for specialists by specialists. This is a competent attempt to deal with a complex subject. It is very useful for non-German speaking readers but it would have been more useful for the non-economist reader if the authors had briefly summarized at the end of the book both the original reforms and then their termination.

449 **Transport and the tertiary sector in the German Democratic Republic.**
Roy E. H. Mellor.   In: *The two Germanies: a modern geography.* Roy E. H. Mellor. London; New York; Hagerstown, Maryland; San Francisco; Sydney: Harper & Row, 1978, p. 405–16. maps. bibliog.
The re-drawing of the boundaries of divided Germany in 1945 paid little heed to existing transport networks. The problems which this presented for the GDR, including the lack of a main port and the need to adjust to radically new patterns of trade, are here clearly presented, with sections devoted to the railways, road haulage, inland waterways, the port problem, and air transport. A brief discussion of the tertiary section is appended.

450 **Combine formation and the role of the enterprise in East German industry.**
Manfred Melzer.   In: *The industrial enterprise in Eastern Europe.* Edited by Ian Jeffries. Eastbourne, England; New York: Praeger, 1981, p. 95–113. bibliog.
A discussion of the role of combines in the attempt to improve the industrial performance of the GDR's economic system. The author asserts that the combines encourage more constructive decision-making than was previously the case but argues that they alone cannot solve all the important problems of the GDR's planning mechanism.

451 **Industrial progress in Poland, Czechoslovakia and East Germany, 1937–1962.**
Alfred Zauberman.   London; New York: Oxford University Press, 1964. 368p. bibliog.

An early pioneering comparative work of immense scholarship which can still be usefully consulted.

Energy

452 **Energiepolitik und Energieforschung in der DDR.** (Energy policy
and energy research in the GDR.)
Werner Gruhn, Günter Lauterbach. Erlangen, FRG: Deutsche
Gesellschaft für zeitgeschichtliche Fragen e.V., 1986. 357p.
bibliog.

The authors treat their subject in two stages. First, there is an outline of the basic
facts of energy policy and its principal constraints in the GDR which considers,
for example, the link between energy and growth, the aims and instruments of
policy, the role of the Council for Mutual Economic Assistance (Comecon) in
energy provision and the structure of consumption. In the second part they
describe the principal fields of energy policy and research under the headings of:
energy saving; consumption of fossil fuels; atomic energy; renewable energy
sources; and research potential and actual research programs. The work provides
a good survey of the available information in these fields.

453 **Die Energiewirtschaft der DDR unter Berücksichtigung
internationaler Effizienzvergleiche.** (Energy provision in the GDR
in the light of international energy comparisons.)
Wolfgang Stinglwagner. Bonn: Gesamtdeutsches Institut, 1985.
241p.

A brief history of energy policy in the GDR is followed by an account of primary
energy sources and of the development of primary energy consumption compared
with other countries. The author goes on to describe the most important fields of
energy conversion, especially electricity, and to analyse energy losses and degrees
of efficiency at the different stages of energy conversion. The work concludes with
an assessment of future choices and constraints in energy policy. A basic source
for all serious students of energy provision in the GDR.

Agriculture

454 **Landwirtschaft in der DDR.** (Agriculture in the GDR.)
Hans Bichler. Berlin (West): Verlag Gebr. Holzapfel, 1981.
159p. bibliog.
This is the second edition of this brief but useful look at the agriculture of the
GDR. It is illustrated with official GDR photographs.

455 **The future of East German agriculture: the feasibility of the
1976–80 plans.**
Ronald A. Francisco. In: *The future of agriculture in the Soviet
Union and Eastern Europe; the 1976–1980 Five Year Plans.* Edited
by R. D. Laird, J. Hajda, B. A. Laird. Boulder, Colorado:
Westview Press, 1977, p. 185–203.
In a detailed numerical analysis of the factors contributing to past performance of
GDR agriculture the author predicts the levels of input needed to produce
particular plan targets and estimates the ability of the GDR economy to supply
these. The account of extensions to vertical and horizontal cooperation and
integration foreshadows later authors' observations on the diseconomies of
specialization. This volume is now of interest to students for its method rather
than its conclusions.

456 **From collectivisation to cooperation: a study of recent trends in East
German agriculture.**
Verna Freeman. *GDR Monitor*, no. 1 (summer 1979), p. 39–49.
Outlines the progress of collectivized agriculture through its different forms of
organization from the completion of collectivization in 1960 to 1978. These years
saw increases in the use of plant, machinery and chemicals. Moreover, the
horizontal integration proceeding from amalgamation and cooperation and
accompanied by specialization was followed by the vertical integration of farms

with both suppliers and customers. A very useful summary, aptly illustrated with tables and diagrams.

457 **Agrarpolitik in der DDR.** (Agricultural policy in the GDR.)
Hans Immler.   Cologne, FRG: Verlag Wissenschaft und Politik, 1971. 207p. bibliog.

A comprehensive description and assessment of GDR agricultural policy prior to 1971. It begins with the Marxist-Leninist idea of socialist agriculture and proceeds to a description of the stages and level of development of GDR agriculture at the time of writing (including the structure of production and productive units, plant and machinery, yields and productivity, management and agricultural incomes). This is followed by a description of the model of socialist agriculture which government policy aims to achieve – a rationalized industrialized and integrated system – designed to realize this. This book remains a fundamental text for any serious study of GDR agriculture.

458 **Playing leapfrog on the people's potatoes: the role of the *Kleingarten* in the GDR.**
Moray McGowan.   In: *Culture and society in the GDR*. Edited by Graham Bartram, Anthony Waine. Dundee, Scotland: GDR Monitor, 1984, p. 71–81. (GDR Monitor Special Series, no. 2).

Considers the origins of the German allotment movement, its rejection as petty-bourgeois by left-wing intellectuals, and its economic, social and ideological roles in the GDR. The private allotment not only provides an essential contribution to soft fruit production in the GDR, but also serves as a safety-valve for aspirations toward autonomy and withdrawal-tendencies which are brought at least formally within public political control by the official Allotment-Holders' Association (VKSK).

459 **Farmer and farm labor in the Soviet Zone of Germany.**
Frieda Wunderlich.   New York: Twayne, 1958. 162p. bibliog.

This book, written before the total collectivization of 1960, describes and analyses the history and performance of East German agriculture as a combination of central planning and direction on the one hand, and largely individual (70 per cent of all land) ownership and management on the other. The work is divided into two parts: the first concerns the farmers, both private and state; while the second deals with the conditions of farm workers. There are useful appendixes on the nationalization of trade and industry.

Trade Unions and Employment Conditions

460 **Degradation or humanization? work and scientific-technical progress in the GDR.**
Mike Dennis. In: *Studies in GDR culture and society 6: selected papers from the eleventh New Hampshire Symposium on the German Democratic Republic.* Edited by Margy Gerber (et al.). Lanham, Maryland; New York; London: University of America Press, 1986, p. 59–80.

Using GDR research undertaken in the 1970s and early 1980s Dennis investigates both the degree to which new technology, automation and management control strategies have alienated and degraded the worker and also the application and success of job-enrichment schemes designed to counter this tendency. Degradation occurs through removal of personal control and discretion and is aggravated in the GDR where technical qualifications are often under-utilized. Centres of such de-skilling are the chemical and automated machine tool industries. Job-enrichment schemes and semi-autonomous work groups intended to make work more creative, however, have not yet been widely introduced and are not always positively received, despite the official long-term commitment to their implementation and to the narrowing of the gap between production workers and the intelligentsia.

461 **Integrating work and personal life: an analysis of three professional work collectives in the German Democratic Republic.**
Marilyn Rueschemeyer. *GDR Monitor*, no. 8 (winter 1982–83), p. 27–45.

Describes trade unions in the GDR as agencies of both representation and control and examines to what extent work collectives fulfil these two functions. The collectives studied were situated in the Academy of Sciences, in a dental clinic and at a provincial university. The conclusions reached stress the importance of compatible personalities, of high mutual regard and of the quality of hierarchic relations and emphasize the crucial supportive role of the work collective for working women.

462 **Job satisfaction and relationship to work.**
Rudhard Stollberg.   In: *Work and technology*. Edited by M. R. Haug, J. Dopy. London: Laye Publications, 1977, p. 107–21.

The author, a researcher in the GDR, reports on research into the relationship between job satisfaction and a socialist attitude to work in the GDR. He concludes that job satisfaction does not necessarily indicate a socialist personality. The latter may even evince 'creative dissatisfaction' with work.

463 **Work in a nationally owned factory.**
Klaus Weise.   Berlin (East): Panorama DDR, 1976. 80p.

An East German look at everyday life and institutions in the NARVA lightbulb factory in East Berlin. The work is useful for its insights into the GDR view of public ownership, plan implementation and the role of the Socialist Unity Party (SED) within the factory. The function of the trade unions as a promoter of productivity is portrayed through programmes such as the 'socialist emulation drive' and the 'innovators movement' as well as through the 'collective bargaining agreements' which link productivity increases with improved wages and conditions. Provision for welfare, working women, education, culture and sport in this large workers' collective is also illustrated.

Statistics

464 **Statistisches Jahrbuch 1986.** (Statistical Yearbook, 1986.)
Edited by Staatliche Verwaltung für Statistik (Central Statistical
Board). Berlin (East): Staatsverlag der Deutschen
Demokratischen Republik 1986. vol. 31. 422p. + appendix 96p. +
index 16p. maps.

The most comprehensive collection of official data relating to all major aspects of
GDR life, such as the economy, the various branches of industry, prices,
education, culture, social services, births and deaths, population structure and the
administration of justice. The appendix provides data on other Council for
Mutual Economic Assistance (Comecon) countries (first section) as well as on the
other major countries of the world (section edition). A useful subject index makes
for easy referencing.

465 **Statistical pocket book of the German Democratic Republic.**
Central Statistical Board, translated from the German by
Intertext. Berlin (East): Staatsverlag. 1959–. annual. approx.
160p.

A useful compilation of statistical data, presented in an easy-to-understand form.

466 **U.N. Statistical Yearbook.**
New York: United Nations, 1948–. annual.

Provides an up-to-date compendium (text in English and French) of economic and
social statistics for many countries in the world, including the GDR. The data
relates to a wide range of subjects from the general to the specific, including, for
example, population, agriculture, manufacturing, energy, building construction,
earnings, prices, beer production, the number of telephones and the total number
of telegrams sent in a year.

467   **Zahlenspiegel Bundesrepublik Deutschland/Deutsche Demokratische Republik. Ein Vergleich.** (Statistics of the Federal Republic of Germany/German Democratic Republic: a comparison.) Bonn: Bundesministerium für innerdeutsche Beziehungen, Sept. 1985. 129p.

A very well presented and most useful slim volume which compares every aspect of life in the two Germanies. The excellent economic section is the work of Doris Cornelsen, Hannsjörg F. Buck, and Bernd Spindler. Ralf Rytlewski deserves special mention for his fine statistical work.

Environment

468 **The environment and Marxism-Leninism: the Soviet and East German experience.**
Joan DeBardeleben.   Boulder, Colorado; London: Westview Press, 1985. 274p. bibliog.

Considers how Marxist-Leninist ideas and concepts structure the environmental debate in the USSR and the GDR. The first part concerns the relation between Marxist-Leninist ideology and environmental issues. It addresses the link between political legitimation, growth and environmental protection, discusses anti-environmental aspects of Marxism-Leninism and establishes categories. The second part deals with Soviet economics, economic policy and the environment, with official rejection of limits to growth. The author presents the Soviet and GDR debates on measures of national economic performance and enterprise performance indicators showing where they sometimes encourage but on occasion also undermine environmental protection. She discusses too, the debate on natural resource pricing. The work brings out clearly differences in approach between the USSR and the GDR. An essential source for the specialist which contains a very full bibliography.

469 **Umweltprobleme und Umweltbewusstsein in der DDR.**
(Environmental problems and environmental consciousness in the GDR.)
Editorial Board of the *Deutschland Archiv*.   Cologne, FRG: Verlag Wissenschaft und Politik, 1985. 253p. maps. bibliog.

Despite considerable legislation and regulation, environmental pollution is a serious problem in the GDR. The country draws 70 per cent of its energy needs from lignite and this results in the production of sulphur dioxide, ash and dust which has disastrous repercussions for vegetation and human health. This volume brings together nine essays on this and other aspects of environmental pollution in the GDR including: the ecological consequences of socialist agricultural policy;

cooperation between the two German states on matters of pollution; official and unofficial ecological debates; the economic dimension to pollution and conservation; and the limited presentation of ecological questions in GDR fiction, poetry and children's literature. Several of the essays have tables, maps and useful additional bibliographical material.

Education

470 **Planning higher and further education in the GDR.**
Douglas Burrington. *GDR Monitor*, no. 6 (winter 1981–82),
p. 1–8.
After providing an introduction to the function of planning in a socialist society,
this article outlines and assesses the procedures by which the demands of the end-
users of trained manpower, the preferences of the education service, and the
requirements of central-planners and longer-range policy-makers in the ruling
Party are approximated to each other.

471 **Knowledge and allegiance: history teaching in the German
Democratic Republic, 1951–1971.**
Douglas Burrington. *Comparative Education*, vol. 19, no. 1
(1983), p. 43–57.
Outlines the methods and aims of history teaching in the GDR between 1951 and
1971 and discusses their relation to the wider policies of the ruling Party. The
author accounts for the transformation of school history during this period from a
largely fact-gathering exercise to a systematic social science of the past.
Burrington concludes that the aim of these changes – a deeper and reasoned
commitment to socialism and the GDR – was not achieved.

472 **Macht durch Wissen.** (Power through knowledge.)
Gert-Joachim Glaessner, Irmhild Rudolph.   Opladen, FRG:
Westdeutscher Verlag, 1978. 331p. bibliog.
Examines higher education and the in-service training of managers and specialists
in the context of the senior staff development and selection policy (*Kaderpolitik*)
of the ruling Socialist Unity Party (SED) in the GDR which took shape under the
economic pressures of the scientific and technological revolution from the late
1950s onwards. As education increasingly reflects manpower planning the authors

164

consider the implications of this for equality of opportunity. A fundamental text for the student and the researcher.

473 Education in the two Germanies.
Arthur Hearnden.   Oxford, England: Basil Blackwell, 1974. 245p. bibliog.

Provides a comparative account of the history of educational provision in West and East Germany from 1945 to the early 1970s prefaced by an outline of the educational heritage. The author places developments in the relevant context of political, ideological, economic and social constraints. He indicates that there was an initial divergence of structures and curricula followed by a restricted convergence in the 1960s. A useful and stimulating contribution for all readers.

474 Education in the GDR.
Brian Holmes.   *GDR Monitor*, no. 2 (Winter 1979–80), p. 43–52.

Presents a thumb-nail sketch of education in the GDR from constitutional provisions to classroom practice. This is followed by a report of the author's visit to educational establishments in the *Bezirk* of Cottbus. A useful first-hand account.

475 Learning for living: education in the GDR.
Helmut Klein, Ulrich Zückert.   Dresden, GDR: Verlag Zeit im Bild, 1980. 64p.

Two GDR educationists outline the history, structure and aims of education in East Germany. There are notes on vocational training and further and higher education, with a short appendix of documents.

476 The challenge of communist education: a look at the German Democratic Republic.
Margaret Siebert Klein.   Boulder, Colorado: East European Quarterly. Distributed by Columbia University Press. 1980. 174p. bibliog. (East European Monographs, no. 70).

This account of education in the GDR, produced by a longer-term Western resident of that country, opens with a brief educational history and some remarks on relevant tenets of Marxist-Leninist theory. The main body of the work concerns the curriculum, polytechnical education, classroom practice, teacher training, and personal impressions gathered from a visit to a school. Contains useful appendixes and an index.

477 Polytechnical training and education in the German Democratic Republic.
Erwin Kohn, Fred Postler.   Dresden, GDR: Verlag Zeit im Bild, 1976. 55p.

This is an information booklet for the general public which is periodically updated. It provides an illustrated account of polytechnical education in the GDR as a system in which practical industrial knowledge and skills are taught as part of the curriculum, both in the classroom and on the one day in the week spent in the factory or other place of work.

478   **Education, employment and development in the German Democratic Republic.**
K. Korn, G. Feierabend, G. Hersing, H.-D. Reuschel.   Paris: Unesco, 1984. 164p. bibliog.

This monograph, produced by senior researchers from the GDR, explores the relationships between education and training, on the one hand, and industrialization and technical progress on the other. As well as an account of the growth of technical and vocational education, together with a survey of the conditions leading to the development of the education system up to the 1980s, the authors consider long-term planning and the new problems confronting policy-makers. The volume is illustrated with useful figures and tables.

479   **Education in East Germany.**
Mina J. Moore-Rinvolucri.   Newton Abbot, England: David & Charles; Hamden, Connecticut: Archon Books, 1973. 117p. bibliog. (World Education Series).

Describes educational provision in the GDR and provides background notes on the country and its educational tasks and policies immediately after 1945. The main body of the work deals with pre-school provision, polytechnical education, post-compulsory education, education of the handicapped, the youth organization, the role of parents, teacher training, higher and further education, educational research and libraries and educational expenditure.

480   **Education under the Honeckers.**
John Page.   In: *Honecker's Germany*. Edited by David Childs. London: Allen & Unwin, 1985. p. 50–65. bibliog.

An excellent summary of educational policy and development from the 1946 Education Act to the 1980s, which mainly focusses on the schools. It includes an account of early disputes arising from the imposition of Soviet educational practice and discusses the significant enactments and changes, both organizational and curricular, over that period. The information on vocational training and higher education is restricted to the period after 1968.

481   **Politische Erziehung in der DDR. Ziele, Methoden und Ergebnisse des politischen Unterrichts an den allgemeinbildenden Schulen der DDR.** (Political education in the GDR: the aims, methods and results of political instruction in schools in the GDR.)
Karl Schmitt.   Paderborn, FRG: Ferdinand Schöningh, 1980. 235p. bibliog.

This is the standard work on civics teaching in the GDR and its effects. It provides a detailed account of the aims of political education, of the training of civics teachers and the materials and methods used and, finally, provides an assessment of the results of such teaching. The author lists and analyses the available survey material published in the GDR and provides a useful appendix of documents.

482   **An investigation of the education system of the DDR.**
       A. Williams.   *German Life and Letters*, vol. 24 (1970–71),
       p. 262–71.
The author characterizes the nature and purposes of the GDR educational system since 1946 and explains the aims of the present system with reference to sections of the 1965 Education Act.

Science and Technology

483 **Technological change in the German Democratic Republic.**
Raymond Bentley, foreword by Christopher Freeman. Boulder,
Colorado; London: Westview Press, 1984. 296p. bibliog.

This study represents the first substantive assessment by a Western scholar of 'the
GDR's capacity to innovate and diffuse technology'. Concentrating on the period
between 1945 and 1975, Bentley argues that the GDR displayed 'a weaker
capacity for technological change' than the FRG (but a stronger one than the
USSR) and that this was a major reason for the gap in productivity between the
two Germanies in the 1960s and 1970s. Separate chapters are devoted to: an
analysis of the technological levels found in the GDR's most important industrial
sectors; the GDR's industrial research and development effort in the 1960s and
1970s; the policy of detailed central planning up to 1962; the New Economic
System and its impact on technological change; the 'offensive strategy' which
aimed at leading the world in certain areas of technology; and the measures taken
to involve the academic sector in industry. The book concludes with 'reflections
towards a model of technological change in the GDR'.

484 **Science in East Germany.**
Vladimir Slamecka. New York; London: Columbia University
Press, 1963. 124p. bibliog.

The author describes this work as 'a brief, non-critical account of present-day
science in East Germany' and as 'a practical guide to the organization, the
research installations, and the information sources of East German science and
technology'. The volume is of particular use to those who require basic
information on the planning, structure, and implementation of science and
technology policies in the GDR. It does not attempt to evaluate scientific
activities, nor to compare them with those of other countries. The education and
training of scientists as well as channels of communication in science are
discussed. Over half of the volume is given over to a series of helpful appendixes

which consider, for example, GDR abstract journals, publishing houses, research institutes and learned societies.

485 **Technology in Comecon: acceleration of technological progress through economic planning and the market.**
J. Wilczynski. New York; Washington, DC; London: Praeger, 1974. 379p.

A most comprehensive, lucid and readable account of the evolution, policies and progress of the Council for Mutual Economic Assistance (Comecon) which is highly recommended for either the specialist or lay reader. It progresses from the historical, institutional and resources background, to approaches towards scientific and technical progress, the application of technology in the main branches of the economy and, finally, international cooperation and rivalry with the capitalist world. The general conclusion is that, while Comecon is a major world economic power block, its prowess is somewhat exaggerated through the presentation of undifferentiated statistics. The author ends with an interesting consideration of social issues and the convergence theory and a consideration of the possibilities of Comecon countries achieving the transition from socialism to full communism.

Language

General

486 **Kleine Enzyklopädie Deutsche Sprache.** (A concise encyclopaedia: the German language.)
Edited by Wolfgang Fleischer (et al.). Leipzig, GDR: VEB Bibliographisches Institut, 1983. 724p. 31 maps. bibliog.

Provides comprehensive and scholarly discussion of the German language from a Marxist-Leninist viewpoint.

487 **East German – a new language?**
Derek Lewis. *GDR Monitor*, no. 1 (summer 1979), p. 50–57.

Considers some of the features which can be held to be distinctive of German as used in the GDR, as opposed to the FRG. Such features include Russian influences in the form of loan-translations and syntactic structures, the lexis of ideology, semantic connotations and re-definitions, neologisms and the complex jargon of economic planning. The language of propaganda, linguistic stereotypes and stylistic characteristics are also considered. It is asserted that, despite a lack of pluralism in the public language in the GDR, there is no evidence for a fundamental linguistic divergence between East and West German, least of all on the level of general communication.

Dictionaries

488 **Trabbi, Telespargel und Tränenpavillon. Das Wörterbuch der
DDR-Sprache.** (Trabant, teleasparagus, and pavilion of tears:
dictionary of the language of the GDR.)
Edited by Martin Ahrends. Munich: Wilhelm Heyne Verlag,
1986. 218p.

The three terms in the title of this book are colloquial expressions for,
respectively, a popular family car, the television tower in East Berlin, and the
Friedrichstrasse crossing point to West Berlin. Their unintelligibility to the
uninitiated demonstrates the need for a German-German dictionary of this kind.
Martin Ahrends explains over a thousand terms and expressions in official and
popular usage which are peculiar to East Germany. He argues, in a thought-
provoking foreword, that a better understanding of the separate language which is
developing in the GDR will lead to a greater understanding of the quite different
realities of life there.

489 **Elaste und Plaste. Ein deutsch-deutsches Wörterbuch.** (Elastic and
Plastic: German-German dictionary.)
Compiled by Theodor Constantin. Berlin (West): Haude &
Spener, 1982. 92p. bibliog.

An indispensable mini-dictionary for those who wish to explore the many
hundreds of new words and different usages which the German language – as it is
written and spoken in the GDR – has acquired. All registers are here, from the
colloquially irreverent ('Erichs Datscha' is popular terminology for the imposing
Palast der Republik in East Berlin) to the sternly official ('Abschnittsbevollmäch-
tigter' is the term for a policeman responsible for a local beat). The entries are
organized alphabetically, each section beginning with a list of abbreviations (for
example, ABF, Arbeiter- und Bauernfakultät). The twenty accompanying
cartoon illustrations ensure that this subject is also viewed from its lighter side.

490 **Handwörterbuch der deutschen Gegenwartssprache.** (A concise
dictionary of the contemporary German language.)
Autorenkollektiv (Authors' collective) led by Günter
Kempcke. Berlin (East): Akademie, 1984. 1,400p.

A useful aid for anyone dealing with contemporary German, particularly as found
in the GDR.

491 **Wörterbuch der deutschen Gegenwartssprache.** (A dictionary of
the contemporary German language.)
Edited by Ruth Klappenbach, Wolfgang Steinitz. Berlin (East):
Akademie, 1980–82. 6 vols.

A major achievement (totalling 4,630p.), which is particularly useful as regards
lexical items which are peculiar to the GDR variety of German, or have a
meaning distinct from that found in the Federal Republic.

Literature

492 **The dialectics of legitimation: Brecht in the GDR.**
David Bathrick. *New German Critique*, issue no. 2 (spring 1974),
p. 90–103.

Bathrick formulates the difficulties Bertolt Brecht and his drama pose for the
GDR by asking the question: Can a theatre created to transform society also be
used to legitimize and affirm a particular social order? The heated debate among
critics in the West as well as the East on Brecht's vexed and complex relationship
to tradition, to the classics and to the bourgeois heritage is seen as rooted in a
larger debate concerning Marxism-Leninism. This has resulted in a 'massive east-
west ideological tug of war' (did Brecht learn his Marxism from Lenin or the
heretic Karl Korsch, for instance?) which has led to much distortion. Bathrick
ranges widely, drawing on the debates on art and politics in the 1920s and 1930s in
the League of Proletarian Revolutionary Writers (a literary and political
organization which represented the German wing of the Moscow-based International Association of Revolutionary Writers), the Expressionism Debate as well
as the controversies about formalism in the arts conducted in the GDR.

493 **Poems and ballads.**
Wolf Biermann, translated from the German by Steve
Gooch. London: Pluto, 1977. 103p.

While Wolf Biermann's own delivery and musical accompaniment is vital to the
impact of his songs and poems, this collection – like *Die Drahtharfe* [The wire
harp], (translated from the German by Eric Bentley, New York: Harcourt, Brace,
Jovanovich, 1968) – provides a good impression of why, until his expatriation in
November 1976, he had been for over a decade such a source of discomfort to the
East German authorities. If most East Germans remain passively contemptuous
of the shortcomings of the régime which controls their lives, Biermann uses his
gadfly political ballads to draw raucous and humorous attention to them.

494 **Einführung in die DDR-Literatur.** (An introduction to the literature of the GDR.)
Christel Blumensath, Heinz Blumensath. Stuttgart, FRG: J. B. Metzlersche Verlagsbuchhandlung, 1983. 235p. bibliog.

This is the second, considerably revised and extended edition of a book written originally to make East German writers more widely-known to a general, and particularly a schools, audience. It is a well-annotated work which examines selected aspects of the development of GDR literature: the anti-fascist period; Socialist Realism; women's literature; divided Germany; and the portrayal of youth, school and the home. The author's aim is to introduce schoolchildren to examples of literature widely-known in the GDR which reflect the realities of life there and which also mirror the goals and aspirations which East German society has set itself. They hope to encourage a fresh approach to the GDR by 'combatting the cultural cold war'.

495 **Zwischen literarischer Autonomie und Staatsdienst. Die Literatur in der DDR.** (Between literary autonomy and service to the state: literature in the GDR.)
Werner Brettschneider. Berlin (West): Erich Schmidt Verlag, 3rd revised ed., 1980. 339p. bibliog.

Brettschneider looks at GDR literature in terms of genres – prose, drama and lyric poetry – and under these headings concentrates on the work of some twenty writers. His analysis of the difficulties encountered by many authors in their dealings with the Party is free of Cold War prejudices and his book is one of the most stimulating and sharply perceptive studies of GDR literature by a Western critic. Its merits are three-fold: dispassionate curiosity about the subject; the author's awareness that his own cultural predispositions may hamper his intention to approach GDR literature on its own terms; and sure-footed literary evaluation and taste. The detailed discussions of individual works are most useful.

496 **Kleine Literaturgeschichte der DDR.** (A brief history of the literature of the GDR.)
Wolfgang Emmerich. Darmstadt, Neuwied, FRG: Luchterhand, 1981. 264p. bibliog.

This is arguably the liveliest and most readable short introduction to the literature of the GDR. It tackles the subject chronologically and in the context of economic and political developments. The volume concludes with a very useful tabular and parallel listing of the principal literary and cultural events since 1945 alongside, by year of publication, the most significant novels and shorter prose fiction, lyric poetry and drama.

497 **Poetry in East Germany: adjustments, visions and provocations.**
John Flores. New Haven, Connecticut; London: Yale University Press, 1971. 354p. bibliog.

In his introduction, Flores briefly outlines trends in GDR literature until the end of the 1960s stressing the separateness of its development and emphasizing that lyric poetry has been the least administered of the genres. In the three central sections of his book he discusses selected poets under the headings of its subtitle. In 'adjustments' Stephan Hermlin and Franz Fühmann he sees as writers who had attempted to modify their writing to meet official demands; in 'visions' Peter Huchel and Johannes Bobrowski are discussed as the GDR's outstanding poets whose work has resisted official pressures; and in 'provocations' he analyses the emergence of a critical, Brecht-influenced poetry with the work of Günter Kunert, Volker Braun, Karl Mickel and Wolf Biermann.

498 **Literatur der DDR in Einzeldarstellungen.** (The literature of the GDR in accounts of individual writers.)
Edited by Hans Jürgen Geerdts. Stuttgart, FRG: Alfred Kröner Verlag, 1972. 571p. bibliog.

This collection of essays by various hands considers twenty-seven GDR writers and is prefaced by an introductory essay on the development of GDR literature. Each essay has a bibliography of primary and secondary literature.

499 **The plebeans rehearse the uprising.**
Günter Grass, translated from the German by Ralph Manheim. London: Secker & Warburg, 1967. 122p.

Irrespective of its setting during the June 1953 Uprising in Berlin, Grass's play cannot be primarily regarded as a source of historical information, any more than most plays can be that might be said to belong to the genre of 'historical drama'. The author's concern is with the role of the intellectual in society, particularly with the perceived negative German tradition of the intellectual standing aside from political events. This is what the Brecht figure in this play does. When approached by participants in the uprising, this character, who is simply called the Boss, will not lend his support to their actions, preferring to regard them as raw material for subsequent aesthetic exploitation. It is of course true that many intellectuals remained loyal to the régime in 1953 and that many, including Brecht, expressed support in one way or another once the uprising was over. Notwithstanding this, it is not by the criterion of 'historical authenticity' that Grass's play should be judged. The volume also contains an introductory address by Grass and historical notes by Uta Gerhardt.

500 **Geschichte der Literatur der Deutschen Demokratischen Republik.**
(A history of the literature of the German Democratic Republic.)
Edited by an authors' collective under the direction of Horst Haase, Hans Jürgen Geerdts, Erich Kühne, Walter Pallus. Berlin (East): Volk und Wissen Volkseigener Verlag, 1976. 908p. bibliog.
(Geschichte der Deutschen Literatur von den Anfängen bis zur Gegenwart – A history of German literature from the beginnings to the present, vol. 11).

An eminent GDR Germanist commented that in this massive volume 'not a single name or title is missing'. This official history of GDR literature from its earliest beginnings to the mid 1970s is indeed remarkable for the amount of factual information it contains about the development of lyric poetry, prose and drama. The Western reader will regard it as an indispensable first introduction to the field

Literature

but will possibly wish to treat its critical judgements with care. The book contains fascinating illustrative material, including, for example: reproductions of book covers and theatre programmes; photographs of drama productions; information about writers' conferences; and manuscript extracts.

501 **East German poetry: an anthology.**
Edited by Michael Hamburger, with poetry translated from the German by Gordon Brotherston, Gisela Brotherston, Michael Hamburger, Christopher Levenson, Ruth Mead, Matthew Mead, Christopher Middleton. Oxford, England: Carcanet, 1972. 213p.

This anthology comprises a selection of poems (in the original German and in an accompanying English translation) by twelve of the GDR's best poets: Bertolt Brecht, Peter Huchel, Johannes Bobrowski, Günter Kunert, Heinz Kahlau, Reiner Kunze, Sarah Kirsch, Karl Mickel, Wolf Biermann, Kurt Bartsch, Volker Braun, Bernd Jentzsch. Michael Hamburger provides an excellent introduction.

502 **The individual in a new society: a study of selected 'Erzählungen' and 'Kurzgeschichten' of the German Democratic Republic from 1965 to 1972.**
Irene Artes Hedlin. Bern: Peter Lang, 1977. 128p. bibliog. (Canadian Studies in German Language and Literature, vol. 16).

Hedlin argues that the relationship between the individual and the new society developing in the GDR has been an increasingly dominant theme in East German literature since 1965. In the first part of her book entitled 'Themes and Directions', she discusses the literary representation of the individual at his place of work and his relation to the collective and to social change. In the second part, 'Types and Situations', she explores various images of the emancipated woman, the outsider figure and the 'positive' hero. Her thesis is that the shorter narrative prose forms have enjoyed an increasingly important role in the development of GDR literature and all her examples are taken, either from the work of representative writers in the genre such as Werner Bräunig, Manfred Jendryschik, Erik Neutsch, Joachim Nowotny and Siegfried Pitschmann, or from individual short stories by other writers – for instance, Volker Braun, Werner Heiduczek, Erwin Strittmatter, Benito Wogatzki and others.

503 **The 'good new' and the 'bad new': metamorphoses of the modernism debate in the GDR since 1956.**
Jost Hermand, translated from the German by Evelyn Torton Beck, Charles Spencer. *New German Critique*, vol. 1, no. 3 (fall 1974), p. 73–92.

Discusses the revival in the GDR of the debates among Marxist theoreticians in the 1920s and 1930s about the 'threat' of modernism. In the 1950s writers and intellectuals such as Peter Huchel (whose journal *Sinn und Form* provided a forum for a more cosmopolitan literature) and Ernst Fischer (who championed the work of Franz Kafka) were constantly embattled with Party officialdom who regarded avant-garde literary techniques as the product of bourgeois decadence and hence incompatible with a socialist, proletarian art. This conflict was the product of resistance to the idea of ideological and cultural coexistence with the West and of a striving for a separate national identity. The article also discusses the GDR view of West German reading habits and GDR attitudes to the classical heritage.

504 **The King David Report.**
Stefan Heym.   London: Quartet Books, 1977. 254p. (The first British edition was published in 1973 in London by Hodder & Stoughton.)

Stefan Heym is arguably the best known of the GDR's internal dissident novelists. A communist of the old guard who returned to (East) Germany in the 1950s from the United States where his first novels were initially published (*The crusaders*, *Hostages*, *Of smiling peace*), he has chosen to remain in the country despite falling foul of the authorities. While *The King David Report* was set sufficiently distant in time and place for its comments on current circumstances to be acceptable, his later novels were not. *5 Tage im Juni* [5 days in June] (London: Hodder & Stoughton, 1977) was a lightly fictionalized mixture of document and contemporary report which provided a balanced account of the June 1953 Uprising in East Berlin. Neither it nor *Collin* [Collin] (London: Hodder & Stoughton, 1980), the story of the psychological struggle between the head of the East German secret police and the eponymous novelist hero, could be published in the GDR, however. Both probe too deeply into taboo areas: the one into the official version of the events of the 17 June 1953, the other into the Stalinist persecutions of the 1950s. This remarkable writer himself produces the English versions of his work.

505 **East is East: six poets from the German Democratic Republic.**
Edited by Konrad Hopkins, Ronald van Roekal, compiled by Edward Mackinnon.   Paisley, Scotland: Wilfion Books, 1984. 63p. bibliog.

A selection of the work of six leading poets – Volker Braun, Karl Mickel, Heinz Czechowski, Sarah Kirsch, Wulf Kirsten, Kito Lorenc – is here presented in English translation. An introduction provides a literary-historical framework, and each of the selections is preceded by a note on the poet in question.

506 **Theater in the planned society: contemporary drama in the German Democratic Republic in its historical, political and cultural context.**
H. G. Huettich.   Chapel Hill, North Carolina: University of North Carolina Press, 1978. 174p. bibliog.

The aim of this book is to trace the development of GDR drama *about* the GDR and to trace and define the sociopolitical function of drama and dramatists in the context of a planned and closely monitored culture. The author reveals an intimate knowledge of the more obscure areas of East German drama as well as of its more obvious peaks. His discussion of numerous individual plays will appeal more to those who see drama as a vehicle for ideas than to those who are interested in 'theatre' as such. His excessively sanguine final chapter on the prospects for drama in the GDR is severely modified by an addendum to the preface which comments on the resurgence, in 1977, of much more hard-line attitudes to artistic and dramatic freedoms.

507 **Literary presentations of divided Germany: the development of a central theme in East German fiction 1945–1970.**
Peter Hutchinson. Cambridge, England: Cambridge University Press, 1977. 204p. bibliog.

A study of East German fiction which has depicted East and West Germany within a single work. The author identifies three major ways in which writers have investigated a divided Germany. Firstly through the figure of the traveller, a traditional device for exploring an alien culture but taking, in this East German manifestation, the form of a hero with a sturdily reflective mind who operates from a firm ideological base. Secondly, through the representative figure who becomes involved in a conflict with ideological implications, and thirdly, by comparing the two Germanies in terms of their relationship to the Nazi past. In an appendix Hutchinson considers the social and ideological factors which have influenced the presentation and reception of the theme of a divided Germany.

508 **Das endlose Jahr. Begegnungen mit Mäd.** (Year without end: confrontations with Mäd.)
Karl-Heinz Jakobs. Düsseldorf, FRG: Claassen Verlag, 1983. 248p.

In 1977 Karl-Heinz Jakobs's life and political outlook were radically changed by meeting Dorothea Garai, known here as Mäd. His shattering book is an account of the years 1937 to 1956 which Mäd – a member of the German Communist Party who had fled to Moscow to escape the Nazis – spent as a political prisoner in a Russian labour camp on Kolyma. Her story of Stalinist atrocities is intercut with Jakobs's blow by blow detailing of his involvement with the protest over the expatriation of Wolf Biermann. These parallel tales are, for Jakobs, a process of political education and disillusionment which culminated in his leaving the Party and moving to the Federal Republic.

509 **A question of perspectives: the literature of the German Republic and its West German critics.**
Martin Kane. *Pen International*, vol. 35, no. 1 (1985), p. 30–36.

Argues that the history, over the last thirty years, of the changing attitudes of West German critics and academics to the literature of the GDR has been as complex and as fraught as the history of the political relations between the two countries in this period. In his review of some ten West German publications on GDR literature Kane concludes, however, that in more recent years a more nuanced and sympathetic stance has developed.

510 **Die Aula.** (The lecture theatre.)
Hermann Kant. Berlin (East): Rütten & Loening, 1965. 466p.

Hermann Kant, erstwhile president of the GDR Writers' Union, achieved celebrity with his first novel, *Die Aula* (there is no English translation). It has been reprinted innumerable times in the GDR and the paperback edition has sold

Literature

some 150,000 copies in the Federal Republic. The novel is a retrospective account of the student days and subsequent successful careers of a group of friends who are the first pupils of the *Arbeiter- und Bauernfakultät* (Workers' and Farmers' Faculty) at Greifswald University. These faculties were established in 1949 to speed the flow of students from working-class backgrounds into a university education. Narrated by the journalist Robert Iswall from a point in the early 1960s when the need for the faculties had become redundant, the novel takes a confident and relaxed view of the development of the GDR, frequently treating its subject with humour and, occasionally, a touch of gentle satire.

511 **The wonderful years.** (Die wunderbaren Jahre.)
Reiner Kunze, translated from the German by Joachim Neugroschel. New York: George Braziller, 1977. 127p.

This collection of brief prose texts documents Kunze's increasing estrangement from life in the GDR (publication of his own literary work had been made increasingly difficult since 1962). As a result of this publication he was excluded from the official writers' organization and he was permitted to emigrate to West Germany in 1977. The particular themes of this volume are growing up in an atmosphere of incitement to hatred towards the West and the tension of youthful originality and exuberance with the stultifying and often hypocritical norms of the state education system. Kunze's personal links with Czechoslovakia (CSSR) are reflected in a special section devoted to the Prague Spring (1968) and Czech poets. Written in a beautifully clear and restrained style, these prose vignettes offer precious and revealing insights into a sensitive human being's perception of the GDR.

512 **Der Vierte Zensor. Vom Entstehen und Sterben eines Romans in der DDR.** (The fourth censor: the origin and death of a novel in the GDR.)
Erich Loest. Cologne, FRG: Edition Deutschland Archiv, Verlag Wissenschaft und Politik, 1984. 96p. bibliog.

Provides a record of the arguments and discussions Erich Loest had with publishers and officials about his novel *Es geht seinen Gang* (Halle, Leipzig, GDR: Mitteldeutscher Verlag, 1978). It identifies the levels of censorship which face writers in the GDR: that which the author operates as he writes; those exerted by the publishing firm and the Ministry of Culture which has to give its seal of approval; and that emanating from the Politbüro which may prevent a work from being published or going into a second edition. This very enlightening account gives a vivid picture of the vast amount of energy which is expended at all levels in the GDR in deciding the fate of a controversial book. It is supplemented by extracts from the novel in question and an interview with its author.

178

513　**Wolf Biermann and 'die zweite deutsche Exilliteratur' (the second German exile literature): an appraisal after nine years.**
Dennis R. McCormick.　In: *Studies in GDR culture and society 6: selected papers from the eleventh New Hampshire Symposium on the German Democratic Republic.* Edited by Margy Gerber (et al.). Lanham, Maryland; New York; London: University of America Press, 1986, p. 187–203.

The author considers whether a GDR-writer now in West Germany, such as Wolf Biermann, can truly be described as 'in exile'. From a long-term and material perspective the answer is probably no, however, an intellectual and ideological sense of exile is a complex question depending on things such as personality, the unresolved issue of the unity of German literature, and on the relevance of convergence (see item no. 426). McCormick reviews the stages of Biermann's output in the West and concludes that he can no longer be regarded as being in exile in the sense of remaining wholly bound to his GDR past. In particular his recent efforts to combine polemical songs with personal elements betoken an attempt to create art beyond the politically short-lived and topical.

514　**Writings beyond the Wall: literature from the German Democratic Republic.**
Edited by Edward Mackinnon, Gina Kalla, John Green.　London: Artery, 1979. 112p.

The editors' aim is to help 'to breach the wall which has been erected in this country [Great Britain] around the socialist culture of the GDR'. Their anthology of short stories and poems in English translation is intended to constitute a cross-section of GDR writers (twenty-one in all) from the older generation to those who emerged in the late 1960s. Also included are four full-page black-and-white reproductions of works by the artist Wolfgang Mattheuer.

515　**Entwicklung und Funktion der Literaturpolitik der DDR 1945–1978.** (The development and function of literary policy in the GDR 1945–78.)
Bernhard Mayer-Burger.　Munich: tuduv-Studien, Reihe Sprach-u.Literaturwiss. Band 17, 1984. 587p. bibliog.

This is a massively scholarly examination of the development of literary policy in the GDR up until 1978. It is aimed at the specialist, not the fainthearted or the casual dabbler in GDR literature. One of its many virtues is to demonstrate with clarity and great detail how the alternating periods of thaw and freeze in the freedoms permitted to GDR writers have been the direct consequence of changing economic, political and social circumstances. The author sees literature as having a vital informative function in a society which has little faith in the official media. While he is primarily concerned with literary policy and the processes whereby the State attempts to steer and manipulate its writers, his discussion is supported with perceptive analysis of specific, representative texts.

Literature

516 **Quartett.** (Quartet.)
Heiner Müller, translated from the German by Karin Gartzke,
Geoffrey Davis. Dundee, Scotland: GDR Monitor, (1984). 16p.
('Literature in Translation' Series, no. 1).
This short, strange play, set unspecifically in time and place, consists of a brutally
erotic dialogue about sexual lust, seduction and bestiality between two languid
French aristocrats Merteuil and Valmont. It is based on *Les liaisons dangereuses*
(1782) by Choderlos de Laclos (see the standard edition of this work edited by M.
Bardon, Paris: Garnier, 1955).

517 **Literature and revolution: a critical study of the writer and
communism in the twentieth century.**
Jürgen Rühle, translated from the German by Jean
Steinberg. London: Pall Mall Press, 1969. 520p. bibliog.
The theme of this book is the conflict – under the harsh realities of Stalinism –
between political power and the world of literature and the intellect. Part 1
documents the 'tragic encounter of literature and revolution' in the Soviet Union.
Part 2 is a discussion of the contributions made by German political writers in the
1920s and 1930s – Thomas Mann, Bertolt Brecht and Anna Seghers in her
correspondence with György Lukacs – to the debates on the relation between
literature and politics. In this part the author also outlines developments in East
Germany after the war; the essays here on Johannes R. Becher's mixed fortunes
as first Minister of Culture and on what the author calls 'literature behind the
wall' will be most useful for students of GDR literature. Part 3 is a study of
miscellaneous fellow-travelling writers and intellectuals from a variety of
European and Asian countries – George Bernard Shaw, H. G. Wells, Romain
Rolland, Ignazio Silone, Jean-Paul Sartre, Jaroslav Hašek, Tibor Déry, Federico
García Lorca, Rabindranath Tagore, Lu Hsun and Milovan Djilas.

518 **Optimistic tragedies: the plays of Heiner Müller.**
Wolfgang Schivelbusch, translated from the German by Helen
Fehervary. *New German Critique*, issue no. 2 (spring 1974),
p. 104–13.
Schivelbusch sees the special quality of Heiner Müller's plays as being the
projection of socialist consciousness 'not as the consciousness of fixed positive
values but as the consciousness of contradictions'. Müller's development as a
dramatist has been from realistic portrayal to a fable form which lends his work
greater universality. His early plays about industrial production – *Der
Lohndrücker* (*The wage shark*), *Die Korrektur* (*The correction*), and *Der Bau*
(*Construction*) – depict the alienation engendered in those who suffer the
drudgery of manual labour entailed in the building of socialism. *Mauser* (The
molting season) is discussed as a continuation of the argument of Brecht's *The
measures taken*. As Fehervary notes in her introductory outline of Müller's life
and work: 'The development from Brecht's dramaturgy to Müller's represents a
historical transition from the individual as the object of history to its subject'.

519 **Wirkungsästhetische Analysen. Poetologie und Prosa in der neueren DDR-Literatur.** (Reader-response analyses: poetics and prose in recent GDR literature.)
Dieter Schlenstedt. Berlin (East): Akademie, 1979. 376p.

One of the country's foremost literary scholars here identifies three main protagonists among the competing tendencies in GDR literature between 1960 and the mid-1970s: 'light' reading; the didactic literature inherited from the 1950s; and what he terms 'Literatur als Selbstverständigung' i.e., a literature which no longer sees the reader as someone to be instructed but as an equal and trusted partner in an open dialogue. It is Schlenstedt's judgement that, while the first of these (still) enjoys the largest readership and the second (still) finds favour in the GDR's official literary politics, it is the third which must be regarded as the dominant mode in terms of its actual and potential contribution to the growth of socialism in the GDR. The book makes for tough reading in places but rewards careful study.

520 **The seventh cross.**
Anna Seghers, translated from the German by James A. Galston.
London: Hamish Hamilton, 1943. 323p.

When Anna Seghers died in 1983 at the age of 82, the GDR lost the most eminent of the group of communist writers who returned from exile in 1945 convinced that they had a vital role to play in the creation of a socialist society. She chose to settle in the GDR because she could 'give expression here to those things for which I have lived my life'. Her masterpieces, however, remain those novels she wrote in exile. *The seventh cross* [Das siebte Kreuz] (which exists in several English translations) is the story of the only one of seven prisoners to escape the Westhofen concentration camp (near Mainz) and survive. The novel gives a gripping account of resistance to Nazism and is a tribute to the indestructibility of the human spirit. *Transit* [Transit visa], translated from the German by James A. Galston (London: Eyre & Spottiswoode, 1945), is set in Marseilles in 1940 and is a less optimistic work. Describing the plight of refugees from fascism who are caught up in a nightmare of bureaucracy in their efforts to secure exit visas, the novel has more in common with certain brands of existentialism than with the sustaining Marxist credo usually associated with its author. The works Seghers produced in the GDR are generally disappointing. *Die Toten bleiben jung* [The dead stay young] (London: Eyre & Spottiswoode, 1950), is an attempt to render the social and political complexities of the period 1918–45 through a bewildering array of characters, and the novel *Die Entscheidung* [The decision] of 1959, which, along with its sequel *Das Vertrauen* [Trust] of 1968, dramatizes the ideological divide of the postwar period, are too heavily partisan in their political sympathies to be entirely convincing.

521 **Literature of the working world: a study of the industrial novel in East Germany.**
Marc D. Silbermann. Bern; Frankfurt am Main, FRG: Peter Lang, 1976. 118p. bibliog.

The world of work is of crucial importance in GDR society: it is the 'formative sphere of social relationships and material productivity'. Silbermann analyses eight representative novels which deal with different manifestations of the working world. He demonstrates their varying points of contact with the programmatic demands of Socialist Realism and examines the extent to which they fulfil the requirement that literature should help to formulate and promote socialist values.

522 **'How did we become as we are?' The treatment of fascism in GDR literature.**
Alexander Stephan, translated from the German by Ian Wallace. *GDR Monitor*, issue no. 3 (summer 1980), p. 5–16.

Stephan argues that, after three decades of antifascist literature with a heavily moralistic tone designed to encourage socialist values, a new generation of younger writers in the GDR began to investigate fascism and its relevance to the present in a more considered and penetrating fashion. Typical of this development, despite leaving certain taboo subjects unspoken, is Christa Wolf's *Kindheitsmuster* with its question: 'How did we become as we are?' Stephan also considers works by Hermann Kant, Helga Schütz and Alfred Wellm.

523 **Bertolt Brecht's adaptations for the Berliner Ensemble.**
Arrigo Subiotto. London: Modern Humanities Research Association, 1975. 207p. bibliog.

The theme of this book is Brecht's concern with literary tradition, his distaste for reverential treatment of the classics, and his own eagerness to adapt them – developing in the process their social and political potential – often with scant consideration for conventional notions of ownership or plagiarism. The author demonstrates how Brecht stamps the authority of his political and dramatic ideas on five plays from the classical repertoire: Jakob Michael Reinhold Lenz's *Der Hofmeister* is adapted in order to dramatize the social and intellectual repression in the transition from feudal to bourgeois society; Gerhart Hauptmann's *Der Biberpelz* and *Der Rote Hahn* are transformed into condemnations of corruption and imperial grandeur; Molière's *Don Juan* becomes a play about feudal exploitation; George Farquar's *The Recruiting Officer* is made into an indictment of colonialism; and Shakespeare's *Coriolanus* becomes an exercise in iconoclasm.

524 **Beyond *Kulturpolitik*: the GDR's established authors and the challenge of the 1980s.**
Dennis Tate. In: *The GDR in the 1980s*. Edited by Ian Wallace. Dundee, Scotland: GDR Monitor, 1984, p. 15–29. (GDR Monitor Special Series, no. 4).

This informative and thought-provoking contribution discusses the East and West German writers' peace conference of 1981 and sets the work of established writers such as Christa Wolf, Irmtraud Morgner and Franz Fühmann in the context of the most pressing issues of the day: the nuclear threat; ecology; and the North/South divide. Wolf's *Kassandra* is seen as an attack on masculine values, Morgner's *Amanda* as a dramatization of socialist feminism and Fühmann's apocalyptic fairy tales and his confrontation with the biography of the poet Georg Trakl (1887–1914) as a continuation of the so-called 'subjective authenticity' which, as a reaction against the aridity of officially favoured 'Socialist Realism', began to characterize many of the best works of GDR literature from the late 1960s onwards. Their use of an historical or mythical dimension makes these authors accessible only to an educated minority which – in the face of official attempts to turn the cultural clock back to the simplicities of Socialist Realism – may explain why their highly critical positions are tolerated.

525   **The East German novel: identity, community, continuity.**
Dennis Tate.   Bath, England: Bath University Press, 1984. 264p. bibliog.

Tate's main concern is with the mainstream development of prose-writing in the GDR and he identifies five major phases, associated respectively with: the work of J. R. Becher; war novels; industrial novels; contemporary biographies; and epic prose. Twenty works of particular importance are analysed.

526   **Aspects of literature in the GDR.**
Frank Trommler.   In: *Contemporary Germany: politics and culture*. Edited by Charles Burdick, Hans-Adolf Jacobsen, and Winfried Kudszus. Boulder, Colorado; London: Westview Press, 1984, p. 353–70. bibliog.

A concise overview of the development of GDR literature prior to the late 1970s. A central theme is the sensitive relationship between the writers and the Socialist Unity Party (SED).

527   **Female roles in East German drama 1949–1977: a selective history of drama in the GDR.**
Katherine Vanovitch.   Frankfurt am Main, FRG; Bern: Peter Lang, 1982. 172p. bibliog. (European University Studies, Series 1: German Language and Literature, vol. 483).

The author considers the roles played by women in GDR drama prior to 1977, concentrating on what they illustrate about the changing lives of women and the changing social attitudes reflected through the dramatist. She deals with the theoretical and historical background to the role of women in 1949 and with the condition of post-war theatre before analysing works by fourteen playwrights, all of them men: Friedrich Wolf; Erwin Strittmatter; Helmut Sakowski; Helmut Baierl; Harold Hauser; Claus Hammel; Rainer Kerndl; Siegfried Pfaff; Rolf Gozell; Rudi Strahl; Peter Hacks; Heiner Müller; Volker Braun; and Stefan Schütz.

528   **The adolescent hero: a theme in recent literature from the GDR, the USSR, Czechoslovakia and Poland.**
Edited by Ian Wallace.   Dundee, Scotland: GDR Monitor, 1984. 98p. (GDR Monitor Special Series, no. 3).

A collection of essays which discusses recent GDR literature within the context of literary developments in the Eastern Bloc as a whole. This is achieved by investigating an area of crucial concern to all of socialist literature: the role of youth. Of the six essays, three are devoted to GDR literature (with particular

Literature

emphasis on Ulrich Plenzdorf and his influence) and one each to the literature of the USSR and Czechoslovakia. In the case of Poland it is Tadeusz Nowak's fiction which is investigated in the final essay.

529   **The writer and society in the GDR.**
Edited by Ian Wallace.   Dundee, Scotland: Hutton, 1984. 151p.

The aim of this book is to show how important literature is in the GDR as a medium through which society reflects critically on its own problems. The opening chapter investigates the role of the writer in the GDR. Subsequent chapters provide individual studies of the work of seven authors: Hermann Kant; Stefan Heym; Peter Hacks; Anna Seghers; Heiner Müller; Christa Wolf; and Volker Braun. A concluding section deals with the 'Biermann affair' of 1976 and its lasting impact on the literary-cultural life of the GDR.

530   **Volker Braun. Forschungsbericht.** (Volker Braun: research report.)
Ian Wallace.   Amsterdam: Rodopi, 1986. 132p. bibliog. (Forschungsberichte zur DDR-Literatur 3 – Research reports on GDR literature, no. 3).

A comprehensive survey of principal aspects of research on the work of the writer Volker Braun (born 1939). The report contains a very full bibliography of 657 items.

531   **Structure and society in literary history.**
Robert Weimann.   London: Lawrence & Wishart, 1977. 273p. bibliog.

Weimann, a member of the Academy of Sciences of the GDR, attempts to overcome the predominance of formalist New Criticism in English and American literary scholarship by examining the structure of literature in the context of its social function. This function is seen in terms of 'genesis' – a dialectical interaction between the author and his social environment – and 'impact', which includes the aesthetics of reception. The theory is developed with reference to the concept of tradition, literary history, metaphor and narrative perspective, with principal reference to English literature, including Shakespeare and the novel. A sensitive and non-dogmatic contribution from a Marxist angle.

532   **The quest for Christa T.**
Christa Wolf, translated from the German by Christopher Middleton.   New York: Farrar, Straus & Giroux, 1970. 185p.

Christa Wolf is the GDR's most celebrated living writer. She is read widely in both German states and internationally. Her first novel, *Der geteilte Himmel* [Divided sky], (translated from the German by Joan Becker; Berlin (East): Seven Seas, 1965), set at the time of the building of the Berlin Wall, tells of a love affair which founders on temperamental but also, and more importantly, ideological differences. As the heroine Rita discovers her identity while working in a carriage-building factory, her lover Manfred departs for the West. Despite the controversy which the book's adventurous narrative technique aroused when it

184

was first published, *Divided sky* is one of the few successful novels to result from the Bitterfeld Conference of 1959 which had urged East German writers to dramatise more energetically the world of work. The theme of self-realization is even more central to Wolf's second novel, *Nachdenken über Christa T.* [The quest for Christa T.], which deals in retrospect with the life of a leukaemia victim. The message here seems to be that GDR socialism is not necessarily the guarantor of happiness and fulfilment. In her masterpiece, *Kindheitsmuster* [A model childhood], (translated from the German by Ursula Molinaro and Hedwig Rappolt, London: Virago, 1982), Christa Wolf brilliantly tackles the problem of Germany's fascist past. Operating on three levels of narration, the novel explores Wolf's own experience of growing up under the Nazis, describes a journey to her home town which is now in Poland and simultaneously reflects on the process of discovery and research which had accompanied the writing of the novel. Wolf's later works reveal feminist preoccupations. *Kein Ort. Nirgends* [No place on earth], (translated from the German by Jan van Heurck, London: Virago, 1983) creates a fictional, but historically and psychologically entirely plausible encounter between Heinrich von Kleist and the poetess Karoline von Günderrode. Her novel *Kassandra* [Cassandra], (translated from the German by Jan van Heurck, London: Virago, 1984) and its accompanying essays are an attack on patriarchal values and reinterpret a classical myth in the light of concerns about the threat of a nuclear holocaust.

533 **Contemporary East German poetry.**
Edited by Richard Zipser. Oberlin, Ohio: Oberlin College, 1980. 191p. (Special Issue of Field).

The editor offers a selection of poems (in the original German and in an accompanying English translation) written in the 1970s by fourteen of the GDR's best poets: Erich Arendt, Thomas Brasch, Volker Braun, Heinz Czechowski, Adolf Endler, Elke Erb, Bernd Jentzsch, Rainer Kirsch, Sarah Kirsch, Wulf Kirsten, Günter Kunert, Reiner Kunze, Kito Lorenc and Karl Mickel. He also provides a brief introduction to GDR poetry in general and a biographical note on each of the poets.

534 **DDR-Literatur im Tauwetter.** (GDR literature in a period of thaw.)
Richard A. Zipser, with Karl-Heinz Schoeps. New York; Bern; Frankfurt am Main, FRG: Peter Lang, 1985. 3 vols. [Vols. I and II *Wandel – Wunsch – Wirklichkeit* (Change – hopes – reality) and Vol. III *Stellungnahmen* (Points of view)]

These three somewhat expensive volumes provide an interesting account of the development of GDR literature in the 1970s and in particular of the period of cultural relaxation between 1971 and 1976. In the first two volumes a short survey of GDR literature precedes extracts from the work of forty-five writers. Each author is introduced with bibliographical and biographical details and is then invited (either by letter or in an interview) to respond to the questions: 'What do you see as the goal of your literary work?', and 'Do you consider this goal achievable?'. The third volume is made up of the responses of these same writers to a series of thirteen further questions on what they regard as the main themes, function and importance of literature in the GDR.

The Arts and Cultural Policy

535   **Culture and Society in the GDR.**
Edited by Graham Bartram, Anthony Waine.   Dundee, Scotland:
GDR Monitor, 1984. 131p. (GDR Monitor Special Series, no. 2).
In their introduction, which concentrates on the earlier, often neglected, period of
GDR culture, the editors attempt to help the general reader by placing the
individual chapters which follow in a broader literary-historical context. These
chapters deal with seven distinct topics: the press in the GDR; Bertolt Brecht in
the GDR; Christa Wolf's work of the 1960s; Ulrich Plenzdorf's sensationally
successful prose/drama *Die neuen Leiden des jungen W.*; the role of the
Kleingarten (allotment) in the GDR; the importance of Georg Büchner's *Lenz* to
contemporary writers in the GDR; and literary developments since Erich
Honecker came to power in 1971. Two appendixes in tabular form present a
chronology of events (1945–79) and place GDR writers and intellectuals in a
historical context.

536   **Film in der DDR. (Film in the GDR.)**
Heiko R. Blum (et al.).   Munich; Vienna: Hanser, 1977. 278p.
bibliog. (Reihe Film (Film Series), no. 13, edited by Peter W.
Jansen, Wolfram Schütte).
Illustrated by numerous monochrome stills, this book has eight sections: an
overview of the development of the film in the GDR; individual chapters on four
leading directors – Kurt Maetzig, Konrad Wolf, Frank Beyer, and Egon Günther;
GDR films after the demise of Ulbricht in 1971; documentary films; a section in
which data on thirty leading directors and on major institutions are included
together with a comprehensive bibliography. This is an indispensable source for
anyone with an interest in GDR cinema.

537 **Die DDR in ihren Spielfilmen. Reproduktion und Konzeption der DDR-Gesellschaft im neueren DEFA-Gegenwartsfilm.** (The GDR in its films: the image and conception of GDR society in the contemporary DEFA-film.)
Harry Blunk. Munich: Profil-Verlag, 1984. 371p. bibliog.

This is one of the few studies in the West of film in the GDR. Although based on a knowledge of 120 GDR films, it is not a history as such. It deals, in an interdisciplinary fashion, with a selection of films the author considers representative of the development of particular trends. He discusses examples of: the filming of literature (Christa Wolf's *The Divided Sky*, for instance); documentary realism; the 'dramatic-emotional' stylistic tendency; Socialist Realism; and of the representation of the problems of youth. Blunk demonstrates that, despite the use of film – 'the most important of the arts' (Lenin) – to win sympathy for the system, it has been done in a subtle and differentiated way and with an often critical presentation of the social realities of the GDR.

538 **Letter to a musician – and others.**
Hanns Eisler, translated from the German by Kay Goodman. *New German Critique*, 2 (spring 1974), p. 63–71.

In the form of an eighteen-part letter to an imaginary friend Eisler sets forth his thoughts on the present 'crisis in music and the world of music' which stems from the contradiction between the development of 'serious' and 'light' music and the contrast between great simplicity and the highest complexity. In its one manifestation music has become reduced to a meretricious commodity, in its other it has become the province of an intellectual élite. Eisler argues the need for a new, popular musical culture, which will close the gap between art and the people. It will have to be a blend of innovation and experimentation with a sense of social purpose and responsibility and will emerge from a process in which composers and audience will listen to, and learn from, each other.

539 **Hans Grundig.**
Günter Feist. Dresden, GDR: Verlag der Kunst, 1979. 352p. bibliog.

Hans Grundig (1901–58), a 'dreamer and fighter', was a Dresden painter closely associated with the German Communist Party in the 1920s and 1930s, the struggle against fascism and with the early years of the GDR. His sociocritical, veristic style was influenced by George Grosz and Otto Dix but fell short of the brutal cynicism of their work. His pro-communist and anti-Nazi drawings and lino cuts led to periods of arrest by the Gestapo in 1936 and 1938 and to imprisonment in Sachsenhausen concentration camp, 1940–45. His reluctance to paint in a naturalistic mode led to criticism and charges of formalism in the early years of the GDR. General recognition of his achievement came only after his death from tuberculosis in 1958. This very detailed and well-documented account of his life and work is generously illustrated.

The Arts and Cultural Policy

540 **Theo Balden.**
Ursula Feist. Dresden, GDR: Verlag der Kunst, 1983. 278p.
bibliog.

Theo Balden is a pseudonym for the sculptor and graphic artist Otto Koehler who was born in 1904 in Brazil of German parents. He was an auto-didact, his craft self-taught. A member of the German Communist Party, he was imprisoned by the Nazis in 1934, and escaped to England in 1939 where he was active in the League of Free German Culture. His work was decisively influenced by Graham Sutherland, John Nash, Henry Moore and Jacob Epstein. In 1947 he returned to East Berlin, and despite some resistance to his work – it was not in the Socialist Realist mould – he was offered a teaching post in 1950. This book provides a detailed portrait of Balden's life and work up until 1980, discusses a selection of his sculptures in particular detail and includes extensive notes by Balden himself on art and the social obligations of the artist.

541 **Kulturpolitik in der DDR.** (Cultural Policy in the GDR.)
Volker Gransow. Berlin (West): Verlag Volker Spiess, 1975.
170p. bibliog.

This book does not make for light reading. It deals with the development of cultural policy in the GDR in two ways. Firstly, it offers a chronological outline. Secondly, it analyses it in the light of three considerations: the attempts to stimulate mass cultural activity; the scientific and technical revolution; and in the context of economic and cultural relations with the Federal Republic.

542 **'Mass cultural activity' in the GDR: on cultural politics in bureaucratically deformed transitional societies.**
Gerd Hennig, translated from the German by Gunner
Huettich. *New German Critique*, issue no. 2 (1974), p. 38–57.

'Mass cultural activity' is seen as a characteristic form of cultural policy in societies in transition from capitalism to socialism or communism. Hennig examines the phenomenon in the context of GDR work brigades and collectives where culture is seen as contributing to the development of the socialist personality and consequently to increased economic effectiveness. He finds that a genuinely proletarian culture has been sacrificed to the pursuit of 'higher' bourgeois cultural activities: attending concerts, the theatre and museums. This he sees as one consequence of a 'bureaucratically deformed socialism' in the GDR. The article contains interesting comments on the Bitterfeld movement (see item no. 48), on the attempts by the Socialist Unity Party (SED) to manipulate artists and writers, and speculates on the possible political consequences of genuine mass cultural activity.

543 **Book collecting and the cultural heritage of the German Democratic Republic.**
Gail P. Hueting. In: *Studies in GDR culture and society 3: selected papers from the eighth International Symposium on the German Democratic Republic.* Edited by Margy Gerber (et al.). Lanham, Maryland; New York; London: University Press of America, 1983, p. 43–55.

Focussing on book collecting as a particular manifestation of the GDR's efforts to preserve its cultural heritage, Gail Hueting points out that the GDR is 'heir to a long tradition of book printing and book collecting' (Leipzig celebrated its 500th year as a city of books in 1981). She discusses the role of the antiquarian book trade and in particular of the *Zentralantiquariat* (the centre of the antiquarian book trade) in Leipzig. She then considers the reprint publishing of facsimile editions, eighty per cent of which are exported, before describing the book collectors' own organization, the Pirckheimer-Gesellschaft (the Pirckheimer Society, founded in 1956), and its quarterly journal, *Marginalien* (Marginalia).

544 **Kultur und Politik in der DDR. Ein historischer Abriss.** (Culture and politics in the GDR; an historical outline.)
Manfred Jäger. Cologne, FRG: Edition Deutschland Archiv, Verlag Wissenschaft und Politik, 1982. 205p. bibliog.

Manfred Jäger identifies seven separate phases in his discussion of the often fraught relationship between culture and politics in the GDR: 1945–49 the *Sturm und Drang* period of new beginnings under anti-fascist auspices; 1949–53 the attempt to manipulate culture through ideology; 1953–58 the crises and uncertain course brought about by the death of Stalin; 1958–64 the repercussions of Bitterfeld (see item no. 48); 1965–70 repressive reaction to attempts to gain greater freedoms for literature and culture; 1971–75 the limited cultural thaw initiated by the 8th Party Congress; and 1976–81 the repercussions of the Wolf Biermann affair. The text of the book is punctuated by short extracts, poems and statements by writers or officials – which illustrate, underpin or move forward its always lively argument.

545 **Kunst der DDR 1945–1959.** (GDR art 1945–59.)
Edited by Ullrich Kuhirt. Leipzig, GDR: Seemann Verlag, 1982. 360p. bibliog.

This history of art in the GDR is divided into two phases corresponding to the pattern which is normally perceived in the country's general history: 1945–49 (art in the period of the antifascist-democratic revolution) and 1949–59 (art in the period of transition from capitalism to socialism). The first phase is presented as a time in which fundamental questions of an ideological and aesthetic kind were debated; the second phase then saw the development of a realistic art based on socialist ideas and ideals. Achievements in the fields of painting, graphic art, sculpture, posters, architecture, town planning, and folk art are discussed and illustrated by 226 photographs. A concluding section lists the major works of art in chronological, tabular form.

546 **Kunst der DDR 1960–1980.** (Art in the GDR 1960–80.)
Edited by Ullrich Kuhirt. Leipzig, GDR: Seemann Verlag, 1983.
464p. bibliog.

This history of the art of the GDR is a continuation of Kuhirt's *Kunst der DDR 1945–1959* (q.v.). The development of painting, graphic art, sculpture, architecture and town planning, the political poster and folk art is viewed against the background of the development of socialist modes of production. The book contains over 400 illustrations and an extensive tabular chronology of what the authors consider to be the most important developments in politics, science, and GDR and international culture.

547 **Rockszene DDR. Aspekte einer Massenkultur im Sozialismus.** (The rock scene in the GDR: aspects of a mass culture in socialism.)
Olaf Leitner. Reinbek, FRG: Rowohlt, 1983. 509p.

This is the first comprehensive study of music for youth in a socialist country. It is written by a journalist and former rock musician and looks at the evolution of popular music in the GDR, from the tentative birth of 'beat' in the 1960s, to a versatile rock movement which is now an acknowledged part of the cultural scene. Despite a recent tendency towards melancholy and mysticism, a new generation of rock artists is characterized by boldness, vitality and wit. Leitner reviews all aspects of rock music, from its themes, organization and language, to its relationship to official cultural policy. Also appended are photographs and a lexicon of rock music personalities, groups and critics along with a 'discography' of record/album titles.

548 **Bernhard Kretschmar.**
Fritz Löffler. Dresden, GDR: Verlag der Kunst, 1985. 216p.
bibliog.

The work of Bernhard Kretschmar (1889–1972) had its beginnings in German Expressionism and in the 1920s developed some similarities with the New Objectivity movement. Kretschmar is regarded first and foremost as a sharp chronicler of the *petite bourgeoisie* in the 1920s and 1930s and also as a landscape and genre painter. His work draws its strength from its identification with the region in and around Dresden where, apart from a prolonged stay in Galicia during World War II and a trip to China in 1954, he lived and worked for most of his life.

549 **An aesthetic debate of 1951: comment on a text by Hanns Eisler.**
Hans Mayer, translated from the German by Jack Zipes. *New German Critique*, issue no. 2 (spring 1974), p. 58–62.

This article comments on the circumstances surrounding the publication at the end of 1951 in *Sinn und Form* under the title 'Letter to West Germany' of Hanns Eisler's 'Letter to a Musician – and Others' (q.v.). Mayer sees the letter as an important contribution to the Marxist aesthetic debates of the immediate postwar period; it is an attempt to 'work out the differences between certain avantgardist trends and his (Eisler's) own concept of progress'. Mayer regards the letter as an eclectic work, detecting the influence of Theodor Adorno and Bertolt Brecht as well as signs of doctrinaire thought; it is seen as the product of Eisler's difficult position at the time of having to 'side either with the GDR or with western cultural production' and is viewed as a cunning and important contribution to the fight against Stalinism in the realm of culture.

550 **Kunstführer durch die DDR.** (Art guide to the GDR.)
Georg Piltz. Leipzig, Jena, GDR; Berlin (East): Urania-Verlag, 2nd ed. 1971. 613p. maps.

A comprehensive listing, with brief commentaries, of the major art treasures to be found in the GDR. Separate chapters are devoted to Berlin and each of the regions. The volume is illustrated with ink drawings, but there are no photographs. A glossary of terms, a register of historical monuments, and an index of place names are appended. The rather small print unfortunately mars the pleasure of using the book.

551 **Johannes R. Becher and the cultural development of the GDR.**
Alexander Stephan, translated from the German by Sara Lennox, Frank Lennox. *New German Critique*, 2 (spring 1974), p. 72–89.

Johannes R. Becher, erstwhile Expressionist poet who became the GDR's first Minister of Culture, was a vigorous participant at all periods in his life in the politics and culture of the day. This article argues that the official eulogization of Becher after his death in 1958 cannot conceal the difficulties and conflicts he encountered with the Party over his 'defence of poetry' vis à vis politics. Stephan corrects the view, widespread in the West, that Becher was merely a hack poet who sold out to communism. In following Becher's involvement in the development of GDR cultural policy from 1943 to 1958 he demonstrates that much criticism of Socialist Unity Party (SED) attitudes to culture was formulated in organizations and journals for which Becher was responsible and that the last thirteen years of his life were punctuated by periods of personal depression and political disillusionment which left him increasingly isolated.

552 **Art in Germany, 1945–1982.**
Karin Thomas. In: *Contemporary Germany: politics and culture.* Edited by Charles Burdick, Hans-Adolf Jacobsen, and Winfried Kudszus. Boulder, Colorado; London: Westview Press, 1984, p. 398–430. bibliog.

A concise, informative essay which, in only five pages (p. 411–15), outlines the evolution of GDR art, emphasizing its gradual liberation from the dictates of Socialist Realism and its developing dialogue with art in West Germany. The 1970s are seen as a decisive turning-point in this respect and as a time when two distinct tendencies become apparent – the socialist, realistic painting associated with Werner Tübke, Bernhard Heisig, Wolfgang Mattheuer and Willi Sitte on the one hand, and the search for new means of expression among the younger generation on the other.

The Arts and Cultural Policy

553   **IX. Kunstausstellung der DDR.** (The 9th Exhibition of GDR Art.)
      Berlin (East): Verband bildender Künstler der DDR, 1982. 478p.

This elaborate catalogue of the 9th Exhibition covers all aspects of GDR art:
painting; drawing; sculpture; architecture; craftwork; industrial and commercial
design; photography; caricature and cartoon; and theatre design. It contains
numerous essays on these various genres, has potted biographies of the several
hundred exhibiting artists, and is very lavishly illustrated.

Sport, Recreation and Festivals

554 The athletic activities of citizens of the GDR: some sociological aspects of their structure and social conditions.
Heidi Bierstedt. *International Review for the Sociology of Sport*, vol. 20, no. 1/2 (1985), p. 39–52.
A general survey of sports participation in the GDR by a leading GDR sports sociologist and official.

555 Sport – a prison of measured time.
Jean-Marie Brohm, translated from the French by Ian Fraser. London: Ink Links, 1978. 185p.
In one of the essays in his book Brohm argues that the penetration of competitive sport into all spheres of life has turned the GDR into a vast sports laboratory, or a sports super-enterprise, in which every worker is a sportsman and every sportsman a worker. Through their performance at work, in their studies and in the stadia, sportsmen and -women must contribute to the strengthening of the GDR. The obsessive preoccupation with sporting productivity has pushed the search for champions into the nursery school; the goal is to turn children into sports robots.

556 The use of sport in the German Democratic Republic for the promotion of national consciousness and international prestige.
G. Carr. *Journal of Sports History*, vol. 1, no. 2 (fall 1974), p. 123–36.
Examines the 'open union of sport and politics' in the GDR with particular reference to sport's contribution towards the search for sovereignty and recognition. Sport is also used as a medium of indoctrination at home: efforts are made to give validity to the growth of socialism in the GDR by tracing it back in time to the sports traditions of the German labour movement prior to 1945. The

demands for patriotic devotion to the GDR and the nationalistic pride associated
with the country's sporting prowess generate a form of sporting nationalism which
is hardly expressive of the brotherhood of Soviet-led socialism.

557 The German Democratic Republic.
David Childs.   In: *Sport under Communism: a comparative study*.
Edited by James Riordan. London: C. Hurst, 2nd ed. 1981,
p. 67–101. bibliog.
Examines not only the organization of sport but also its social and political
importance for the GDR. Although many people are not as enthusiastic about
sport as the authorities would like them to be, the country's sports efforts and
successes have been used to help the GDR gain a measure of recognition and to
enhance its prestige both at home and abroad. The international achievements of
the GDR's sportsmen and -women can be explained, in part, by the rivalry
between the two German states, the German tradition of allying medicine and
science to sport, the concentration of talent in a few specialist clubs and
organizations, and the financial security enjoyed by top performers.

558 Sports participation in the GDR.
Michael Dennis.   *GDR Monitor*, 7 (summer 1982), p. 10–22.
An examination of the varying levels of sports participation according to variables
such as age, gender, region and occupation. The topic is treated in greater detail
in two books, both by Dieter Voigt – *Soziale Schichtung im Sport* (Berlin (West):
Verlag Bartels und Wernitz, 1978) and *Soziologie in der DDR. Eine
exemplarische Untersuchung* (Cologne, FRG: Verlag Wissenschaft und Politik,
1975).

559 The politics of leisure in the GDR.
Volker Gransow.   In: *The GDR under Honecker, 1971–1981*.
Edited by Ian Wallace. Dundee, Scotland: GDR Monitor, 1981,
p. 21–28.
Considers whether the collectivization of leisure by political means overcomes the
loneliness of individuals in industrial societies. The author outlines the official
attitudes toward leisure, goes on to consider relevant statistics and argues that the
GDR has not overcome the antagonism between work and leisure which is typical
of capitalism.

560 Sport and political ideology.
John M. Hoberman.   London: Heinemann, 1984. 315p. bibliog.
Chapter 9 analyses the sport culture of East Germany, the scientific cultivation of
high performance, and the 'overestimation' of sport in the pursuit of the man-
machine symbiosis.

561 **German festivals and customs.**
Jennifer M. Russ. London: Oswald Wolff, 1982. 153p. bibliog.

A good account of German festivals and customs, mostly within the borders of the pre-1938 *Reich*, this book contains some reference to those practised in the present-day GDR. However, there is no quick and easy way of abstracting these from the work as a whole.

562 **Track and field.**
Edited by Gerhard Schmolinsky. Berlin (East): Sportverlag, 1983. 2nd ed. 416p.

A sports textbook written by a team of authors; it assesses the pedagogic, psychological, physiological, and technical aspects of all track and field events. The emphasis is on the techniques of training and the book is aimed at coaches and sports teachers. Sportverlag publishes many other similarly well-designed textbooks: Gerhard Hochmuth, *Biomechanics of Athletic Movement* (1984); Autorenkollektiv unter der Leitung von Theodor Körner und Peter Schwanitz, *Rudern* (1984); and Autorenkollektiv unter der Leitung von Wolfgang Lohmann, *Leichtathletik. Trainingsprogramme*, parts 1-111 (1985).

563 **Diplomats in track suits: the role of sports in the foreign policy of the German Democratic Republic.**
Andrew Strenk. *Journal of Sport and Social Issues*, vol. 4, no. 1 (spring-summer 1980), p. 34–45.

Argues that the 'choice of sports as a method to force international recognition was a stroke of brilliant genius and one for which the West was totally unprepared'. The GDR athletes were well prepared, well trained and highly motivated, ideologically as well as materially, to accomplish the Socialist Unity Party's (SED) goal of international prestige and recognition for the GDR. Two FRG contributions to this debate are: Peter Kühnst's *Der missbrauchte Sport. Die politische Instrumentalisierung des Sports in der SBZ und DDR 1945–1957* (Cologne FRG: Verlag Wissenschaft und Politik, 1982); and Günter Holzweissig's *Diplomatie im Trainingsanzug* (Munich, Vienna: Oldenbourg, 1981).

564 **Politics only?: sport in the German Democratic Republic.**
Jürgen Tampke. In: *Sport in history: the making of modern sporting history*. Edited by Richard Cashman, Michael McKernan. Queensland, Australia: University of Queensland Press, 1979, p. 86–98. bibliog.

The author denies that the GDR's diplomatic breakthrough can be traced back to its sporting successes. The large number of people participating in sport provide the essential basis for the achievements at international level. The author rejects attempts to explain the GDR's successes on the grounds of misuse of drugs, brutal training methods and the expenditure of vast sums of money.

Sport, Recreation and Festivals

565 **Soziologie in der DDR: Eine exemplarische Untersuchung.**
(Sociology in the GDR: an investigation exemplified by the
sociology of sport.)
Dieter Voigt.   Cologne, FRG: Verlag Wissenschaft und Politik,
1975. 333p. bibliog.

This is the standard work on the sociology of sport in the GDR. It is prefaced by
an introductory survey recounting the emergence of academic sociology and
empirical sociological research in the GDR from its beginning in 1963. The author
outlines the history of the sociology of sports, defines the concept of sport and
relates social functions of sport in the GDR. In addition, he analyses the
determinants of attitudes towards sport, among both young and old. This work
contains valuable introductions to the sociology of leisure and of medicine as well
as a survey of small group research in the GDR, with some notes on the social
stratification of participants in sport. The book is illustrated with forty-one tables
and fourteen diagrams.

566 **Die Freizeit der Jugend.** (Youth and leisure.)
Edited by Peter Voss.   Berlin (East): Dietz Verlag, 1981. 267p.

A standard GDR publication on the nation's youth and leisure. The authors place
youth in its social context, define the main function of leisure as 'reproduction of
labour power' and go on to discuss: time-budget studies (the ways in which young
people divide their time); social activity (i.e. in official organizations); leisure and
further education; attitudes to (approved) culture; the role of youth clubs; sport;
tourism; the formation and function of unorganized leisure groups; and the place
of young people's leisure in the overall 'socialist way of life'. A useful work for all
readers.

Museums and
Galleries

567   **Literarische Museen und Gedenkstätten in der Deutschen
Demokratischen Republik.** (Literary museums and memorials in
the German Democratic Republic.)
Edited by Max Kunze.   Berlin, GDR: Nationaler Museumsrat der
DDR, 1981. 160p. bibliog.

This attractively produced book lists in alphabetical order all seventy-six of the
literary museums which have been set up in the GDR. Most of the listings are
illustrated by at least one photograph, and each includes a useful description of
the museum and its holdings. A brief biography of the particular writer in
question as well as the address of the museum and the times when it is open are
also provided. A valuable companion for anyone with an interest in the literary
geography of the GDR.

568   **Der Zwinger in Dresden.** (The Zwinger in Dresden.)
Fritz Löffler, with photographs by Willy Pritsche.   Würzburg,
FRG: Verlag Weidlich, [n.d.]. 188p. bibliog.

This is a licenced edition of a book originally published in Leipzig, GDR, in 1976
by E. A. Seemann Verlag. It is beautifully produced and combines an informative
and well-written history of the Zwinger Museum and Palace with over 100
excellent pictorial illustrations.

569   **The Dresden Gallery.**
Henner Menz, translated from the German by Daphne
Woodward.   London: Thames & Hudson, 1962. 320p.

This volume, written by the director of the Dresden Art Gallery, begins by
describing the history of the Gallery, with particular attention being paid to its
golden age in the first part of the 18th century. There then follow almost a
hundred colour plates of some of the Gallery's most precious paintings, each

197

accompanied by a brief but informative and scholarly interpretation. In its third part the book presents miniature photographs (in monochrome) of a further series of paintings. A list of illustrations and a useful index of names are appended. All in all, an excellent guide to one of Europe's most important galleries.

570   **State museums of Berlin.**
Introduction by John Russell.   London: Thames & Hudson, 1964.
269p.

Illustrated with 195 plates of which twenty-eight are in colour, this splendid volume introduces the reader to East Berlin's state museums, which, as John Russell notes in an introduction written in 1964, 'might as well be on the moon for all the impact they have made, these last years, on the majority of the English-speaking public'. Happily, the museums' many treasures are now being seen by increasing numbers of visitors, and this book can serve as an excellent first guide for both layman and expert.

The Media and Propaganda

571 **To win the minds of men: the story of the propaganda war in East Germany.**
Peter Grothe. Palo Alto, California: Pacific Books, 1958. 241p.

A severely anti-communist account of the official socialization and resocialization of the population of the Soviet Zone and the GDR during the 1940s and 1950s. It includes observations on the police, the press, radio and television and the arts, as well as on agitation and propaganda both in schools, the youth organization the Free German Youth (FDJ) and elsewhere. Some notes on the resistance of the churches and on Western counter-propaganda are also included. A highly readable sketch for the non-specialist, containing interesting interview material and some first-hand observations.

572 **Abends kommt der Klassenfeind: Eindrücke zwischen Elbe und Oder.** (The class enemy comes in the evening: impressions between Elbe and Oder.)
Lothar Loewe. Frankfurt am Main, FRG; Berlin; Vienna: Ullstein, 1977. 139p.

In the wake of the normalization of intra-German relations Lothar Loewe became in 1974 the first accredited national West German television correspondent in East Berlin. Two years later, and after extreme difficulties, he was expelled for allegedly hostile reporting and contraventions of the Basic Treaty (1972). Loewe documents this period, during which he concentrated on street interviews with ordinary citizens despite extreme difficulties of access. Of particular interest is his team's influence in forcing the government to make social policy concessions at the 9th Party Conference, his reporting of the first citizens' rights group formed under Dr Karl-Heinz Nitschke and the events surrounding the expulsion of Wolf Biermann; an interview with Robert Havemann is also described. Loewe paints a picture of a paranoid Socialist Unity Party (SED) scared stiff of its own citizens' interest in his first-hand reportage.

573 **Das kleine Massenmedium.** (The small mass medium.)
Anita Mallinckrodt, translated from the English by Kornelia
Mrowitzky. Cologne, FRG: Verlag Wissenschaft und Politik,
1984. 324p. bibliog.

This work is an important contribution to the study of popular culture and
political socialization in the GDR. The author has undertaken an exhaustive
contents analysis of five popular cheap paperbacks (*Blaulicht, Das Neue
Abenteuer, Meridian, Tatsachen, Erzählerreihe*) which specialize in tales of
adventure, crime, war and politics-history; they are aimed mainly at teenagers
and young adults. The total circulation of these and other 'dime novels' is
500,000. In addition to sampling the publications during the years 1969–78, the
author has analysed short stories about women in two GDR magazines, *Für Dich*
and *Das Magazin*. On the basis of her analysis of well over 9,000 entries the
author concludes that the stories have a clear socialist orientation in their contents
(40.6 per cent of the stories took place in the socialist system; the persons
exhibiting positive characteristics conformed to the model of the socialist
personality; the significance of work and top performance was stressed; and the
GDR is depicted as the true heir to the German labour movement). On the other
hand: there was a clear stereotyping of gender roles; self-criticism was rarely
mentioned; most of the characters were white; and the significance of the Third
World received little attention. Over 90 per cent of the authors were men, sexual
issues were neglected, and the portrayal of the FRG was milder in the 1978 stories
than in the earlier ones.

574 **Nachrichten in der DDR. Eine empirische Untersuchung über** *Neues
Deutschland.* (News in the GDR: an empirical investigation of
'New Germany'.)
Elmar Dieter Otto, foreword by Werner Kalterfleiter. Cologne,
FRG: Verlag Wissenschaft und Politik, 1979. 191p. bibliog.

An empirical investigation of the role of the mass media as agents of propaganda
and agitation with particular reference to the Socialist Unity Party (SED) daily
organ's treatment of political and economic issues and the considerable degree to
which *Neues Deutschland* draws upon material in Soviet newspapers.

575 **The mass media of the German-speaking countries.**
John Sandford. London: Oswald Wolff, 1976. 235p. bibliog.

Sandford's aim is to provide an introduction to the history and present
organization of the press and broadcasting in the two Germanies, Austria and
Switzerland. The last of his seven chapters is devoted to East Germany
(p. 184–209). Here he analyses Marxist-Leninist press theory, the origins of the
socialist press in Germany, the development of the press in East Germany, and
the question of how it is coordinated and controlled. In a shorter section on
broadcasting, Sandford first outlines the growth of socialist radio in Germany
before presenting the main features of radio and television in the GDR. An
appendix includes a brief description of the GDR's most important newspaper,
Neues Deutschland (p. 215).

576   **The press in the GDR: principles and practice.**
John Sandford.   In: *Culture and Society in the GDR*. Edited by
Graham Bartram, Anthony Waine. Dundee, Scotland: GDR
Monitor, 1984, p. 27-36. (GDR Monitor Special Series, no. 2).
The GDR press is organized on the basis of Lenin's statement that a newspaper is 'not merely a collective propagandist and collective agitator, it is also a collective organizer'. The function of the GDR media is to give people what they need, that is 'social information' which will enable readers to see how the various events in the world around them fit into the overall pattern of historical necessity as interpreted by the Party. The overall structure of the GDR press reflects not only the dominant influence of the Socialist Unity Party (SED) and its specialist organizations (for example, the Department of Agitation and Propaganda) but also the deep-rooted German tradition of provincialism. Sandford argues that if propaganda is the raison-d'être in the GDR, profit is undeniably the motor force behind the press in the Federal Republic.

Newspapers, Magazines and Periodicals

GDR newspapers and magazines

577 **Bauern-Echo.** (Farmers' Echo.)
Berlin (East): Deutscher Bauernverlag, 1948–. daily.
The organ of the Democratic Farmers' Party of Germany. The paper had a circulation of 91,000 in 1981.

578 **Berliner Zeitung.** (The Berlin Newspaper.)
Berlin (East): Berliner Verlag, 1945–. daily.
The daily newspaper of the Socialist Unity Party (SED) in the GDR capital. The evening edition is entitled *BZ am Abend* (Berlin Newspaper, Evening Edition). As in all the regional (*Bezirk*) newspapers, the reports on political, cultural and sporting events have a local flavour. The other SED regional newspapers bear their own title, for example, *Freiheit* (Liberty) in Halle and *Sächsische Zeitung* (Saxon Newspaper) in Dresden.

579 **Deutsches Sportecho.** (German Sports Echo.)
Berlin (East): Sportverlag, 1947–. 5 issues per week.
A good sports daily which covers a wide range of sports both at home and abroad. It is the organ of the German Gymnastics and Sports Federation and had a circulation of 178,000 in 1981.

580 **Eulenspiegel.** (Eulenspiegel.)
Berlin (East): Berliner Verlag, 1946–. weekly.
The GDR's satirical magazine which spares neither GDR red-tape nor capitalist exploitation. The numerous cartoons are a noteworthy and delightful feature. Its circulation was 371,000 in 1980.

Newspapers, Magazines and Periodicals. GDR newspapers and magazines

581   **Für Dich.** (For You.)
      Berlin (East): Berliner Verlag, 1964–. weekly.
The country's main illustrated magazine for women. Its coverage includes political commentaries, extracts from novels, fashion advice, the upbringing of children, women's issues, readers' letters and economic developments.

582   **Glaube und Heimat.** (Faith and Home.)
      Jena, GDR: Verlegerische Arbeitsstelle, 1946–. weekly.
This weekly newspaper of the evangelical church in Thuringia has a counterpart in most of the other regional church organizations of the GDR. The contents include reports on theological matters as well as controversial social and political issues.

583   **Horizont.** (Horizon.)
      Berlin (East): Berliner Verlag, 1968–. monthly.
This magazine, which focuses on international affairs, has appeared monthly since April 1983 and enjoyed a circulation of 116,800 in 1980.

584   **Junge Welt.** (Young World.)
      Berlin (East): Verlag Junge Welt, 1947–. daily.
The organ of the Central Council of the Free German Youth Movement (FDJ) with a circulation of 1.1 million in 1981. Its broad coverage includes FDJ activities, pop music, youth criminality, fashion, philately, crosswords, cartoons, sport, new technology, the arts, political news and young people's personal problems (the 'Unter vier Augen' column).

585   **Kultur im Heim.** (Culture in the home.)
      Berlin (East): Verlag Die Wirtschaft, 1955–. 6 issues per year.
A popular magazine full of tips for improving the home and the environment in general. The publication is liberally illustrated with photographs.

586   **Der Morgen.** (Morning.)
      Berlin (East): Der Morgen, 1945–. daily.
The organ of the Liberal Democratic Party of Germany (LDPD). In 1981 it had a circulation of 50,900.

587   **National-Zeitung.** (The National Newspaper.)
      Berlin (East): Verlag National-Zeitung, 1948–. daily.
The daily newspaper of the National Democratic Party (NDPD) of Germany with a circulation of 58,800 in 1981.

588   **Neue Zeit.** (New Era.)
      Berlin (East): Verlag Neue Zeit, 1945–. weekly.
The central organ of the Christian Democratic Union party (CDU) of the GDR. It enjoyed a circulation of 86,100 in 1981.

Newspapers, Magazines and Periodicals. GDR periodicals in German

589   **Neues Deutschland.** (New Germany.)
      Berlin (East): Verlag Neues Deutschland, 1946–. weekly.
The Socialist Unity Party's (SED) daily newspaper with a circulation of over one million in 1982. Whilst a considerable proportion of the paper is devoted to Party affairs, it does not neglect sport and the arts.

590   **Neues Leben.** (New Life.)
      Berlin (East): Verlag Junge Welt [n.d.]. monthly.
This is the GDR's most important youth magazine and it had a circulation of 558,000 in 1980. It is quite attractively presented and its regular feature articles concern pop music and stars in the West and the East, travel, fashion, film and book reviews, sport, cartoons, adverts for pen friends, short stories, sexual problems and political events.

591   **Sport und Technik.** (Sport and Technology.)
      Berlin (East): Militärverlag, 1953–. monthly.
A magazine for young people issued by the paramilitary *Gesellschaft für Sport und Technik* (Society for Sport and Technology). Founded in 1952, the Society is responsible for preparing fourteen to eighteen-year-olds for military service; it has about 600,000 members (1982). The magazine's contents range from military technology through depictions of historical conflicts, to socialism's contribution to the 'defence' of peace.

592   **Tribüne.** (Tribune.)
      Berlin-Treptow (East): Tribüne Verlag, 1945–. daily.
The organ of the Confederation of Free German Trade Unions with a circulation of 404,500 in 1982. Its coverage reflects not only trade union interests (trade union activities in the enterprises, discussions of Labour Code regulations, the advantages of new technologies) but also matters of general interest.

593   **Wochenpost.** (Weekly Post.)
      Berlin (East): Berliner Verlag, 1954–. weekly.
The GDR's major mass circulation (1.2 million in 1981) weekly magazine. It covers a wide range of topics: East German television programmes; a cultural review; foreign affairs; adverts for marriage partners; and reports on the nation's crime.

GDR periodicals in German

594   **Arbeit und Arbeitsrecht.** (Labour and Labour Law.)
      Berlin (East): Verlag Die Wirtschaft, 1946–. monthly.
The coverage includes brief reports on academic research into labour relations in the combines and enterprises as well as commentaries on recent labour legislation.

595   **Beiträge zur Geschichte der Arbeiterbewegung.** (Contributions to
      the History of the Labour Movement.)
      Berlin (East): Dietz, 1959–. 6 issues per year.
Edited by the Institute for Marxism-Leninism of the Central Committee of the
Socialist Unity Party (SED), the journal contains articles and documents on the
history of the German labour movement in the 19th and 20th centuries, including
the development of the SED.

596   **Berufsbildung.** (Vocational Training.)
      Berlin (East): Volk und Wissen, 1947–. monthly.
This periodical contains programmatic statements by state officials as well as short
reports on theoretical and practical aspects of the country's vocational training
system.

597   **Bildende Kunst.** (Fine Arts.)
      Berlin (East): Henschelverlag, 1953–. monthly.
This is the GDR's most important fine arts journal and an essential guide to
recent developments in an area whose practitioners have aroused a growing
interest and respect in the West.

598   **Chemische Technik.** (Chemical Technology.)
      Leipzig, GDR: Deutscher Verlag für Grundstoffindustrie, 1949–.
      monthly.
Each issue contains brief technical articles on specific aspects of chemical
engineering. The chemical industry is one of the GDR's major industries and new
scientific methods and processes are expected to make a significant contribution to
the intensification and up-grading strategy. The periodical is published by the
Chemical Technology Association of the Chamber of Technology.

599   **Deine Gesundheit.** (Your Health.)
      Berlin (East): Verlag Volk und Gesundheit, 1955–. monthly.
A popular presentation of individual and public health problems.

600   **Deutsche Zeitschrift für Philosophie.** (German Journal of
      Philosophy.)
      Berlin (East): Deutscher Verlag der Wissenschaften, 1953–.
      monthly.
This well-established periodical provides a forum not only for philosophers but
also for sociologists.

601   **edv-aspekte.** (Aspects of Electronic Data Processing.)
      Berlin (East): Verlag Die Wirtschaft, 1965–. quarterly.
This publication enables readers to keep abreast of the latest research into, and
the applications of, data processing in the GDR.

602 **Einheit.** (Unity.)
Berlin (East): Dietz, 1946–. monthly.
The official journal of the ruling Socialist Unity Party (SED). Each issue contains book reviews, short commentaries on topical events and, above all, lengthy articles on important political, economic, social and international issues.

603 **Elternhaus und Schule.** (Parental Home and School.)
Berlin (East): Volk und Wissen, 1952–. monthly.
A periodical which seeks to provide parents with guidance on how to bring up and educate their children at home and in cooperation with the school. A supplement is published each year on the choice of a career.

604 **Die Fachschule.** (The Technical College.)
Berlin (East): Deutscher Verlag der Wissenschaften, 1953–.
monthly.
Articles appear regularly on how technical education is affected by changes in the GDR's economic and educational policies and how colleges can contribute to the training of a more efficient and creative workforce.

605 **Fertigungstechnik und Betrieb.** (Production Engineering and Enterprise.)
Berlin (East): Verlag Technik, 1951–. monthly.
Although the journal's main concern lies in publishing details of recent applications in production and electrical engineering, attention is also paid to the social implications of modern technology.

606 **Film und Fernsehen.** (Film and Television.)
Berlin (East): Henschelverlag, 1973–. monthly.
The organ of the Association of Film and Television Freelance Artists and Writers.

607 **Forschung der sozialistischen Berufsbildung.** (Research into Socialist Vocational Training.)
Berlin (East): Zentralinstitut für Berufsbildung der DDR, 1967–.
six issues per year.
The research areas covered include vocational training theory, careers guidance, the planning and organization of research, syllabus content, teaching methods, and vocational training in other countries.

608 **Geschichtsunterricht und Staatsbürgerkunde.** (History Lessons and Civics.)
Berlin (East): Volk und Wissen, 1959–. monthly.
This journal is mainly concerned with the contents of schools' history and civics syllabuses but it also includes major policy statements and reinterpretations of the historical record. An example of the latter is the article by H. Meier and W.

Newspapers, Magazines and Periodicals. GDR periodicals in German

Schmidt (no. 9, 1984), on the Socialist Unity Party's (SED) revision of the GDR's historical heritage and tradition.

609 **Gesetzblatt der Deutschen Demokratischen Republik.** (The Law Gazette of the German Democratic Republic.)
Berlin (East): Staatsverlag, 1952–. published occasionally.
All the GDR's laws and decrees are published in this gazette.

610 **Finanzwirtschaft, Sozialistische.** (Socialist Financial Management.)
Berlin (East): Verlag Die Wirtschaft, 1947–. bimonthly.
In this journal, state officials, enterprise managers and university economists discuss the function of the financial and credit system and consider the most effective use of the country's financial resources.

611 **Das Hochschulwesen.** (Higher Education.)
Berlin (East): Deutscher Verlag der Wissenschaften, 1953–. monthly.
Issued by the Ministry for Higher Education. The journal's contributors examine all aspects of higher education from Socialist Unity Party (SED) policy to the encouragement of students' creative work.

612 **Humanitas.** (Humanity.)
Berlin (East): Verlag Volk und Gesundheit, 1961–. fortnightly.
This publication, presented in newspaper format, specializes in short reports on all aspects of the public health service.

613 **Informatik.** (Informatics.)
Berlin (East): Verlag Die Wirtschaft, 1954–. 6 issues per year.
The journal enables readers to keep abreast of the latest theoretical and practical developments in GDR informatics.

614 **Informationen zur soziologischen Forschung in der Deutschen Demokratischen Republik.** (Information Bulletin on Sociological Research in the German Democratic Republic.)
Berlin (East): Akademie für Gesellschaftswissenschaften beim ZK der SED, 1965–. 6 issues per year.
Although this bulletin is the GDR's only specialist sociology journal, sociological research also finds an outlet in the university journals as well as in *Sozialistische Arbeitswissenschaft* (Socialist Labour Science), *Deutsche Zeitschrift für Philosophie* (German Journal of Philosophy) and the important *Jahrbuch für Soziologie und Sozialpolitik* (Yearbook of Sociology and Social Policy). The bulletin concentrates on conference reports, the activities of the Scientific Council of Sociological Research and the most recent sociological research projects. The periodical and book review sections occasionally draw attention to Western publications. For example, there is a positive review (no. 6, 1985) by Professor Artur Meier of G. Edwards's *GDR Society and Social Institutions* (q.v.).

615 **IPW-Berichte.** (IPW Reports.)
Berlin (East): Staatsverlag, 1972–. monthly.

This publication of the Institute for Politics and Economics (IPW), which was founded in 1971, provides regular reports on political and economic developments in capitalist countries, especially the Federal Republic. A quarterly periodical, *IPW – Forschungshefte* (IPW – Research Journal), undertakes more detailed and scholarly investigations, from a Marxist-Leninist perspective, of one specific problem per issue.

616 **Junge Generation.** (The Young Generation.)
Berlin (East): Verlag Junge Welt, 1947–. monthly.

The organ of the Free German Youth Movement (FDJ). Its reports on FDJ meetings and policy, the education of young people, sport, education, and the capitalist world are mainly aimed at FDJ functionaries. The publication's circulation in 1980 was 71,300.

617 **Kooperation.** (Cooperation.)
Berlin (East): Deutscher Landwirtschaftsverlag, 1967–. monthly.

Its broad coverage of GDR agriculture includes articles on scientific labour organizations, different types of production, wages and bonuses, improvements in efficiency, and changes in the organization of production units.

618 **Körpererziehung.** (Physical Education.)
Berlin (East): Volk und Wissen, 1951–. monthly.

Although scholarly articles on sociological and social-psychological topics appear in the journal, the emphasis is on providing physical education trainers and teachers with practical advice. The political function of physical education and sport also receives attention.

619 **Neue deutsche Literatur.** (New German Literature.)
Berlin (East): Aufbau, 1953–. monthly.

The journal of the Writers' Union of the GDR. It publishes original work by members of the Union and, occasionally, by socialist writers from other countries. In addition, each issue includes book reviews and a brief section of news items.

620 **Neue Justiz.** (New Justice.)
Berlin (East): Staatsverlag, 1947–. monthly.

The journal is subdivided into critical assessments of GDR legislation, a survey of recent laws, practical issues arising from the application of GDR laws, and law in capitalist countries.

621 **Neuer Weg.** (New Way.)
Berlin (East): Dietz Verlag, 1946–. 2 issues per month.

A pamphlet issued by the Socialist Unity Party (SED) Central Committee for Party activists and functionaries. Articles on general Party policy are followed by readers' letters and reports on the activities of local Party organizations and cadres.

622 **Der Neuerer.** (The Innovator.)
Berlin (East): Verlag Die Wirtschaft, 1952–. monthly.

The emphasis is on publicizing the major discoveries and applications of the ideas of the GDR's innovators. In 1983 the value to the economy of the 1.9 million ideas which were taken up and acted on was put at 5.3 billion GDR Marks.

623 **Pädagogik.** (Education.)
Berlin (East): Volk und Wissen, 1946–. monthly.

Contributors to the periodical concentrate on theoretical and practical aspects of secondary school education in the GDR. A separate supplement appears quarterly.

624 **Petermanns Geographische Mitteilungen.** (Petermann's Geographical Bulletin.)
Gotha, GDR: Hermann Haack, 1856–. quarterly.

This is the GDR's main academic geographical journal and it covers all aspects of geographical studies.

625 **Psychologie für die Praxis.** (Practical Psychology.)
Berlin (East): Deutscher Verlag der Wissenschaften, 1983–. quarterly.

This journal, which replaced *Probleme und Ergebnisse der Psychologie* which had first been published in 1960, focuses on the practical application of psychological research in the economy, education and medicine. It is the official publication of the Society for Psychology of the GDR.

626 **Der Schöffe.** (The Lay Assessor.)
Berlin (East): Staatsverlag, 1954–. monthly.

Issued by the Ministry of Justice, this slim publication concentrates on the practical aspects of the work of lay assessors and arbitration courts.

627 **Sinn und Form.** (Meaning and form.)
Berlin (East): Rütten & Loening, 1949–. 6 issues per year.

This is the journal of the Academy of Arts of the GDR and it contains original work by GDR writers, writers from other socialist countries, and, occasionally, left-wing writers from capitalist countries. In addition it regularly includes extensive essays by leading literary critics as well as a section of book reviews.

628 **Sozialistische Arbeitswissenschaft.** (Socialist Labour Science.)
Berlin (East): Verlag Die Wirtschaft, 1957–. bimonthly.

One of the GDR's most important social scientific journals. Although reports on current research projects and conferences tend to adopt an optimistic view of the application of modern technologies in socialism, authors frequently admit to social and organizational problems. In general, labour sciences are expected to assist the Socialist Unity Party (SED) in promoting the more rational and productive utilization of labour and machinery.

629   **Staat und Recht.** (State and Law.)
      Berlin (East): Staatsverlag, 1952–. monthly.

This journal is concerned with all aspects of law in the GDR but it also provides a forum for political scientists.

630   **Standpunkt.** (Point of View.)
      Berlin (East): Union Verlag, 1973–. monthly.

This Protestant monthly is closely linked to the Christian Democratic Union Party (CDU) and exhibits a clear political orientation. Its Catholic counterpart is entitled *Begegnung* (Meeting).

631   **Temperamente.** (Temperaments.)
      Berlin (East): Verlag Neues Leben, 1976–. quarterly.

This journal was founded in 1976 in order to provide young writers with an outlet for their work. After a troubled start, which may have been related to the uncertainties following the contentious expulsion from the GDR of Wolf Biermann in November 1976, the entire editorial board was changed from issue 2 in 1978. Since then the journal has appeared regularly.

632   **Theorie und Praxis der Körperkultur.** (The Theory and Practice of Physical Culture.)
      Berlin (East): Sportverlag, 1952–. bimonthly.

The GDR's most important sports periodical. Articles and conference reports appear on a variety of topics: the level and determinants of sports participation; state and Party policy; sports legislation; the organization of GDR sport at central and local level; socialist sport and the history of sport in the GDR; and the manipulation of sport for political purposes by imperialist countries.

633   **Vergleichende Pädagogik.** (Comparative Education.)
      Berlin (East): Volk und Wissen, 1965–. quarterly.

The contributors to this periodical analyse education in socialist, capitalist and Third World countries.

634   **Weimarer Beiträge.** (Weimar contributions.)
      Berlin (East); Weimar, GDR: Aufbau, 1955–. monthly.

Contains articles on literary and cultural topics as well as book reviews, reports and interviews with leading writers. Each issue includes a summary of contents in Russian, English and French.

635 **Wirtschaftswissenschaft** (Economics.)
Berlin (East): Verlag Die Wirtschaft, 1953–. monthly.

This is the GDR's most prestigious economics journal. In addition to scholarly articles concerning the theory and practice of Marxist economics, the periodical publishes detailed reports on economics conferences and a guide to research in progress, or recently completed. Latterly, contributors have focused on key technologies, such as microelectronics, CAD/CAM and robotics, energy saving measures, and specialization and cooperation in foreign trade. Another important economics journal, which unexpectedly ceased publication in 1983, was *Die Wirtschaft* (The Economy) [Berlin (East): Verlag Die Wirtschaft, 1946–83. monthly]. This publication specialized in reports on economic practice in the state enterprises, although it also covered other economic developments at home and abroad.

636 **Wissenschaft und Fortschritt.** (Science and Progress.)
Berlin (East): Akademie-Verlag, 1951–. monthly.

This popular scientific publication of the Academy of Sciences of the GDR covers recent scientific discoveries and the social implications of modern science.

637 **Wissenschaftliche Zeitschrift der DHfK.** (Scientific Journal of the German College of Sports.)
Leipzig, GDR: Deutsche Hochschule für Körperkultur, 1960–. 3 issues per year.

The house journal of Leipzig's world-famous Sports College. Scholarly articles are published on a wide range of topics, for example, sports medicine and the sociology of sport.

638 **Wissenschaftliche Zeitschrift der Hochschule für Ökonomie.**
(Scientific Journal of the College of Economics.)
Berlin (East): Hochschule für Ökonomie, 1956–. quarterly.

The College, founded in 1956, is the GDR's only economics institution in the higher education sector. The journal issues articles on the college's special research areas, for example, foreign trade, labour economics, planning and management problems.

639 **Wissenschaftliche Zeitschrift der Humboldt Universität zu Berlin.**
(Scientific Journal of the Humboldt University, Berlin.)
Berlin (East): Humboldt Universität zu Berlin, 1952–. 10 issues per year.

This scholarly journal is subdivided into a social-scientific and a mathematics/natural-scientific series. All other universities and institutions of higher education publish their own journal and, except where they are specialist colleges of education, economics and architecture, tend to issue two series. The journals are relatively expensive.

Newspapers, Magazines and Periodicals. GDR magazines and periodicals in English

640 **Zeitschrift für Alternforschung.** (Journal for Gerontology Research.)
Berlin (East): Verlag Volk und Gesundheit, 1946–. bimonthly.

The organ of the Society of Gerontology of the GDR, this journal deals with a broad range of topics, including the health, institutional care, and the leisure activities of older people.

641 **Zeitschrift für Germanistik.** (Journal of Germanistics.)
Leipzig, GDR: VEB Verlag Enzyklopädie, 1980–. quarterly.

This periodical publishes articles in German on all aspects of Germanistics and it has included particularly useful work on the theory and methodology of literary interpretation. Each issue contains an annotated listing of recently completed dissertations on relevant themes at GDR universities.

642 **Zeitschrift für Geschichtswissenschaft.** (Journal of Historical Science.)
Berlin (East): Deutscher Verlag der Wissenschaft, 1953–. monthly.

The most prestigious of the GDR's historical journals. All periods of history are covered but the emphasis is on German history since the late 15th century. The journal represents a valuable source for tracking Socialist Unity Party (SED) reinterpretations of major historical figures (including, for example, Luther, Frederick the Great and Bismarck) and social and political movements (such as the non-communist opposition during the Third Reich). The book review section is extensive and space is also provided for the proceedings of historical conferences.

GDR magazines and periodicals in English

643 **Bulletin of the National Olympic Committee of the GDR.**
Berlin (East): National Olympic Committee of the GDR, 1956–. quarterly.

A most disappointing periodical which contains little more than excerpts from official statements and superficial assessments of the function and development of the Olympic movement. In 1984 it was used as a vehicle to explain the GDR's withdrawal from the Los Angeles games. Issue 2 reported a speech by Manfred Ewald, the President of the Deutscher Turn- und Sportbund (German Gymnastics and Sports Federation) justifying the GDR's actions as follows: 'But the protection of their (GDR athletes') honour, their dignity and lives has absolute priority. This is, however, not guaranteed under present conditions, in which hatred and calumny, political and criminal attacks would imperil the safety and health of our team.'

212

Newspapers, Magazines and Periodicals. GDR magazines and periodicals in English

644   **FDGB Review.**
Berlin (East): Verlag Tribüne, 1956–. bimonthly.
This English edition of the trade union magazine also appears in six other languages. Whilst it tends to depict labour relations and the activities of the FDGB (Confederation of the Free German Trade Unions) in an uncritical manner, it does at least disseminate some useful factual information about the Labour Code and workers' theoretical rights.

645   **Foreign Affairs Bulletin.**
Berlin (East): Staatsverlag, 1957–. every ten days.
The bulletin provides translations of articles from the GDR press. Although the emphasis is on foreign affairs, it devotes some space to important domestic matters, such as Socialist Unity Party (SED) congresses, economic plans and elections to the organs of state. Like the German edition entitled *Aussenpolitische Korrespondenz*, it is issued by the Press Department of the Ministry of Foreign Affairs.

646   **GDR Export. Journal of GDR Foreign Trade.**
Berlin (East): Verlag Die Wirtschaft. [n.d.] monthly.
An attractively presented brochure which seeks to provide potential customers with information about the latest GDR products. The journal also appears in French, German and Spanish.

647   **GDR Review.**
Berlin (East): International Friendship League of the GDR, 1956–. monthly.
A glossy magazine whose attempts to present a foreign audience with a picture of life within the GDR rarely rise above the superficiality of a holiday brochure.

648   **German Democratic Report.**
Berlin (East): John Peet, 1952–75. fortnightly.
The main aim of this publication through the twenty-four years of its existence was to provide information in English on developments in the GDR. This was seen as a way of counteracting a tendency hitherto in the English-speaking world to take its news about the GDR largely from the hostile West German press. In addition, attention was drawn to the alleged resurgence of militarism and Nazism in the Federal Republic. The English-born journalist, John Peet, was the editor and guiding spirit of the Report.

649   **German Foreign Policy.**
Berlin (East): Deutscher Verlag der Wissenschaften, 1962–74. bimonthly.
An organ of the Institute for International Relations containing articles and reviews focussing on all aspects of GDR foreign policy.

650 **Law and Legislation in the German Democratic Republic.**
Berlin (East): Staatsverlag, 1959–. biannual.
This is the organ of the Lawyers' Association of the GDR. The journal is subdivided into an extensive documentation section and includes articles assessing topics such as the criminal procedure code, international commercial contracts, the family code and the social courts.

651 **Prisma.**
Berlin (East): Panorama, 1977–. quarterly.
A GDR *Reader's Digest.* Translations are provided of articles on a wide range of topics from GDR magazines, newspapers and periodicals.

652 **Sports in the GDR.**
Berlin (East): Deutscher Turn- und Sportbund. [n.d.] bimonthly.
An attractively presented magazine which was designed to present GDR sport in a favourable light. It ceased publication in 1986.

FRG magazines and periodicals in German

653 **Aus Politik und Zeitgeschichte.** (From Politics and Contemporary History.)
Bonn: Bundeszentrale für politische Bildung, 1951–. weekly.
This periodical is a supplement to *Das Parlament* which is a weekly record of the activities of the West German parliament. The supplement is issued by the Federal Office for Political Education. GDR items appear quite frequently. Number 27 (1986) carried three articles on GDR youth and youth policy, and number 20–21 (1986) contained Johannes Kuppe's analysis of the changes in the GDR's interpretation of Prussian history. Other important contributions in 1986 included Ulrike Ender's examination of women's employment (no. 6–7) and Doris Cornelsen's clear and perceptive evaluation of the 1981–85 Five-Year Plan (no. 4).

654 **DDR heute. Berichte Erfahrungen Kommentare.** (GDR today. Reports, Experiences, Commentaries.)
Frankfurt am Main, FRG: Internationale Gesellschaft für Menschenrechte, Deutsche Sektion (International Society of Human Rights, German Section), 1985–. 5 issues per year.
This periodical presents texts, photographs and cartoons on GDR topics which are all selected and edited by former political prisoners in that country.

Newspapers, Magazines and Periodicals. FRG magazines and periodicals in German

655   **Die DDR – Realitäten Argumente.** (The GDR: realities arguments.)
       Edited by the Friedrich-Ebert-Stiftung (Friedrich Ebert Foundation). Bonn: Verlag Neue Gesellschaft, 1983–. Irregular.
By 1986 over eighty titles had appeared in this series of booklets devoted to a wide variety of aspects of GDR affairs. Recent titles include: *Wehrpflicht in der DDR* [Conscription in the GDR], (1984); *40 Jahre Sozialistische Einheitspartei Deutschlands* [40 years Socialist Unity Party of Germany], (1985); and *Zur Geschichte der DDR* [The history of the GDR], (1986).

656   **DDR Report.** (GDR Report.)
       Bonn: Verlag Neue Gesellschaft, 1968–. monthly.
A journal which provides a comprehensive coverage of the GDR press in the form of short extracts from newspapers, magazines and learned journals; topics range from political, legal, economic and military affairs to the arts, literature, history, the churches, science and education. The periodical also carries book reviews and articles on important current issues.

657   **Deutsche Studien.** (German Studies.)
       Lüneburg, FRG: Ost-Akademie Lüneburg, 1963–. quarterly.
An important journal covering all aspects of GDR studies. The following themes have been examined in recent numbers: economic growth versus environmental protection (no. 90, 1985); the German question and the history of the GDR (no. 92, 1985); the churches (no. 88, 1984); the structural problems of the economy (no. 84, 1983); historical tradition and the armies of the two German states (no. 72, 1980); and youth (no. 76, 1981).

658   **Deutsches Institut für Wirtschaftsforschung. Wochenbericht.**
       (German Institute for Economic Research: Weekly Report.)
       Berlin (West): Deutsches Institut für Wirtschaftsforschung, 1934–. weekly.
Although the bulletin (now available in English) concentrates on the FRG, it is an indispensable source for any student of the GDR economy. The institute's quarterly publication, *Vierteljahreshefte zur Wirtschaftsforschung* (Quarterly for Economic Research), is also of interest for GDR researchers.

659   **Deutschland Archiv.** (Germany Archive.)
       Cologne, FRG: Verlag Wissenschaft und Politik, 1968–. monthly.
This journal, which superseded *SBZ Archiv*, is absolutely essential for anyone engaged in GDR studies. Each issue usually includes scholarly articles on a variety of topics, reviews of GDR periodicals and books, short reports on recent events, a selection of documents, and conference reports.

Newspapers, Magazines and Periodicals. FRG magazines and periodicals in German

660   **FS-Analysen.** (FS-Analyses.)
Berlin (West): Forschungsstelle für gesamtdeutsche wirtschaftliche und soziale Fragen, 1974–. 5 to 6 issues per year.

This research agency's research reports are an indispensable guide to the economic development of the GDR. Much criticized by the GDR for its pro-market orientation, the agency concentrates on up-to-date assessments of the GDR's economic policy, foreign trade (notably the reports by Maria Haendke-Hoppe), agriculture (Karl Hohmann), economic organization (Kurt Erdmann), and science and technology (Klaus Krakat).

661   **Informationen.** (Information Bulletin.)
Bonn: Bundesministerium für innerdeutsche Beziehungen in Zusammenarbeit mit dem Gesamtdeutschen Institut, 1971–. 2 issues per month.

This news bulletin, which superseded *Gesamtdeutsche Fragen* (All-German Questions), is published by the Federal Ministry for Intra-German Relations in conjunction with the All-German Institute in Bonn. It includes: a chronological survey of the main political events in the GDR; articles on current social, cultural, political and economic issues; a documentation section; and a list of the most recent publications about the GDR. In short, it is a most useful guide for keeping in touch with the latest developments in the GDR.

662   **Kirche im Sozialismus.** (The Church in Socialism.)
Berlin (West): Wichern-Verlag, 1975–. bimonthly.

This journal is essential for following the most recent developments in GDR church affairs, the autonomous peace and ecology groups, youth problems, and relations between churches in the East and the West. There is also a helpful survey of articles published in GDR and FRG periodicals and in church newspapers.

663   **Politik und Kultur.** (Politics and Culture.)
Berlin (West): Colloquium Verlag. 1974–. bimonthly.

Carries articles concerning GDR education, law, politics, culture and social issues.

664   **Pressespiegel.** (Mirror of the Press.)
Berlin (West): Gesamtdeutsches Institut, Bundesanstalt für gesamtdeutsche Fragen, 1969–. 2 to 3 issues per month.

A digest of the GDR press published by the All-German Institute. Its former titles reflect changing attitudes to the GDR: *Hinter dem eisernen Vorhang* (Behind the Iron Curtain), 1951–61; and *Pressespiegel der Sowjetzone* (Mirror of the press of the Soviet Zone), 1962–68.

Newspapers, Magazines and Periodicals. Periodicals published outside the GDR and the FRG

665 **Der Spiegel.** (The Mirror.)
Hamburg, FRG: Spiegel Verlag, 1947–. weekly.
This West German magazine regularly carries features on GDR politics. In January 1978 the publication became the centre of an East-West controversy when it published the Manifesto of the so-called BDKD (League of Democratic Communists of Germany) [see *Manifesto* (BDKD, translated from the German by Karl Reyman) (q.v.)].

666 **Wir in Ost und West.** (We in East and West.)
Wiesbaden, FRG: Universum Verlagsanstalt, 1985–. occasional.
A new magazine aimed primarily at young people and supplying them with details of everyday life in the GDR. The publication is a vigorous supporter of the thesis of a common German national identity. Links binding the FRG and the GDR, according to the first issue in September 1985, are Frederick the Great, the cultural heritage as represented by the Semper Opera House in Dresden, and the exploits of the tennis star, Boris Becker.

Periodicals published outside the GDR and the FRG

667 **ABSEES: Abstracts Soviet and East European Series** (Soviet and East European abstracts series.)
Oxford, England: Pergamon Press, 1970–. 3 issues per year.
Each issue contains printed brief summaries of items as well as detailed abstracts presented on microfiches. The major subject areas include agriculture, Comecon, economic planning, finance, foreign trade, industry, labour, management, and scientific and technical progress. GDR coverage tends to be limited to a small selection of journals (*Wirtschaftswissenschaft*, Trade Technical Review) and one daily newspaper, *Neues Deutschland*.

668 **Business Eastern Europe.**
Geneva: Business International, 1972–. weekly.
Aimed at businessmen, this eight-page bulletin, formerly entitled *Eastern Europe Report*, gives up-to-date reports on the state of the individual East European economies and on market opportunities.

669 **Connaissance de la RDA.** (Knowledge of the GDR.)
Paris: Université de Paris VIII, 1975–. 2 issues per year.
Set up with the express purpose of increasing knowledge of the GDR in France, this journal publishes articles, book reviews, bibliographies and important documents (including original contributions by GDR writers). Contributions appear in French or German. The journal is generally sympathetic towards the

GDR but not uncritical of its faults. There have been special issues on literature (nos. 6 and 7, 1978), the economy (no. 8, 1979), Ulrich Plenzdorf (no. 11, 1980), fine arts (no. 12, 1981) and music (no. 14, 1982).

670 **East Central Europe.**
Irvine, California: Charles Schlacks, 1974–. 2 issues per year.
The journal has already published two special volumes on the GDR (in 1979 and 1984) and further GDR special issues are expected in the near future. In addition, a bibliographical review of GDR books and articles appears in the periodical once a year.

671 **East European Markets.**
London: Financial Times Business Information, 1981–. 2 issues per month.
Surveys current economic developments and business prospects in Eastern Europe and includes brief reports on the GDR. The GDR economy was described in the first issue of the 1986 volume as 'the healthiest economy in CMEA'.

672 **East/West Technology Digest.**
Washington, DC: Welt Publishing, 1975–. monthly.
An information leaflet on GDR and other East European products. For the benefit of potential Western purchasers, addresses are given of the GDR suppliers.

673 **Economic Bulletin for Europe. The Journal of the United Nations Commission for Europe.**
Oxford, England; New York; Toronto: Pergamon Press, 1945–. quarterly.
This publication concentrates on regional problems and themes. Its regular surveys of East-West trade contain valuable data on the GDR's foreign trade. An essay by Professor Harry Maier, formerly at the Institute for Theory, History and Organization of Science at GDR's Academy of Sciences, on the role of biotechnology for future economic development has recently appeared (no. 1 1986).

674 **Economic Intelligence Unit: Quarterly Economic Review of East Germany.**
London: Economist Intelligence Unit, 1977–. quarterly.
A short introduction to the business outlook is followed by a detailed business-orientated analysis of the latest economic indicators, especially foreign trade and the balance of payments.

Newspapers, Magazines and Periodicals. Periodicals published outside the GDR and the FRG

675 **END. Journal of European Nuclear Disarmament.**
London: European Nuclear Disarmament, 1982–. 5 issues per year.
Each issue normally contains at least one short article, or a document, relating to the unofficial peace movement in the GDR.

676 **GDR Bulletin.**
Saint Louis, Missouri: Washington University, 1975–. 2 issues per year.
An American newsletter for the dissemination of information about GDR studies in the United States. There is also an extensive periodical and book review section.

677 **GDR Monitor.**
Edited by Ian Wallace. Dundee, Scotland: GDR Monitor, 1979–84; Loughborough, England: GDR Monitor, 1984–86; Amsterdam: Editions Rodopi, 1986–. 2 issues per year.
This publication defines itself as 'an independent forum for discussion of all aspects of the life of the GDR' from a plurality of viewpoints. It is the only English-language academic journal devoted entirely to GDR studies.

678 **GDR Peace News.**
London: GDR Working Group of END, 1985–. quarterly.
A four-page bulletin produced under the aegis of the European Nuclear Disarmament organization with news items and documents on peace and disarmament issues in the GDR.

679 **Index on Censorship.**
London: Writers and Scholars International, 1972–. 10 issues per year.
Material about the GDR appears occasionally either in the form of work by GDR writers themselves, such as Lutz Rathenow for example (no. 1, 1986) or as critical commentaries by Western authors on literature and the nature of censorship in the GDR such as Tim Garton Ash's short report on the peace movement (no. 1, 1984).

680 **International Affairs.**
Guildford, England: Butterworth Scientific, 1922–. quarterly.
A publication of the Royal Institute of International Affairs. Recent contributions on the GDR are the articles by Eberhard Schulz on the German question and Ronald Asmus on the GDR and the German nation (no. 1, 1984).

Newspapers, Magazines and Periodicals. Periodicals published outside the GDR and the FRG

681 **International Organization.**
Cambridge, Massachusetts: MIT Press, 1947–. quarterly.
Articles on matters specifically, or less directly related to the GDR appear infrequently; examples are Thomas Baylis's excellent analysis of the GDR's economic strategy (no. 1, 1986) and Valerie Bunce's lengthy evaluation of whether Eastern Europe is a Soviet asset or liability (no. 1, 1985).

682 **International Review of Sport Sociology, superseded by International Journal for the Sociology of Sport.**
Warsaw: Polish Scientific Publishers, 1966–72. annual; 1973–83, quarterly; Munich: R. Oldenbourg, 1983–. quarterly.
Translations from the German of articles by GDR sports sociologists and functionaries appear regularly in the journal.

683 **Labour Focus on Eastern Europe.**
London: Labour Focus on Eastern Europe and Verso, 1978–85, bimonthly; 1986–. 3 issues per year.
This bulletin seeks to provide information about the activities and the repression of socialists and the labour movement in Eastern Europe and the Soviet Union. Numerous articles have appeared on Rudolf Bahro, Robert Havemann, and the autonomous peace groups. One invaluable service is the translation of GDR documents such as, for example, the letter on human rights signed by, among others, Pastor Rainer Eppelmann (no. 2, 1986).

684 **New German Critique.**
Milwaukee, Wisconsin: University of Wisconsin, 1973–. triannual.
A journal of interdisciplinary studies. Although the Federal Republic receives more attention, the GDR is not entirely neglected. Christa Wolf and Rudolf Bahro have been subjected to critical analysis and excerpts from I. Morgner's novel *Life and Adventures of Trobadora Beatriz* (Berlin (East): Weimar, GDR: Aufbau, 1974) appeared in another issue (fall, 1978).

685 **Newsletter. GDR Studies Association of the USA.**
Storrs, Connecticut: University of Connecticut, 1985–. occasional.
This publication provides news on the activities of the GDR Studies Association in the United States as well as notices of publications, research activities and conferences.

686 **Orbis. A Journal of World Affairs.**
Pennsylvania: Foreign Policy Research Institute, 1957–. quarterly.
Although the GDR does not figure prominently in the pages of this international relations journal, recent articles on GDR-related issues include Ronald Asmus's discussion of the GDR peace movement and James McAdams's study of inter-German relations.

Newspapers, Magazines and Periodicals. Periodicals published outside the GDR and the FRG

687 **Problems of Communism.**
Washington, DC: United States Information Agency, 1952–. bimonthly.

Although the emphasis is on the current social, economic, political and international problems of the Soviet Union, book reviews and articles occasionally deal with the GDR. For example, Hartmut Zimmermann's impressive survey of the GDR appeared in one issue (March-April, 1978) – see item no. 19.

688 **Religion in Communist Lands.**
Keston, Kent, England: Keston College, 1973–. quarterly.

The college is an educational charity whose publications cover the activities of religious groups in the Soviet Union and Eastern Europe. Articles and documents have, on occasions, highlighted the GDR's autonomous peace initiatives.

689 **Revue d'Études Comparatives Est-Ouest; Économie, Planification, Organisation.** (Journal of East-West Comparative Studies: Economy, Planning, Organisation.)
Paris: Centre National de la Recherche Scientifique, 1970–. quarterly.

The GDR economy is often examined in a comparative framework and, albeit more rarely, as a topic in its own right.

690 **Soviet Studies: a Quarterly Journal on the USSR and Eastern Europe.**
Harlow, England: Longman, 1949–. quarterly.

The coverage of GDR economic, social and political affairs is sporadic. A recent contribution is Pieter Boot's assessment of the growing importance of the combines (no. 3, 1983).

691 **Studies in Comparative Communism.**
Guildford, England: Butterworth Scientific, 1968–. 3 issues per year.

This journal is valuable for its contribution to the methodology of communist studies as well as for the occasional publications on the GDR. Among the latter are the essays by Henry Krisch on political culture (no. 1, 1986), Joyce Mushaben on the peace movement (no. 2, 1984), and Joan Ecklein and Janet Giele on women and social policy in the GDR and the United States (no. 2–3, 1981).

692 **Studies in GDR Culture and Society.**
Edited by Margy Gerber (et al.). Washington, DC: University Press of America, 1981–. annual.

The annual proceedings of the New Hampshire Symposium on the German Democratic Republic have appeared under this title (since 1981). Contributions

Newspapers, Magazines and Periodicals. Periodicals published outside the GDR and the FRG

cover all the major aspects of GDR studies but literary and cultural themes are particularly well represented.

693 **Survey: a Journal of East and West Studies.**
London: Survey, in association with the Institute for European Defence and Strategic Studies, 1955–. quarterly.

Current affairs and historical topics represent the major focus of the journal. Ronald Asmus on the Socialist Unity Party's (SED) reinterpretation of Martin Luther and Roger Woods on opposition in the GDR are recent articles worthy of mention.

694 **Telos.**
Saint Louis, Missouri: Telos Press, 1968–. quarterly.

Papers on socialism in Eastern Europe help to put individual countries into a comparative Marxist perspective. Articles on the GDR appear sporadically but recent contributions include Klaus Ehring on the peace movement (no. 56, 1983) and Herbert Ammonn/Peter Brandt on Germany and the peace movements (no. 51, 1982).

695 **World Marxist Review.**
Toronto: Progress, 1958–. monthly.

This self-styled 'Theoretical and Information Journal of Communist and Workers' Parties Throughout the World' frequently publishes translations of articles by GDR historians and political scientists and statements by Socialist Unity Party (SED) officials.

696 **World Politics: a Quarterly Journal of International Relations.**
Princeton, New Jersey: Princeton University Press, 1948–. quarterly.

The GDR is sometimes catered for by an individual entry such as Pedro Ramet's article on dissent (no. 1, October 1984) or is placed within a broad comparative framework as in Stephen White's analysis of economic performance and the legitimacy of Communist régimes in no. 3, April 1986.

Reference Works

697   **ARTbibliographies MODERN.**
Oxford, England; Santa Barbara, California: Clio Press, 1972–.
2 issues per year.
An abstracting service covering the history of art, architecture and design from 1800 to the present day. Full documentation of current books, dissertations, exhibition catalogues and periodical articles is provided. The East German periodicals which are covered by this service include *Bildende Kunst* (Visual Art), *Dresdener Kunstblätter* (Dresden Art Notes), *Jahrbuch der Staatlichen Kunstsammlungen in Dresden* (The Yearbook of the State Art Collections in Dresden) and *Kunst und Literatur* (Art and Literature). For information on publications discussing works of art produced before 1800 and held in GDR museums the standard service is *RILA (Répertoire International de la Littérature de l'Art)* (Williamstown, Massachusetts: Getty Art History Information Program, 1975–. 2 issues per year).

698   **Wörterbuch der marxistisch-leninistischen Soziologie.** (A dictionary of Marxist-Leninist sociology.)
Edited by Georg Assmann (et al.).   Berlin (East): Dietz, 1983.
3rd ed. 758p.
Sociology is a science which the GDR has taken more time to come to terms with than the relatively much more open societies of the West (there is, for instance, no entry under 'sociology' in the *Kleines politisches Wörterbuch* (q.v.)). This volume provides an invaluable guide towards an understanding of how Marxism-Leninism has sought to integrate sociology into the socialist system of the GDR.

Reference Works

699 **Ökonomisches Lexikon.** (Economic lexicon.)
Autorenkollektiv. (Authors' collective.)   Berlin (East): Verlag
Die Wirtschaft, 1979. 3rd ed. 3 vols. (A–G, H–P, Q–Z).

These large volumes (totalling 2,332p.) are interesting for what they leave out as well as for what they include. Lenin's New Economic Policy is there, so is the Nippon Steel Corporation, the Nissan-Konzern, the New Deal, and the Nixon-Doktrin but the GDR's own New Economic System introduced in the 1960s is omitted. V. I. Lenin and Karl Marx are there too, but not Joseph Stalin, M. Varga or Y. Liberman.

700 **Wörterbuch der Geschichte.** (An historical dictionary.)
Edited by Horst Barthel (et al.).   Berlin (East): Dietz, 1984. 2 vols. 2nd ed. 1,237p.

An important volume for those wishing to gain an appreciation of the Marxist-Leninist interpretation of history. Many of the concepts discussed here are also found in the *Kleines politisches Wörterbuch* (q.v.) which may therefore be usefully consulted for comparative purposes.

701 **Kulturpolitisches Wörterbuch.** (Dictionary of cultural policy.)
Edited by Manfred Berger (et al.).   Berlin (East): Dietz, 1978. 2nd ed. 904p.

An indispensable reference guide to cultural policy in the GDR which includes a chronological table of the major events which took place within the sphere of cultural policy from 1945 to 1976 (p. 789–887).

702 **Kleines politisches Wörterbuch.** (Concise political dictionary.)
Edited by Waltraud Böhme (et al.).   Berlin (East): Dietz, 1983. 4th ed. 1,133p.

An essential reference work for those interested in the GDR's political system. According to the editor's introduction, the intention is to help the East German reader towards a deeper understanding of political concepts which he may encounter daily at work or in his social activities, in the hope that he will in this way better comprehend the policies pursued by the Socialist Unity Party (SED). Western readers may find the book difficult to read, but it does provide useful insights into the political theory and practice of Marxism-Leninism in the GDR.

703 **Namen und Daten wichtiger Personen der DDR.** (Names and data of important people in the GDR.)
Günther Buch.   Berlin (West); Bonn: J. H. W. Dietz Nachf., 1982. 3rd ed. 384p.

An invaluable reference book which provides basic facts on over 2,000 leading figures in GDR life. No comparable book is published in the GDR. For more detailed and comprehensive information on GDR diplomats, see item no. 326.

704 **Wörterbuch des wissenschaftlichen Kommunismus.** (Dictionary of scientific communism.)
Edited by Rudolf Dau (et al.). Berlin (East): Dietz, 1986. 3rd ed. 427p.

Scientific communism is defined in the GDR and in the socialist bloc as a whole as an essential ingredient of Marxism-Leninism. In essence, its task is to investigate the historical laws governing the preparation and development of communist society and the realization of the world-historical mission of the working class. This reference book can be regarded as an authoritative source of information on the subject.

705 **Scholars' guide to Washington D.C. for Central and East European studies. Albania, Austria, Bulgaria, Czechoslovakia, Germany (FRG & GDR), Greece (Ancient and Modern), Hungary, Poland, Romania, Switzerland, Yugoslavia.**
Kenneth J. Dillon. Washington, DC: Smithsonian Institution Press, 1980. 329p. bibliog.

Published under the auspices of the Woodrow Wilson International Center for Scholars, this guide presents a survey of resources available in the Washington DC area to scholars interested in Central and Eastern Europe. The guide is comprehensive, detailed and easy to use. An invaluable research tool.

706 **GDR society and social institutions: facts and figures.**
G. E. Edwards. London: Macmillan, 1985. 244p. bibliog.

Examines GDR society and its social institutions under four main headings: the family; the position and role of women outside the family; youth; and the elderly. The aim is to demonstrate that, over the years, the welfare of the population has been promoted by progressive legislation in child care and crèche facilities, expanded opportunities for women, education, health care and provision for the elderly. The author's argument is supported by a wealth of data, including some 104 statistical tables of varying significance. There are figures, for instance, on the number of new dwellings constructed since 1960, as well as on the 'relationship between social contact and acceptance of teachers' instructions during second year of apprenticeship, as percentage' (sic.). The use, however, of 'almost exclusively East German sources' means that there is little room in this account for anything beyond the image which the society wishes to project of itself.

707 **A bis Z. Ein Taschen- und Nachschlagebuch über den anderen Teil Deutschlands.** (A to Z: a paperback reference book on the other part of Germany.)
Edited by the Federal Ministry for All-German Affairs. Bonn: Deutscher Bundes-Verlag, 1969. 11th revised and expanded ed. 832p. maps. bibliog.

An invaluable reference book, the first edition of which appeared in 1953. The entries are listed in alphabetical order and cover all major aspects of the GDR. Also included are: a section of biographical sketches of leading GDR personalities; a chronological table of the main events in the GDR's history and immediate pre-history (1945–68); and a useful bibliography organized around fourteen major themes.

708 **Historical Abstracts.**
Santa Barbara, California; Oxford, England: ABC-Clio
Information Services, 1955–. Published in two parts, each of 4
issues per year.

This is a major international undertaking which provides a comprehensive bibliographical service for the control of the world's periodical, book and dissertation literature in history (post-1450) and related fields. *Historical Abstracts* covers, for example, approximately 1,800 journals (including all of the most important GDR historical periodicals) published in over eighty countries in almost forty languages. This is an essential reference tool for anybody wishing to keep up-to-date with the latest published research concerning GDR historiography and the history of East Germany.

709 **Wörterbuch Philosophie und Naturwissenschaften.** (Dictionary of
philosophy and natural sciences.)
Edited by Herbert Hörz (et al.). Berlin (East): Dietz, 1983. 2nd
ed. 1,044p.

An invaluable reference work, packed with closely-typed information on the Marxist-Leninist view of all aspects of philosophy and the natural sciences.

710 **Area handbook for East Germany.**
Edited by Eugene K. Keefe. Washington, DC: US Government
Printing Office, 1972. 329p. bibliog.

Designed as a compact and informative reference manual for military and other personnel, this handbook aims to present an objective description of the GDR and foresee the possible, or probable, changes for the future. Apart from the GDR's natural and geographical resources and settlement patterns, the language and also the social values of its people are sensitively considered. The conclusion is that East Germans have accommodated themselves to the socialist system and have developed attitudes of upward social mobility within a new social structure which has incorporated some elements of the old. Education, religion, public communication, culture, government and political values are also reviewed, alongside the functioning of the economy and the military system. The authors conclude that, despite earlier repression, popular support for the state has increased. A notable work for its factual approach and objective interpretation of data. It has been up-dated and superseded by *East Germany: a country study* (q.v.) but remains a useful reference work for understanding the GDR at the beginning of the 1970s.

711 **Dichters Ort. Ein literarischer Reiseführer.** (A writer's place: a
literary guide.)
Werner Liersch. Rudolstadt, GDR: Greifenverlag, 1985. 384p.
A useful reference work which provides a full and informative account of the
places in the GDR where some of Germany's greatest writers lived and worked.
Readers who are looking for a compact tourist guide on the same theme,
attractively illustrated and provided with maps, are referred to item no. 37.

712 **Wörterbuch der marxistisch-leninistischen Philosophie.** (A
dictionary of Marxist-Leninist philosophy.)
Alfred Kosing. Berlin (East): Dietz, 1985. 616p.
An important aid to an understanding of the intricacies of Marxist-Leninist
philosophy. Readers may refer to the *Wörterbuch Philosophie und Naturwissenschaften* (q.v.) and the *Kleines politisches Wörterbuch* (q.v.) for further helpful
explanation of many of the concepts which are listed here alphabetically.

713 **Kulturpolitisches Wörterbuch. Bundesrepublik Deutschland/DDR
im Vergleich.** (Dictionary of cultural politics: Federal Republic of
Germany/GDR; a comparative view.)
Edited by Wolfgang R. Langenbucher, Ralf Rytlewski, Bernd
Weyergraf. Stuttgart, FRG: Metzler, 1983. 828p. bibliog.
This volume adopts a comparative approach in dealing alphabetically with a wide
selection of topics and concepts which are of central importance in the cultural
sphere in both German states. An invaluable reference book.

714 **Who's who in the socialist countries: a biographical encyclopedia of
10,000 leading personalities in 16 communist countries.**
Edited by Borys Lewytzkyj, Juliusz Stroynowski, translated from
the German and edited by Stephen Pringle, Ulla Dornberg. New
York; Munich: Saur, 1978. 736p.
A carefully assembled listing of 'leading figures in all spheres of life in all socialist
countries'. Each entry is provided with a useful and reliable annotation.

715 **Research on the GDR 'auf englisch': researchers of East German
affairs and their studies in English-language countries.**
Anita M. Mallinckrodt. Washington, DC: Mallinckrodt
Communications Research, 1984. 47p.
Presents the results of a survey conducted by the author in 1983, with the support
of the Ministry for Intra-German Relations in Bonn, into the research activities of
scholars working on the GDR in English-speaking countries. She includes a listing
of English-language conferences and publications on the GDR, the principal
subject matters researched, and the names and addresses of almost 300
researchers with their areas of specialization.

716 **Zeittafel zur Militärgeschichte der Deutschen Demokratischen Republik 1949–1984.** (A chronological table of the military history of the German Democratic Republic 1949–84.)
Autorenkollektiv (Authors' collective) led by Toni Nelles.   Berlin (East): Militärverlag, 1986. 571p.

A useful reference book which presents in straightforward tabular form the way in which the GDR sees the development of its own military history, the emphasis being firmly placed on the 'struggle for peace and socialism'.

717 **DDR Handbuch.** (GDR handbook.)
Edited by Hartmut Zimmermann with Horst Ulrich, Michael Fehlaner.   Cologne, FRG: Verlag Wissenschaft und Politik, 1985. 3rd ed. 1,559p. 2 vols. bibliog.

These volumes constitute the most comprehensive and detailed account of all aspects of the GDR to be found in one work. They include over 1,000 contributions, of which ninety are extended articles, illustrated with maps, diagrams and a large number of tables. An essential companion to any serious study of the GDR.

Bibliographies

718 **A working bibliography for the study of the GDR.**
Jim Brewer (et al.). *New German Critique*, no. 2 (1974),
p. 124–51.
This bibliography was produced in response to the growth of interest in the GDR
shown by American academia in the early 1970s. Only books are listed, and each
is annotated with particular emphasis on its value as a source of information and
on the clarity of its organization and analysis. Only a small selection of books with
a hostile, 'Cold War' approach to the GDR is included.

719 **A selected bibliography of articles and books in the social sciences
published in the German Democratic Republic in 1983.**
Compiled by Mike Dennis, Martin McCauley. *East Central
Europe*, 1–2 (1984), p. 129–45.
Some 180 items are listed here, usually followed by a brief annotation. The
articles are drawn from twenty-two of the GDR's major journals of interest to
social scientists. The areas covered are economics, law, occupational sciences and
sociology, sport, history, foreign policy, the military and ideology.

720 **A selected bibliography of articles and books in the social sciences
and humanities published in the German Democratic Republic in
1984.**
Compiled by Mike Dennis, Martin McCauley, Martin
Watson. *East Central Europe*, 1 (1985), p. 65–98.
Over 3,000 items are listed and each is followed by a useful annotation. The
articles are drawn from thirty-six of the GDR's leading periodicals. The areas
covered are economics, foreign affairs, history, ideology, law and criminology,
literature, the military, occupational sciences and sociology, and sport.

721   **Literature of the German Democratic Republic in English translation: a bibliography.**
Margy Gerber, Judith Pouget.   Lanham, Maryland; New York; London: University Press of America, 1984. 134p. (Studies in GDR Culture and Society: A Supplementary Volume).

This bibliography lists eleven English-language anthologies of GDR literature and works in English translation by no fewer than 128 GDR authors. The compilers very sensibly decided to include only those works by GDR authors published in German after 1945 and to exclude writers such as Uwe Johnson who left the GDR at an early age and established themselves as writers in the West (but to include writers who left the GDR after 1976, the year in which Wolf Biermann's expatriation became a cause célèbre). What is surprising therefore when consulting this volume is that samples of the work of so many GDR writers should be available in English, albeit often only in the form of an occasional poem or piece of short prose.

722   **A bibliography of German studies, 1945–1971.**
Compiled by Gisela Hersch.   Bloomington, Indiana; London: Indiana University Press, 1972. 603p.

A massive unannotated listing of works, usually in German, on post-war Germany up to the year of Erich Honecker's accession to power in the GDR. One of the book's sections is devoted entirely to the GDR (p. 374–498).

723   **East Germany: a selected bibliography.**
Compiled by Arnold H. Price.   Washington, DC: Library of Congress, 1967. 133p.

Emphasis is placed in this useful and exhaustive bibliography on works published between 1958 and 1966, the period up to 1958 having been covered previously by Fritz T. Epstein's *East Germany: a selected bibliography* (Washington, DC: Library of Congress, 1959). The book is primarily concerned with works examining conditions in the GDR itself, including its external relations, rather than with international or general German problems. Publications in German, English and other West European languages are included, the exceptions being one Russian bibliography and a few publications in Sorbian. The 833 entries are arranged by subject and, within each subject, alphabetically.

Document Collections

724 **Briefe aus einem anderen Land. Briefe aus der DDR.** (Letters from another country: letters from the GDR.)
Edited by Hildegard Baumgart, foreword by Carola Stern.   Hamburg, FRG: Hoffmann & Campe, 1971. 334p.

Published at a time when 'unfiltered', first-hand information on life in the GDR was still relatively rare, this volume attempts to fill the gap by presenting a generous selection of letters sent by GDR citizens to correspondents in West Germany over a period of twenty-five years, with a particular emphasis on the time of the building of the Berlin Wall in the early 1960s. The letters were written by a wide cross-section of correspondents from a variety of viewpoints, but the general impression is of a people who accept the GDR as their state while not being slow to criticize its shortcomings. The book makes fascinating reading for the outsider who wants to gain an insight into the impact of major historical events on the lives of ordinary individuals in divided Germany.

725 **Friedensbewegung in der DDR. Texte 1978–1982.** (The peace movement in the GDR: texts 1978–82.)
Edited by Wolfgang Büscher, Peter Wensierski, Klaus Wolschner with Reinhard Henkys.   Hattingen, FRG: Scandica Verlag, 1982. 327p.

A collection of documents pertaining to the unofficial GDR peace movement. It includes essays, letters and declarations from churchmen, writers and others as well as interviews with dissident intellectuals and other individuals on both general and particular issues of peace and disarmament, together with official government statements rebutting the position of the protesters. A useful initial source for researchers.

Document Collections

726 **The Federal Republic of Germany and the German Democratic Republic in international relations.**
Edited by Günther Doeker, Jens A. Brückner with the assistance of Ralph Freiberg. Dobbs Ferry, New York: Oceana, 1979. 3 vols. bibliog.

The purpose of this three-volume compilation is twofold: to provide 'not only a documentary analysis of the problems and issues raised by the participation of both German states in international politics, but also a problem-oriented study of issues' raised by Germany's position between East and West. It covers the period up to, and including, June 1978. Volume 1, entitled 'Confrontation and Cooperation', traces the development of both states from occupied territory to participating states in international politics; Volume 2 stresses, in addition to all-German problems, the issue of Berlin's political and legal status; and Volume 3 focuses on intra-German relations. Each volume contains relevant documents (in English) as well as problem-oriented study texts/complementary reading. The three volumes are sub-divided into eight parts, each of which concludes with a selected bibliography. See also item no. 369.

727 **Sozialistische Landesverteidigung. Aus Reden und Aufsätzen Juni 1978 bis Mai 1982.** (Socialist defence of the country: from speeches and essays, June 1978 to May 1982.)
Heinz Hoffmann. Berlin (East): Militärverlag, 1983. 511p.

A selection of pronouncements by the man who for over twenty years was Minister for National Defence.

728 **The German Democratic Republic.**
Erich Honecker, foreword by Henry Winston. New York: International Publishers, 1979. 256p.

This useful selection of excerpts from key addresses and interviews by the East German Party Leader, Erich Honecker, covers the period 1971–78. The most significant are his reports as Central Committee Chairman to the 8th and 9th Socialist Unity Party (SED) Party Congresses, outlining national and Party policies and revealing not only the change from the Ulbricht era to more realistic economic planning but also the commitment to managerial and technological rationalization. Relations with the Federal Republic are normalized by international agreement, but despite the GDR's accession to the United Nations and the 'breaking' of the 'imperialist blockade', irritation remains over the issue of recognition. East-West détente, the arms race, and the post-Helsinki human rights controversy are both major themes of this period for which this volume provides an interesting collection of background documents.

729 **Die Kulturpolitik unserer Partei wird erfolgreich verwirklicht.**
(The cultural policy of our Party is being successfully implemented.)
Erich Honecker. Berlin (East): Dietz, 1982. 339p.

A selection of statements on cultural policy since Honecker's accession to power in 1971.

232

730 **Zur Jugendpolitik der SED. Reden und Aufsätze von 1945 bis zur Gegenwart.** (The youth policy of the SED: speeches and essays from 1945 to the present.)
Erich Honecker. Berlin (East): Verlag Neues Leben, 1985. 3rd ed. 2 vols.

Erich Honecker's close involvement with the youth policy of his Party after 1945 (when he became youth secretary in the central committee of the Communist Party) is documented in this comprehensive collection.

731 **Erich Honecker. Reden und Aufsätze.** (Erich Honecker: speeches and essays.)
Edited by Institut für Marxismus-Leninismus beim ZK der SED. Berlin (East): Dietz, 1975–86. 10 vols.

A definitive collection in the original German of Honecker's official pronouncements.

732 **East Germany – A new German nation under socialism?**
Edited and translated from the German by Arthur W. McCardle, A. Bruce Boenau. Lanham, Maryland; New York; London: University Press of America, 1984. 364p.

This reader, primarily designed for university students, consists in the most part of texts, in English translation, written by East Germans themselves or former East German citizens. Not all are adherents of the régime – there is a piece by Robert Havemann – but, by design, the volume contains almost nothing by critical outsiders. Among the luminaries whose words are reproduced are Erich and Margot Honecker and the GDR foreign minister Oskar Fischer. In all there are twenty-three chapters, each briefly introduced by the editors, which are subsumed under the general headings 'Germany and the GDR', 'The Political System of the GDR', and 'The Society of the GDR'. Topics dealt with include the law and the role of literature, whilst some of the chapters consist of documents, for instance the 1974 constitution. This is a valuable collection, particularly for non-German speakers, although the decision not to include more critical material may not have been entirely wise.

733 **Documents on Germany under occupation 1945–1954.**
Selected and edited by Beate Ruhm von Oppen. London: Oxford University Press, 1955. 648p.

This collection, produced under the auspices of the Royal Institute of International Affairs, includes a considerable number of documents relating to the Soviet Zone and the GDR. These range from decrees of the Soviet Military Administration to declarations by political parties. The documents also include statements by the various powers, either singly or jointly, relating to Germany and Berlin. All the documents are of an official or quasi-official nature; they do not include, for example, newspaper reports on specific events.

Document Collections

734 **Dokumente zur Kunst-, Literatur- und Kulturpolitik der SED.**
(Documents on the art, literature and cultural policy of the
Socialist Unity Party.)
Edited by Elimar Schubbe. Stuttgart-Degerloch, FRG: Seewald
Verlag, 1972. 1,813p.

This is the first of three volumes in a series. The other two volumes are:
Dokumente zur Kunst-, Literatur- und Kulturpolitik der SED 1971–1974, edited
by Gisela Rüss, (Stuttgart-Degerloch: Seewald Verlag, 1976. 1,145p.) and
Dokumente zur Kunst-, Literatur- und Kulturpolitik der SED 1975–1980, edited
by Peter Lübbe, (Stuttgart-Degerloch, FRG: Seewald Verlag, 1984. 1,071p.).
Together they constitute a mammoth attempt to give a comprehensive picture of
the cultural, intellectual and artistic life of the GDR by bringing together official
speeches, directives and statements, interviews and articles on literature, cinema,
the theatre and the other arts. The third volume differs somewhat from its
predecessors which covered the years 1946–74 in that it includes amongst its 254
items contributions from GDR writers which could be published only in West
Germany. This is a vital addition since the years covered here have seen some of
the most abrasive confrontations between writers and the Party since the founding
of the GDR; the Wolf Biermann affair, for instance, and its widespread
repercussions for dissident artists and writers. The voluminous collections and
their respective introductions are indispensable reading for the serious student of
GDR culture.

735 **Documents in communist affairs, 1977.**
Edited by Bogdan Szajkowski. Cardiff: University College
Cardiff Press in association with Christopher Davies, 1978. 363p.

This collection of documents, all of which are dated 1977, includes English
translations of Erich Honecker's interview with Erich Voltmer of the *Saarbrücker
Zeitung* (excerpts) and part four of the controversial *Manifesto* allegedly written
by dissident Socialist Unity Party (SED) members and first published in the West
German magazine *Der Spiegel* (p. 291–316). A brief commentary by the editor is
included on p. 34–35.

736 **Whither Germany?**
Walter Ulbricht, foreword by Stefan Doernberg. Berlin (East):
German Institute of Contemporary History, 1966. 440p.

This volume contains extracts from speeches and articles by Ulbricht from the
period 1933 to 1966. The theme of the book is the national question, which
acquired an immediate and somewhat embarrassing importance to the GDR
leadership given the sudden and unexpected prospect of positive dialogue with
West Germany during the mid-1960s, and the tone is set in Professor Doernberg's
foreword: 'If the West German Federal Republic embodies the fatal past, the
German Democratic Republic represents the new, real Germany. The GDR
embodies the peaceful future of the whole German nation, its social progress and
its new relations with all peoples.'

737   **On questions of Socialist construction in the GDR.**
Walter Ulbricht.   Dresden, GDR: Verlag Zeit im Bild, 1968.
709p.

This selection of speeches and essays by Walter Ulbricht, published to coincide with his 75th birthday and at a time when he was at the peak of his power and influence in the GDR, is devoted to the theme of the 'socialist construction of the GDR' and covers the period of the anti-fascist democratic order after 1945, through the beginning of the construction of socialism in the early 1950s up to the shaping of the 'developed social system of socialism'. Apart from economic questions, of special interest are perhaps Ulbricht's specifications of the 'New Type Party' in 1948, the programme of youth education and the emergence of the final and fateful trend towards the claim that the developed socialist system had evolved on German soil – the arrogance of which would contribute to his downfall in Soviet eyes.

738   **Guten Morgen, du Schöne. Frauen in der DDR.** (Good morning, beautiful: women in the GDR.)
Maxie Wander, with a foreword by Christa Wolf.   Darmstadt, Neuwied, FRG: Luchterhand, 1978. 216p.

A celebrated collection of seventeen texts, based on taped interviews conducted by Maxie Wander with GDR women of varying ages, background and experience. Taken as a whole, the texts confirm the growing, and much discussed, emancipation of women in the GDR, but they show too that in some areas (notably in the behaviour of many men towards women) much remains to be done if that emancipation is to be more than partially realized.

739   **DDR Dokumente zur Geschichte der Deutschen Demokratischen Republik.** (GDR documents on the history of the German Democratic Republic.)
Edited by Hermann Weber.   Munich: DTV, 1986. 472p.

This new collection of documents consists of eight chapters which are arranged chronologically; in each case, the documents are preceded by a short introduction by Weber. The greater part of the volume is devoted to the Ulbricht era, the Honecker years only occupying ninety pages of text and documents. The final part of the book is a table of events. Because of Weber's expertise, this collection is a most useful additional resource for studying the GDR.

Index

The index is a single alphabetical sequence of authors (personal and corporate), titles of publications and subjects. Index entries refer both to the main items and to other works mentioned in the notes to each item. Title entries are in italics. Numeration refers to the items as numbered.

246

248

I

261

274

290

Map of East Germany

This map shows the more important towns and other features.

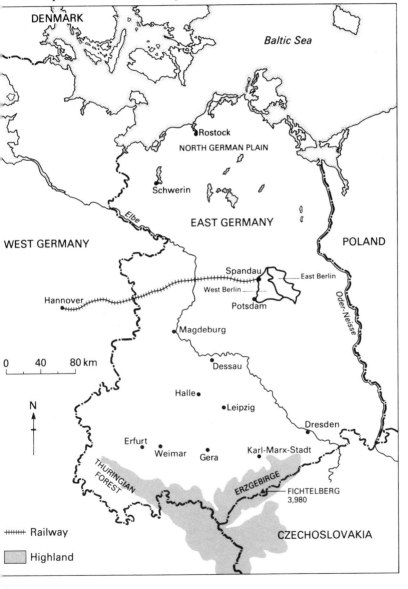

DENMARK

Baltic Sea

Rostock

NORTH GERMAN PLAIN

Schwerin

Elbe

EAST GERMANY

WEST GERMANY

POLAND

Spandau

East Berlin

West Berlin

Hannover

Potsdam

Magdeburg

0   40   80 km

Dessau

N

Halle

Leipzig

Dresden

Erfurt

Weimar   Gera   Karl-Marx-Stadt

Oder-Neisse

THURINGIAN FOREST

ERZGEBIRGE

FICHTELBERG
3,980

Railway

Highland

CZECHOSLOVAKIA